Piedmont

Nicola Williams, Duncan Garwood

Contents

Highlights	6	Health	154
Getting Started	9	World Time Zones	157
Itineraries	12	Language	158
The Authors	15	Glossary	160
Snapshot	16	Behind the Scenes	161
History	17	Index	164
The Culture	23	Legend	168
Environment	29		
Piedmont Outdoors	33		
The Winter Olympics	37		
Food & Drink	46		
Turin	54		
Valle di Susa & Val Chisone	90		
Southern & Eastern Piedmont	100		
Northern Piedmont & the Lakes	121		
Directory	142		
Transport	150		

Northern Piedmont
& the Lakes p121

Turin p54

Valle di Susa
& Val Chisone p90

Southern &
Eastern Piedmont
p100

Destination Piedmont

Forget any preconceived notion you have of a grey, smoke stack–filled industrial region: although it has a great industrial heritage and a wealth of cutting-edge industries, Piedmont (Piemonte in Italian) is pretty, green and fabulous. Natural treasures abound, its cultural portfolio is stunning and the gastronomic orgasms cooked up in the kitchen are mouthwatering and memorable.

Piedmont *is* Italy's land of good food and wine. Dogs snuffle around the roots of oak, beech, chestnut and hazelnut trees in the gently rolling Langhe hills to sniff out the world's richest crop of white truffles. In Turin confectioners craft elegant chocolate fit for kings, while city-slick coffee lovers sit on designer bar stools sipping orange cappuccinos or espressos in chocolate-lined cups. Ferrero rolls out its golden *rocher* (rocks) in Alba, the southern Piedmontese town where the sweet superpower was conceived in 1946. In villages nearby, Barbaresco reds wait an age in oak and chestnut barrels to become seductive wines to die for; while 75-year-old Romano Levi passes the day doing what he has done for the past five-and-a-bit decades – painting highly sought-after bottle labels to stick on his family-distilled grappa.

Pedal-power is just one way to appreciate this fertile land's sinful pleasures. For James Bond–style action seekers, there are outdoor adventures galore to gorge on in a playground set at the feet of Europe's highest mountain peaks. And for the green-fingered, pearly lakes proffer waterside gardens embellished with magnificent 19th-century villas. Boating, boarding or *belle époque* beauties – it's all part of Piedmont's big and brilliant surprise.

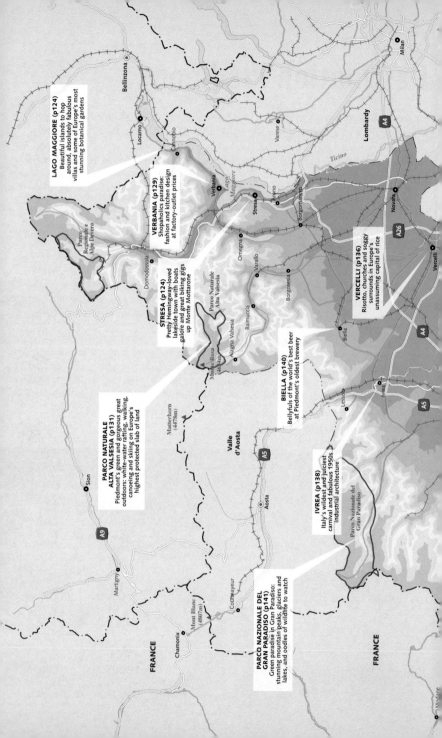

LAGO MAGGIORE (p124)
Beautiful islands to hop around, absolutely fabulous villas and some of Europe's most stunning botanical gardens

VERBANIA (p129)
Shopaholics paradise: fashion and kitchen design at factory-outlet prices

STRESA (p124)
Pretty Hemingway-loved lakeside town with boats galore and great biking gigs up Monte Mottarone

PARCO NATURALE ALTA VALSESIA (p131)
Piedmont's green and gorgeous great outdoors: white-water rafting, walking, canoeing and skiing on Europe's highest protected slab of land

VERCELLI (p136)
Risotto, churches and soggy surrounds in Europe's unassuming capital of rice

BIELLA (p140)
Bellyfuls of the world's best beer at Piedmont's oldest brewery

IVREA (p138)
Italy's wildest and juiciest carnival and fabulous 1950s industrial architecture

PARCO NAZIONALE DEL GRAN PARADISO (p141)
Green paradise in Gran Paradiso: stunning mountain peaks, glaciers and lakes, and oodles of wildlife to watch

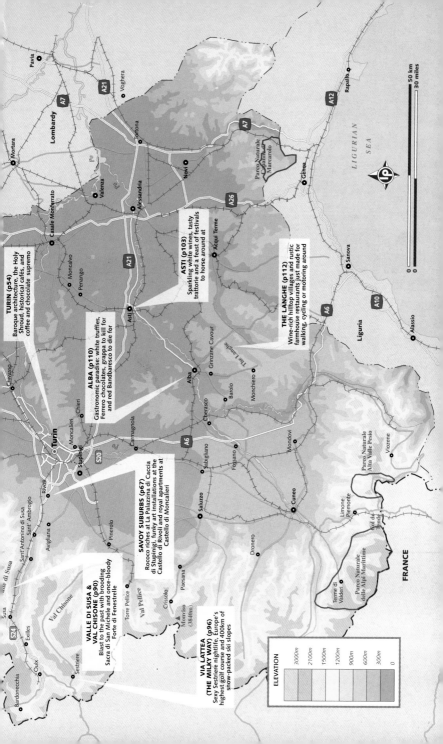

TURIN (p54)
Baroque architecture, the Holy Shroud, historical cafes, and coffee and chocolate supremo

ALBA (p110)
Gastronomic paradise: white truffles, Ferrero chocolates, grappa to kill for and red Bandbaresco to die for

ASTI (p103)
Sparkling white wines, tasty trattorie and a feast of festivals to horse around at

THE LANGHE (p112)
Wine-rich hilltop villages and rustic farmhouse restaurants just made for walking, cycling or motoring around

SAVOY SUBURBS (p67)
Rococo riches at La Palazzina di Caccia di Stupinigi, funky installations at the Castello di Rivoli and royal apartments at Castello di Moncalieri

VALLE DI SUSA & VAL CHISONE (p90)
Blast to the past with brooding Sacra di San Michele and once-bloody Forte di Fenestrelle

VIA LATTEA (THE MILKY WAY) (p96)
Sexy Sestriere nightlife, Europe's highest golf course and 400km of snow-packed ski slopes

ELEVATION
3000m
2100m
1500m
1200m
900m
600m
300m
0

50 km
30 miles

LIGURIAN
SEA

FRANCE

LIGURIA

LOMBARDY

There's much more to Piedmont than Turin, with its baroque **architecture** (p26), the **Holy Shroud** (p64), **coffee** (p48), **chocolate** (p48) and **FIAT cars** (p22). Stick so much as your little toe outside the regional capital and you'll be hit by a stunning collection of royal **castles and palaces** (p67); **sacred mountains** (p30) topped with fabulous **religious sanctuaries** (p98); **vineyards** galore (p103); wet and soggy **paddy fields** (p126); the world's richest white **truffle crop** (p112); and feisty fiestas of **orange-pelting** (p138), **horse-racing** (p105) and **cinema** (p66).

MARTIN MOOS

View Turin from the top of the Mole Antonelliana (p66)

Experience two favourites flavours of Piedmont – Grappa and coffee (p48)

ALAN BENSON

A panoramic view of the Turin skyline (p54)

NEIL SETCHFIELD

MARTIN MOOS

Cycle through towns such as Neive (p113) in the Langhe

Savour highly prized Piedmont truffles (p112)

ALAN BENSON

MARTIN MOOS

Journey across Lago Maggiore
to the Borromean Islands
(p124)

ALAN BENSON

Vines in the Langhe (p112)

Cattedrale di San Lorenzo, Alba (p111)

MARTIN MOOS

Snails – a Cherasco speciality (p115)

ALAN BENSON

Getting Started

Be it cultural, natural or gastronomic treasures you are after, Piedmont has it all. Visit the region once and you'll be returning time and time again to take in yet another royal castle, gourmet feast, green wonder or cultural festival. An easy place to travel to and around, Piedmont requires little forward planning – beyond deciding in which order you'll feast on which tasty spot.

WHEN TO GO

Piedmont is alluring at any time of year, although those hoping to cheer on a champion at the XX Winter Olympic Games need to be there from 10 February to 26 February 2006 (p37).

City lovers would do well to steer clear of Turin in July and August, when the weather boils, locals flee the city for the cooler coast or countryside, and many shops, restaurants and art galleries close down. Warm and sunny April, May, June and September are among the most attractive months to stroll its streets – those planning a city break should plump for a weekend when mid-range and top-end hotels empty of mid-week business travellers and lower their rates to lure guests in. Shoppers with serious splurge aspirations could consider January and its sales.

See Climate Chart (p144) for more information.

Alpine winters are long and severe, with the first snows falling sometime in November and continuing as late as May or June in some high-altitude spots. Skiers and snowboarders fly down Piedmont's slopes from late December to early April, while summertime walkers and outdoor-sport enthusiasts are best off hitting the road in July or September: trails can be horribly overcrowded in August.

Piedmont boasts oodles of cultural festivals (p11) and gastronomic temptations around which to plan a trip. Food fanatics wanting to taste (or hunt for) Alba's legendary white truffles need to come between September and December; the less-rare black truffle can be sought and sampled in spring, winter and autumn. Grapes are harvested in southern Piedmont in September or October, as is eastern Piedmont's rice crop (p126). Autumn is the season for game (also making it the best time of year to sample the region's robust red wines), while soft cheeses such as *taleggio*, *Toma Piemontese* and Gorgonzola (p130) taste best in winter.

COSTS & MONEY

Piedmont isn't cheap, although compared with the UK and northern Europe, the situation is not so bad. What you spend on accommodation (probably your single greatest expense) will depend on various factors, such

---

DON'T LEAVE HOME WITHOUT...

- A whetted palate and a hearty appetite (p46)
- A set of smart casual clothes for evenings out: turning up to restaurants and bars in grimy T-shirts, shorts and dusty sandals doesn't cut the mustard in fashion-conscious Turin
- Warm windproof clothing, sun glasses, sun protection and a good set of mountain hiking shoes
- Valid travel insurance (p146)
- Your ID card or passport and visa, if required (p149)
- If driving, a driving licence and car documents, along with appropriate car insurance (p152)

as location (Turin is pricier than Cuneo), season, the degree of comfort you want and old-fashioned luck. At the bottom end you will pay around €10.50 per night in youth hostels, where meals cost around €8. The cheapest *pensione* (small hotel) in Turin is unlikely to cost much less than €25/35 for a basic single/double with shared bathroom, while comfortable rooms with en suite bathroom clock in at around €45/70. Mid-range hotels in the regional capital charge anything from €70/100 to €150/180 for a single/double.

Eating out is also variable and is not necessarily location-led. Dining in some of rural Piedmont's farmstay restaurants costs just as much as in the centre of Turin: on average you'll pay €20 to €30 for a full meal with house wine, although you can still have set-lunch menus for as little as €10.

A backpacker sticking religiously to hostels, snacking for lunch and travelling slowly could scrape by on €40 per day. Your average mid-range daily budget, including a sandwich for lunch and a solid but not fancy dinner, as well as budgeting for a couple of sights and travel, might come to anything from €100 to €150 a day.

Public transport is reasonably priced, but car hire is expensive (as is petrol) and may be worth organising before you leave home (p153). On trains it is cheaper to travel on the *regionale* (slow local train) and *diretto* (slow direct train) rather than the faster InterCity and Eurostar Italia trains.

LONELY PLANET INDEX

Litre of gas/petrol €1.10

Litre of water €0.60

Bottle of Peroni beer €1.50

Souvenir T-shirt €15

Pizza slice to eat in €3

TRAVEL LITERATURE

Several 'grand Italian tour' classics by literary greats such as Johann Wolfgang von Goethe, Charles Dickens, Henry James and DH Lawrence pass through the Piedmontese capital ('city of arcades, pink and yellow stucco, innumerable cafes' wrote James in *Italian Hours*). For books on history and society see History (p17); for other classics by local writers, see The Culture (p24); for tasty food and wine titles, see Food & Drink (p46).

The Dust Roads of Monferrato (Rosetta Loy) Life on a farm in Monferrato is the setting for this fabulous tapestry, spanning three generations, of 19th-century rural Piedmont.

A Farewell to Arms (Ernest Hemingway) A tragic tale of love and war, this starts near the Italian-Slovenian border but moves swiftly to a hospital in northern Italy and later Stresa on Lago Maggiore.

The Moon and the Bonfires (Cesare Pavese) No book depicts the Langhe hills better than this short novel – the tale of an Italian peasant who, after WWII, returns from the USA to the countryside farm where he grew up.

The Name of the Rose (Umberto Eco) Investigate a spate of deaths in a monastery in northern Italy with Piedmont's best-known writer, thanks in part to Sean Connery's celluloid portrayal of Eco's medieval Franciscan sleuth.

Nietzsche in Turin (Lesley Chamberlain) For an alternative perspective of the regional capital, read this fascinating study of how Nietzsche saw Turin and allowed the city to seep into his work (1888–89).

Numbers in the Dark (Italo Calvino) The Cuban-born essayist, journalist and novelist brilliantly depicts Turin ('straight streets that never end') in this collection of stories and fables.

Other People's Trades (Primo Levi) This collection of essays by Levi, a suicidal Turin Jew, includes an account of the house on Corso Re Umberto in Turin, where he was born in 1919.

HOW MUCH?

Espresso standing up/ sitting down €0.80/1.50

Bicerin (coffee, chocolate & milk blend) €4

One-hour's city parking €0.50-2

City bus or tram ride €0.90

10-minute taxi ride €8

Packet of 20 cigarettes €3

Local/foreign newspaper €0.90/2.50

Two-scoop ice-cream cone €1.50

Bottle of 1998 Barolo wine €25-156

INTERNET RESOURCES

Art Itineraries Index (www.piemonte-emozioni.it) Discover 14 different itineraries around Piedmont by car, bicycle or on foot – complete with comprehensive accommodation and cultural-event listings, gastronomic tips, and a ticket-booking service for museums, shows and exhibitions en route.

Discovering Piedmont: Extratorino (www.extratorino.it) Food and wine, famous people, spot-on reviews of the latest clubs, bars and restaurants; shopping recommendations and walking tours are tuned-in highlights of this cutting-edge city guide.

Lonely Planet (www.lonelyplanet.com) One of the best places to start your web explorations; you'll find concise information, postcards from other travellers, and the Thorn Tree bulletin board, where you can ask questions before you go or dispense advice when you return.

Regione Piemonte (www.regione.piemonte.it) Click on Languages/English to reach the tourism arm of the Piedmont Region website – gastronomy, art and culture, a daily weather report and more.
Torino 2006 (www.torino2006.com) This is the spot to find anything and everything about the 2006 Winter Olympics, including event schedules, venue info and job opportunities.
Trenitalia (www.trenitalia.it) Plan train journeys, check timetables and prices, and book tickets on Italy's national railways website.

TOP FIVES
FESTIVALS & EVENTS

Piedmont's tip-top festivals revolve, happily so, around the region's two great passions – food and film. The following list is our top five; for a list of regional festivals see p145. Destination-specific events are listed in the regional chapters.

- Battaglia delle Arance (Battle of Oranges; Ivrea) February (p138)
- CioccolaTò (Piedmont) March (p145)
- Douja d'Or, Festival delle Sagre & Il Palio di Asti (Asti) September (p105)
- Fiera Nazionale del Tartufo Bianco d'Alba (National Alba White Truffle Fair; Alba) October (p112)
- Turin Film Festival (Turin) November (p71)

MUST-SEE MOVIES

Pre-empt your trip with a pre-departure celluloid tour of Piedmont. Our top five range from horror to Italian cinema classics.

- *The Italian Job* (1968) Director: Peter Collinson
- *Deep Red* (1975) Director: Dario Argento
- *La Donna della Domenica* (1975) Director: Luigi Comencinci
- *Così Ridevano* (1998) Director: Gianni Amelio
- *Sleepless* (2001) Director: Dario Argento

TOP TASTES

Several hundred very tasty meals later, our top five taste bud ticklers looked like this. For the full munching monty see p51.

- *Bicerin* (a blend of coffee, hot chocolate, milk and whipped cream) with a gold-wrapped *gianduiotti* (velvety hazelnut chocolate) on the side (p49)
- Barolo and Barbaresco wine (p112)
- An early-evening aperitif Turin-style (p81)
- *Lumache al Barbera* (p52)
- *Tartufi bianchi* (white truffles; p112)

TOP TOURS

The region offers far more than your conventional museum and art gallery. For a taste of industrial Piedmont, make time for a tour on the quirky side.

- Cascina Venaria rice farm (p126)
- Factory museum and archive of design king Alessi (p128)
- FIAT's car-manufacturing plant at Mirafiori (p68)
- Lavazza's coffee-roasting plant (p70)
- Martini & Rossi's distillery (p114)

Itineraries

CLASSIC ROUTES

ROYAL CASTLES

One week / Turin to Garéssio

This regal route stretches 330km from the regional capital to the it's most southeastern realms: one week is enough to see the Savoy side of things, but for those with time on their hands, there is plenty more to entertain along the way.

The House of Savoy left behind a treasure trove of architectural gems, which have all been protected as World Heritage sites since 1997.

Turin (p54), Savoy capital from 1563, bursts with absolutely fabulous pads. Palazzo Reale, at the heart of the Savoy 'command area', reveals lavish room after lavish room. Palazzo Madama, Palazzo Carignano, Castello del Valentino and Villa della Regina are other wonders in the city.

After that, head to **Aglié** (p139), home to a 13th-century fortress adopted by the Savoys in the 18th century. Then it is off to **Venaria Reale** (p68) with its twin set of royal castles. From here, a drive around Turin takes you to **Rivoli** (p67) with its art-filled castle; **Stupinigi** (p67), where the Savoys hunted; and **Moncalieri** (p68), a 13th-century defensive outpost.

Fleeing the Savoy suburbs, motor southeast past **Govone** (p113) to **Barbaresco** (p113). Then wiggle west through winemaking villages to **Racconigi** (p116), with its ravishing royal abode, and on to **Saluzzo** (p115). From here, the castle at **Manta** (p116) makes a great half-day trip. Still not castled-out? Continue south to Castello Reale di Casotto in **Garéssio** (p120) in the **Valle Tanaro** (p120) on Piedmont's most southeastern tip.

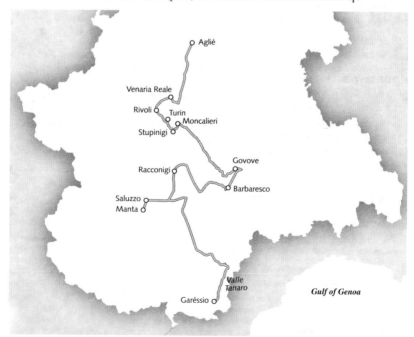

Aglié

Venaria Reale

Rivoli

Turin

Moncalieri

Stupinigi

Govove

Racconigi

Barbaresco

Saluzzo

Manta

Valle Tanaro

Gulf of Genoa

Garéssio

GREEN PIEDMONT

Two weeks / Valle di Susa to Monte Rosa

Pick a mountain resort in the legendary **Via Lattea** (Milky Way; p96): **Sestriere** (p96), **San Sicario** (p97) and **Clavière** (p97) are fine choices for some sporting action. Passing by **Turin** (p54), pick up a list of farmstays and stock up on cheese and salami in the farm shop at **Agriturismo Piemonte** (p142).

Heading north, admire herons and other bird species around **Lago di Candia** (p139), Piedmont's most important bird-watching wetland. Then move east, stopping off around **Vercelli** (p136), to view its paddy fields, or in **Novara** (p134) to see its Baroque basilica. After this, head north to **Lago Maggiore** (p124).

On the lake shore, **Stresa** (p124) is your place. Hike (or ride the cable car) up **Monte Mottarone** (p124) to discover Alpine flora in the Giardino Botanico Alpinia, then mountain bike or ski down. Another day, take a boat to **Verbania** (p129) to visit the Villa Taranto gardens and take in the sun on Piedmont's cleanest lakeside beach. **Isola Bella** (p127) and **Isola Madre** (p127) are both worth the boat trip.

Motoring west towards **Lago d'Orta** (p130), you hit **Orta San Giulio** (p130). Stroll around the 20 chapels dotted on its **Sacro Monte** (p130) then continue west to the **Sacro Monte di Varallo** (p131). Some of Piedmont's most breathtaking mountain scenery laces the **Valsesia** (p131). Canoe the rapids in **Varallo** (p131), visit the Germanic Museo Walser in **Pedemonte** (p132), and ski or hike in **Alagna** (p132), fabulously nestled at **Monte Rosa's** feet.

From the Valle di Susa to the foot of Europe's second highest mountain is a 360km-long route (partly along wiggly mountain roads) that deserves time: two weeks allows you to spend several days skiing or snow-boarding, before moving on to savour Piedmont's northern natural treasures.

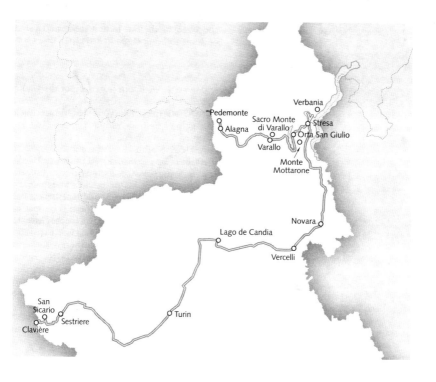

TAILORED TRIPS

TASTEBUD TOUR

If you take tummy matters more seriously than seriously, Piedmont is your place. This is gourmet paradise, after all.

Kick off your movable feast in **Turin** (p54) with an *aperitivo* (aperitif). Consider a Martini from **Cinzano** (p114), sparkling **Asti** (p103) or a best-in-the-world Menabrea beer from **Biella** (p140) to accompany that titillating banquet of complimentary hors d'œuvres. But leave room for your *antipasto* (starter): snails from **Cherasco** (p115); *tartufi bianchi* (white truffles) from **Alba** (p110); or **Nizza Monferrato** (p109) thistles perhaps.

For the *primo piatto* (first course) it's off to **Vercelli** (p136) for some *risotto alla Piemontese* (home-grown Arborio rice with shaved black truffles) or to **Novara** (p134) for *panissia alla Novarese* (Piedmontese rice with onion, sausage and a vegetable soup). For the *secondi piatto* (second course), there is nothing better than *brasato al Barolo* (beef in Barolo wine) in **Barolo** (p115) with a glass of red **Barbaresco** (p113).

Finish off with *torta di nocciole* (hazelnut cake) oozing **Langhe** (p112) hazelnuts; a Lavazza *caffè* with a *gianduiotto* (velvety hazelnut chocolate) on the side in **Turin** (p54); and a shot of Romano Levi grappa in **Neive** (p113).

KIDDING AROUND

With its mountains, lakes and big city, Piedmont is perfect for the young and young-at-heart.

Children are spoilt for choice in **Turin** (p54); take your pick from a clutch of museums, nip outside for a gulp of fresh air with a river-boat tour or funicular ride, and finish off with a sweet mug of chocolate *bicerin*.

Hours can be whiled away kidding around on the snowy slopes of the **Valle di Susa** (p98) and **Val Chisone** (p93) ski resorts. Some have ice-skating rinks and supervised snow-play areas for toddlers, and there is a military fort at **Exilles** (p98) and **Fenestrelle** (p94) to peek at en route. The southern ski slopes of the valleys around **Cuneo** (p116), **Limone Piemonte** (p120), **Frabosa Sottana** and **Frabosa Soprana** (p120), are equally effective energy burners.

Then it is off to **Lago Maggiore** (p124) for a summer stroll around the Parco Zoologico di Villa Pallavicino in **Stresa** (p124) or the doll museum in **Arona** (p127). The Parco della Fantasia in **Omegna** (p130), on **Lago d'Orta** (p130), will capture of the imagination of every child, as will helping out on the farm in **Ponzone** (p109). Come carnival, orange-pelting in **Ivrea** (p138) is a must.

The Authors

NICOLA WILLIAMS Coordinating Author

A Latin leap for love, from the Lithuanian capital of Vilnius to Lyon in France in 1997, proved a strategic move for travel writer Nicola Williams, who has nipped through the Fréjus tunnel numerous times since to feast on Piedmont's extraordinary cuisine, ski its slopes and shop Turinese style. In 2001 Nicola researched the 1st edition of Lonely Planet's tri-city guide, *Milan, Turin & Genoa*. As coordinating author of this guidebook, Nicola wrote all the introductory chapters, including Itineraries, History, The Culture, Environment and Food & Drink as well as the Directory chapter.

My Piedmont

Coming from France, lunch at Ristorante Biovey (p99) in Bardonecchia is a must after driving through the Fréjus tunnel. Then it's straight to Turin (p54) for shopping, *aperitivo* and dinner; or – if I have bags of time – a mountainous wiggle through the Val Chisone (p93). The end-of-the-earth Val Pellice (p93) also makes a great detour. For me, Piedmont means food and nothing beats Monferrato (p106) and the Langhe (p112) with its fabulous *agriturismi* (p142), multitude of *enoteche* (p113) and truffle hunters (p112). In season, *Tra Arte e Querce* (p112) in Monchiero is just my cup of tea for breakfast.

DUNCAN GARWOOD Contributing Author

Duncan lives in the wine-rich hills overlooking Rome, and divides his time between writing and teaching English. An Italian-speaker, he has travelled extensively throughout the peninsula, enjoying the country's disarming beauty and hidden complexities. As contributing author, Duncan wrote Piedmont Outdoors and the Turin, Valle di Susa & Val Chisone, Southern & Eastern Piedmont, Northern Piedmont & the Lakes and Transport chapters.

Snapshot

Piedmont, it seems, has stopped mourning. In January 2003, when Giovanni Agnelli, legendary head of the once-almighty FIAT, succumbed to prostate cancer, aged 83, it seemed the very soul of Turin had died with him. Hot on the heels of his death, the firm, which his grandfather founded in 1899, announced job cuts of 12,300 worldwide and the closure of 12 factories, in a last-ditch attempt to save a car-manufacturing company that had seen two straight years of billion-euro losses. It really seemed to be the final nail in the coffin.

Yet Piedmont is moving again. Under the left-wing leadership of Turin city mayor Sergio Chiamparino, whose party landed a third term in office in 2001, the drive has never been more towards industrial innovation. Entrepreneurial energies are being directed towards technical-scientific sectors (rather than traditional manufacturing), while the hot-shot likes of Omnitel and Telecom Italia Mobile feature in its economic portfolio. Piedmont exports clock up 13% of national exports.

After years of braking on a proposed high-speed rail link between Turin and Lyon in neighbouring France, Regione Piemonte president, right-wing Enzo Ghigo (b 1953), gave his €100-million blessing for the primarily EU and Italian-French government financed project in early 2004. Costing €13 billion in all, by 2012 the Turin-Lyon link will whisk train travellers at lightning speed along the Valle di Susa and through a 52km-long trans-Alpine tunnel into France.

Behind the scenes Piedmont punters are enjoying light relief in the dashing form of daredevil Italian royal prince Emanuel Filiberto, grandson of Italy's last king (Umberto II). Since his family's return from exile in 2002 (the Savoys were banned from Italy in 1946), the handsome young prince has raised eyebrows with his marriage to a French actress, and his appearance in TV ads for olives and jet-set jaunts.

Elections to Piedmont's *consiglio regionale* (regional assembly) in December 2002 ushered in Lega Nord (Northern League; p21) party member Roberto Cota as president. The Novara-born politician's push for more genuine autonomy from the central government is a sentiment shared by many politicians countrywide. The next regional elections are in 2005.

In 2006 Piedmont will host the Winter Olympics. This means big bucks. Not counting investments from within the region, €2.6 billion in Olympic and government funds is being ploughed into Piedmont. For every €1 million spent, 15 new jobs will be created – peaking at 9700 by 2005. New state-of-the-art sporting venues and hotels are being built at competition venues in Turin, the Valle di Susa and Val Chisone; and transport infrastructure is being improved. Unemployment will fall by 0.3% a year and annual GDP will rise by 0.3% to 0.4% – an increase in value of €1425 million between 2004 and 2007 – according to Toroc (Torino Organising Committee, p45), the brain behind Piedmont's Olympic extravaganza.

FAST FACTS

Population: 4,289,731

Area: 25,640.1 sq km

Provinces: Alessandria, Asti, Biella, Cuneo, Novara, Turin, Verbania & Vercelli

GDP: €92.3 billion

GDP per head: €18,748

Unemployment: 6.3%

Highest point: Dufour summit, Monte Rosa (4633m)

Area above 3000m: 101.7 sq km

Mobile phone users: 58.2% of people aged 11 or more (of whom 33.6% call every day)

Pasta consumption: just 55kg per person per year (southern Italians wolf down 129kg a year each)

History

TRIBAL CLASHES

Tribal Palaeolithic Neanderthals pitched up in Piedmont 70,000 years ago. By 1800 BC, the region was settled by a pack of pre-Indo European Italic tribes, including the bold Ligurians and the powerful Etruscans, who had their sticky fingers in the Po Plain. From 300 BC, the Insubres settled north of the River Po in Cisalpine Gaul, only to be turfed out by Roman legions a century later.

During the Second Punic War (218–202 BC), fought between the Romans and Carthage (a kingdom of traders based in North Africa), Piedmont's mountains proved the mightiest enemy. Carthaginian general Hannibal crossed the Italian Alps in 15 days during his march from Spain to Rome, only to lose 15,000 of his 40,000 troops and all but one of his war elephants to Alpine snowstorms and landslides. The feisty war warrior's mountain crossing was sufficiently noble nonetheless to win the support of local Celts and Ligurians in his subsequent anti-Rome military campaign. En route, Hannibal stumbled across Taurasia (Turin) on the River Po, home to the Taurini tribe since between 500 and 400 BC. Hannibal burnt their village to the ground.

Revengeful Romans defeated the Celts once and for all in 197 BC, conquering all of Cisalpine Gaul six years later.

ROMANS TO HOLY ROMAN EMPIRE

Victorious Romans plumped for the confluence of the Po, Stura and Tanaro Rivers to build Pollentia (present-day Pollènza in southern Piedmont), the first Roman settlement founded in the region, between 173 and 125 BC.

Derzona (Tortona), at the crossroads of Via Postumia and Via Fulvia, followed in 120 BC. The remains of Via Fulvia, a road constructed under Quintus Fulvius in 179 BC to link Piacenza in present-day Emilia-Romagna with France, are preserved at the archaeological park in Alessandria (p107). In 89 BC, the Romans colonised Hasta Pompeia (Asti) and built walls around the ancient wine-making settlement.

Julius Caesar founded Colonia Giulia (Turin) in 58 BC, granting Roman citizenship to its inhabitants. During the 40-year rule of Roman Emperor Augustus (from 43 BC), the Roman *castrum* was refounded as Augusta Taurinorum and fortified with 6m-high walls, pierced by four gates. The eastern city gate (incorporated into the facade of Palazzo Madama; p59) and its northern counterpart (Porta Palatina; p63) still stand. You can view the remnants of Turin's amphitheatre and theatre in its Museo d'Antichitá (p63).

This period was known for its flourishing arts. Alba Pompeia (Alba) sprung up with magnificent marble temples, public baths, arenas and amphitheatres. Picture yourself watching a gladiator combat in the amphitheatre at the Riserva Naturale Speciale dell'Area Augusta Bagiennorum (p115), or wallow like a Roman god in the warm and salty thermal waters of Acquae Statiellae (Acqui Terme, p108), an illustrious Roman spa fed with water from the River Erro by a 10km-long aqueduct (four arches still stand).

TIMELINE	c70,000–400 BC	58 BC
	Palaeolithic hunter-gatherers roam across Piedmont; the Taurini tribe settles Taurasia (Turin) on the River Po	Julius Caesar founds the military colony of Colonia Giulia (Turin) and grants Roman citizenship to its inhabitants

With the end of the Roman Empire in 476, Piedmont fell from one barbaric invader to another. In 570 it tumbled into the hands of the Lombards, a Swabian people from neighbouring Lombardy, who created duchies out of Turin, Ivrea, Asti and San Giulio d'Orta. The Lombards were chucked out in 773 by the Franks, who threw Piedmont into the melting pot, with hitherto Byzantine-controlled lands, to create the Papal States. On Christmas Day 800, Frankish king Charlemagne (742–814) was crowned emperor of the Holy Roman Empire – of which much of present-day Piedmont thus became a part of.

A FAMILY AFFAIR

Charlemagne's successors struggled to hold together his empire, so much so that the Franks were kicked out of Piedmont in 888, leaving the region to degenerate into a battlefield of duchies, counties and marquisates ruled by a soap opera–style bunch of oligarchies in which one family prevailed.

Under Manfred II (r 1002–35), Turin became an independent county in 1002, only to vie for supremacy with its powerful rival, Ivrea, under whose marquisate yoke it had been since 892. Saluzzo and Monferrato were other prominent marquisates in northwestern Italy at this time. When Manfred II's daughter, Bertha, died in 1091, a system of city-states ruled by communes – town councils, free from feudal control or autonomous but protected by the pope or emperor – evolved.

In southern Piedmont, Asti remained a free republic until the mid-14th century and the stronghold of Saluzzo remained independent until 1601. In eastern Piedmont, Monferrato was ruled by the Aleramici family from the 10th to 14th centuries, the Paleologo dynasty until 1633, and then the Gonzagas, who spent the next century squabbling with the French House of Savoy over the Piedmontese marquisate.

The immensely influential Savoy dynasty had gained a foothold in Piedmont as early as 1046 with the marriage of Adelaide, heiress of Turin County, to Oddone of Savoy (1010–60). In 1248 the Savoys scored complete control of Turin and – with the exception of a brief interlude between 1255 and 1274 (when rebellious Turinese sided with the Republic of Asti to oust the Savoys) – ruled the Piedmontese capital almost exclusively until the 19th century. From the end of the 14th century, they also controlled the Valle di Susa, Valle di Lanzo, Ivrea, the Canavese and Cuneo.

In northeastern Piedmont, the towns of Novara, Vercelli and Asti were ruled by the viscounts of Milan. The fortress town of Alessandria was founded in 1168 as a military base for the Lega Lombardia (Lombardy League), a coalition of northern Italian cities set up to fight Swabian duke Frederick Barbarossa I. Barbarossa, made advances on Lombardy and eastern Piedmont from 1154. In 1155 he became emperor of the Holy Roman Empire. The Italians sent 'Red Beard' (as Barbarossa was known) packing once and for all in 1176, and Alessandria remained an important military town for centuries to come.

NEW HORIZONS

In 1347 the bubonic plague tore through Europe, killing off half of Turin's population and leaving economic depression and famine in its wake. The Black Death, as the disease was otherwise known, didn't thwart Savoy growth however.

Considered positively Machiavellian in his diplomacy by some historians, Vittorio Amedeo II comes under lively discussion in *War, Diplomacy and the Rise of Savoy 1960–1720* by Christopher Storrs.

Lombards invade Piedmont and create duchies out of Turin, Ivrea, Asti and San Giulio d'Orta – forming part of the Papal State in 773

The French Savoy dynasty takes control of Turin; Northeastern Piedmont is ruled by the viscounts of Milan from Lombardy

Piedmont's first university, the Università degli Studi di Torino, opened in 1404. The Renaissance ushered in the city's white-marble Duomo di San Giovanni (1491–98). Hydraulic and irrigation projects converted the Po Plain from swampy woodland into an extremely productive agricultural collective, with some of Italy's most fertile farmland. Rice was cultivated in eastern Piedmont.

But trouble hovered on the horizon. A convenient stepping stone for armies crossing the Alps into the Italian peninsula, Turin was visited in 1494 by a war-waging Charles VIII of France, en route south to Naples. In 1533 French troops returned again, this time forcing the Piedmont duke, Charles III, to flee Turin. Three years later the French seized Piedmont, maintaining control of it throughout the Italian Wars (1494–1559). The Treaty of Câteau-Cambrésis (1559) restored peace and made France give Piedmont back to the House of Savoy. Saluzzo remained in French hands.

As if to reaffirm its rightful place on the European map, Duke of Savoy Emanuele Filiberto (1553–80) shifted the Savoy capital from Chambéry in present-day France to Turin in 1563, and set about building a star-shaped citadel, elegant palaces and a rash of public buildings. Emanuele Filiberto, incidentally, is the sweet soul held responsible for introducing chocolate to Piedmont (p76). The duke's glorification of the city was continued by Carlo Emanuele I (1580–1630), Vittorio Amedeo II (1666–1732) and Carlo Emanuele II (1638–75). Under the latter the city's wealth of baroque palaces and sprawling hunting lodges was created by royal architect Filippo Juvarra.

In 1578 the sacred Holy Shroud, the cloth in which Jesus was supposedly buried, was brought from Chambéry to Turin. The Shroud had already been moved to the region for safekeeping twice before – during the 1533 French invasion of Savoy, and again during the Italian Wars. Both times the cloth was hidden in the Cattedrale di Sant'Eusebio in Vercelli.

The War of the Spanish Succession broke out in 1701. Allied with Austria, Turin was besieged by French and Spanish troops in 1706, inciting its population to seek refuge in the citadel and prompting Turinese miner Pietro Micca to blow up a tunnel – and himself – to stave off French advances and pre-empt their eventual defeat.

The Treaty of Utrecht (1713) that ended the War of the Spanish Succession saw Vittorio Amedeo II become king of Sicily – a title and territory he held onto until 1720, when the Spanish took it from him and gave him Sardinia and its crown instead. In 1714 the Savoys also secured sovereignty of Monferrato, a Piedmont marquisate, where Savoy troops had being fighting since 1691.

Immerse yourself in 1950s Piedmont with *Le Amiche* (The Girlfriends, 1955) and *Il Grido* (The Outcry, 1957), two classic films by Italian film director Michelangelo Antonioni of *Blow-Up* fame.

NAPOLEON

Italy had been the source of many enlightened political ideas, but the concept of national sovereignty had not been one of them until Napoleon Bonaparte, a 27-year-old Corsican-born French general, came along.

Napoleon acceded to the nationalist calls of Italian deputies in Lombardy, Bologna, Emilia and Modena, and in 1797 proclaimed the Cisalpine Republic, a nominally independent republic with its own government, constitution and capital city (Milan). Napoleonic troops fought battles in Mondovì and Rivoli, and in 1798 marched into Turin and forced the

1536–59	1861
A period of French rule ends with the Treaty of Câteau-Cambrésis, which sees Piedmont returned to the Duchy of Savoy	House of Savoy's Vittorio Emanuele II, proclaimed king of a newly united Italy; Turin serves as its capital until 1865

Savoys into exile. Two years later, Austrian troops keen to conquer the region were defeated by Napoleon at the bloody Battle of Marengo (1800), in which 7000 French and 14,000 Austrian soldiers were wounded. Relive the battle at Alessandria's Museo della Battaglia (p108).

By 1802 Napoleon's Cisalpine Republic had been superseded by the Italian Republic and in 1805 the Kingdom of Italy came into being. But in 1815 Napoleon was defeated at Waterloo, dashing any hopes of independent constitutional rule, and at the Congress of Vienna, Turin was annexed back to the House of Savoy.

UNIFICATION

The events of 1815 were a step backwards but it bred one of Italian history's greatest figures, Giuseppe Garibaldi (1807–82). After an unsuccessful uprising in Piedmont in 1834 the revolutionary, who was a champion of the nationalist Risorgimento (literally 'Revival') movement, who spent most of his life exiled from his homeland, was tried in absentia and sentenced to death.

In *Il Risorgimento,* one of several publications to spring up in 1847 out of the growing Italian nationalist movement, Turin-born Camillo Benso di Cavour (1810–61) and nationalist writer Cesare Balbo (1789–1853) pressed for a constitution. In 1848, they published their *Statuto* (Statute), advocating a.two-chamber parliament, with the upper chamber to be appointed by the Crown and the lower chamber to be elected by educated taxpayers. In 1861, *Statuto* was to become the constitutional basis of the Kingdom of Italy, but not before 13 more years of warring between the various European princes had resulted in the deaths of many more Italians.

Cavour fought side by side with Garibaldi to break the stranglehold of foreign domination. His brilliant diplomacy, coupled with the independent efforts of Garibaldi and his popular base, finally caught the attention of European communities, which became staunch supporters of a free and united Italy. The palace in Turin where Cavour was born and died can be visited (p65), as can his fabulous family home in Grinzane Cavour (p114).

When King Carlo Alberto (r 1831–49), the sympathetic Piedmont monarch, granted a constitution based on *Statuto* in March 1848, Cavour stood for election. In 1850 he was given three ministries in the government headed by Massimo d'Azeglio – only to join his centre-left forces with the centre-right behind d'Azeglio's back, prompting the prime minister to resign and Cavour to take his place. As prime minister, Cavour focused on forging an alliance with the French emperor Napoleon III, in a move destined to overthrow Austrian domination of Piedmont.

The Kingdom of Italy was declared on 17 March 1861. Victor Emmanuel II became the first king of Italy, and Turin became the kingdom's capital, a status it kept until 1865, when the parliament and capital shifted to Florence.

INDUSTRIALISATION

Turin's answer to its loss of political significance was industrialisation. In 1899, the Fabbrica Italiana di Automobili di Torino (FIAT; Italian Automotive Manufacturer of Turin) was founded, followed by rival car manufacturer, Lancia, in 1906. Out in the countryside – linked by rail to

1899	**1915–18**
Industrial Piedmont is conceived with the birth of Fabbrica Italiana di Automobili di Torino (FIAT) in Turin	Italy joins Allies against Germany and Austria in WWI

ANOTHER COUNTRY

Utopia for the Lega Nord (Northern League) is Padania – another country, separate from poor old southern Italy, with its own government and nobody to subsidise.

Padania was proclaimed in 1996 – to the joy of two million 'Padanians', who gathered along the River Po to mark the occasion – by Umberto Bossi, the political party's outspoken leader who was born a stone's throw from the Piedmont-Lombardy border on the eastern bank of Lago Maggiore. The autonomous political entity has since come to spearhead the Lega Nord's right-wing secessionist ideology. Padania would be governed by a federal assembly, and further split into a national and regional assembly. Popular vote would elect the national assembly, comprising 200 deputies, every five years.

Since the Lega Nord's foundation in 1991, it has been criticised for its blatantly anti-Semitic and anti-foreigner stance. 'I want to hear cannons roar', declaimed Bossi in response to the boatloads of illegal immigrants arriving in Italy in summer 2003.

Under Bossi's leadership the Lega Nord enjoys strong support in Piedmont: indeed, the party was borne out of a marriage between Bossi's Lombard League (which called for autonomy for Lombardy) and Piemonte Autonomista, a movement, founded by Turin politician Giuseppe Farassino detto Gipo, calling for Piedmont autonomy.

In March 2004 Bossi was rushed into a Varese hospital after suffering a mild heart attack.

Turin since the 1860s – two enterprising young men, Martini and Rossi (p114), were making great strides with their distillery, founded in 1879.

Growing social and economic unrest in Europe in the late 1890s was reflected in Italy's political arena by constant fluctuations between socialist democrats and right-wing imperialists, who gained then lost the support of the discontented populace. One man who bridged the political extremes was Mondovì-born politician Giovanni Giolitti (1842–1929), a Turin university graduate who headed five governments between 1892 and 1921, making him one of Italy's longest-serving prime ministers. He granted male suffrage in 1913, resigned in 1914, watched his country go to war in 1915, and became prime minister again in 1920.

WWI & WWII

Fascism's rise after WWI was paralleled by that of trade unionism. In Turin, FIAT had profited enormously from WWI, increasing its 4000-strong workforce 10-fold by 1918. But soaring living costs, coupled with lousy wages after WWI, saw the membership of the dissident Unione Sindacale Italiana (Italian Trade Union) grow from 300,000 members in 1919 to over 800,000 by September 1920, when workers countrywide decided to strike. In Turin alone, over 150 factories were occupied, including Michelin's rubber-tyre plant, which had been churning out tyres since 1906. (Today Michelin employs more than 27,000 at its Cuneo plant.)

Industrial unrest on the factory floors of FIAT spawned the Italian Communist Party in 1921 under the leadership of Antonio Gramsci (1891–1937), a Turin university graduate. The same era saw the emergence of the Juventus football club as a force to be reckoned with, thanks to Giovanni Agnelli (p68), who took the club under his wealthy wing from 1923. The great old industrialist had built the Sestriere ski resort

Juventus FC players originally wore pink on the pitch. It was only after a wrong shipment of shirts arrived from England, where they were manufactured, in 1903 that the side made the switch to today's black-and-white striped strip.

1940–45

Fascist Italy enters WWII on Nazi Germany's side; Allied bombings destroy much of central Turin; Northern Italy is liberated in May 1945

1960s

Large-scale migration of southern Italians to northern Italy as Turin's FIAT becomes the driving force of Italian industry

Keep abreast with policies, events and political happenings with the Lega Nord (Northern League) at www.leganord.org, www.padania.to.it and www.naz-piemonte. leganord.org.

in the 1930s, and in the late 1960s he demonstrated his passion for fast cars by buying a chunk of the Ferrari company.

During WWII, allied bombings destroyed vast areas of Turin. The city was liberated from the Germans and Italian fascists in May 1945, after Allied troops broke through German lines. In Alba, citizens declared an independent republic, after partisans liberated it from the Germans. It lasted 23 days.

War-torn Turin was struck by tragedy again in 1949 when the plane carrying the Grande Torino football team crashed into the Basilica di Superga near Turin in thick fog, killing all 31 on board, including the national footballer of the day Valentino Mazzola (1919–49).

INDUSTRIAL PIEDMONT

Swift postwar economic recovery hailed the dawning of a new era. At FIAT, output leapt from 425,000 cars in 1960 to 1.7 million by 1970. The company bought Ferrari in 1969, and in 1978 it swallowed up the financially troubled Lancia car manufacturer. Its takeover of Milan-born Alfa Romeo in 1986 gave FIAT a monopoly on the Italian car-manufacturing market. With such a boom, southern Italians flocked to the cold and cloudy north to find factory work in the wealthy regional capital.

The construction of large exhibition centres, such as Turin's Lingotto Fiere, signalled the birth of northern Italy's trade-fair industry. The 11.7km-long Mt Blanc Tunnel opened in 1965, prompting an immediate and dramatic increase in tourism and traffic in the formerly quiet Valle d'Aosta, west of Turin, as the road tunnel became a major road-freight thoroughfare between Italy and France. When a second road tunnel, the 12.9km-long Fréjus Tunnel, was burrowed out between the two countries in 1980, there was no escaping Turin's continuing growth as a transport hub. Trains between Paris and Turin have whizzed beneath Piedmont, courtesy of the Mt Cenis Tunnel (built between 1857 and 1871), since the end of the 19th century.

POLITICAL POWER-PLAY

With the waning of economic muscle in the late 1960s, social unrest spawned the terrorist group, Brigate Rosse (Red Brigades). Brigate Rosse operated throughout the so-called *Anni di Piombo* (Years of Lead; 1973–80), with 1977 seeing a major recruiting campaign inject new zest into the movement. One of the region's more unfortunate sons, General Carlo dalla Chiesa from Saluzzo, was appointed to wipe out the terrorist group. His implacable pursuit of the Mafia-like Brigate Rosse led to his assassination in 1982.

The 1990s were marred by Tangentopoli (literally 'kickback cities'), a political scandal that broke in early 1992 when a functionary of the Partito Socialista Italiano (PSI; Italian Socialist Party) was arrested on charges of accepting bribes in exchange for public-works contracts. Thousands of top politicians and businessmen were implicated in the scandal, which wiped out the centre of the Italian political spectrum and paved the way for new political parties to emerge. In 2000 a right-wing coalition won the regional elections, with Enzo Ghigo becoming president of the Piedmont region. Left-wing Sergio Chiamparino was appointed mayor of Turin in 2001.

DID YOU KNOW?

In 1986 Turin-born developmental biologist Rita Levi-Montalcini won the Nobel Prize in Physiology for her discovery of growth-nerve factor (GNF) based on experiments she'd carried out with mice and chicken embryos in the 1950s.

1999	2003
Piedmont is picked as host city for the XX Winter Olympic Games in 2006	FIAT crisis: Turin mourns the death of its auto godfather, Giovanni Agnelli; 12,300 jobs axed in a bid to save the company

The Culture

REGIONAL IDENTITY

Cold, closed and as proud as punch are characteristics piled on Piedmontese by other Italians – and invariably by Piedmontese too, should one be so pertinent as to ask.

Piedmont completely contradicts the stereotypical sun-loving, work-shy Italian image. In this chilly northern neck of the woods, it is far too cold to linger on the streets or leave front doors open. People are accustomed to hard work and working hard. They are resilient and resourceful, with an almost brutal determination and independence spawned by their region's great industrial heritage.

Caginess toward and suspicion of anyone not from Turin is a result of the mass immigration of workers from southern Italy to the regional capital in the 1960s.

The entrepreneurial energy and creativity that many Turinese possess was also kindled by industry, which prompted people to dream up new means of making money.

Within the region, people from Asti are considered the most exuberant. Always armed with a glass of wine and slice of salami in hand, they welcome outsiders and bear a happy-go-lucky attitude towards life. The Cuneo crowd is less forthcoming, but a jolly bunch nonetheless, albeit the butt of regional jokes: simple country folk, who always drive with their headlights on, say scornful Turinese (who, in turn, allegedly have a *braccio corto* – literally, a 'short arm', meaning to be stingy). Few dare mock Piedmont's mountain inhabitants, for whom everyone has a deep-rooted respect.

Optimistic and with a good sense of humour, passionately loyal to their friends, and passionate about wine, food, football and cars, are classic labels worn across the region. *Piemontese falso e cortese* (literally 'false and kind', meaning appearing to be generous but actually the contrary) is a common expression.

Piemonte Magazine Online at www.piemonte-online.com is just that – an online magazine devoted to regional culture, history and tradition.

LIFESTYLE

Strolling beneath the porticoes of Turin's Via Roma on Sunday is an eye-opener. First come the well-dressed and well-heeled, out to buy cake for traditional family Sunday lunch. Next come the Juve fans, en route to the football stadium for the Sunday match. Then there's the afternoon horde, a younger crowd that hails from suburbia and hits the centre to hang out.

THE OTHER FACE OF PIEDMONT

Gianduja is not just a hazelnut chocolate paste to die for. It is a stock character in the 16th-century comedy, *Commedia dell'Arte*, and in the late 18th century Turinese puppeteer Gian Battista Sales turned the cheery chap into a marionette. Today, it's the face of Piedmont – albeit in the shape of a mask – at carnival.

Conservative, good humoured, naive and honest are characteristics embodied by Gianduja, the Piedmontese puppet peasant, whose original name in local dialect was Giöan d'la douja (*douja* being a terracotta wine jug unique to Asti). The plucky little fellow has three big loves in life – food, wine and his girlfriend Giacometta. Recognise him by his red-trimmed brown jacket, yellow waistcoat, pea-green knickerbockers and tomato-red stockings.

Springtime carnival aside, Gianduja appears at the traditional celebrations held in Turin on 24 June to honour San Giovanni (St John), the city's patron saint.

In a city where one family owns everything from the football club and newspaper to one of Europe's biggest car manufacturers, it comes as no surprise that some people call Turin 'FIAT ville'. For decades, shop opening hours, cinema schedules and so on in Turin were dictated solely by FIAT working-shift hours. Come the 1960s, FIAT expansion brought waves of southern Italians who, along with their cheap factory labour, brought tomato sauce, pizza and a sun-inspired flamboyancy previously unheard of.

Yet traditional dynamics have shifted. FIAT is no longer the global power it was in the 1980s, and scores of multinational companies have set up shop and paved the way for new cultural and economic creativity. A new generation, prepared to reinvent the traditional wheel in a multicultural context, does account for a chunk of contemporary urban society.

Women constitute 42% of Piedmont's workforce (compared to 39% in 1995 and 37.5% nationally) and unemployment in the region is low at 4% (compared with 8.5% nationally and 17% in southern Italy). Around 25% of people feel, nonetheless, that they are financially worse off than a year ago, with 5% struggling to pay the monthly bills.

Gays and lesbians can walk with ease in Turin, but might encounter discrimination in more rural climes (p146).

Discover how often people in Piedmont drink fizzy drinks, how many eggs they eat a day or how often they eat greens with Piemonte in *Cifre* (www.piemonteincifre .it), the regional statistical yearbook.

POPULATION

While people in Turin live in each other's pockets (6909 people per sq km), the surrounding region has lots of empty space with 170 inhabitants per sq km. Piedmont is home to 7% of Italy's populace.

Northern Italy's foreign population rose by 20% in 1999 (compared to 15% in central and southern Italy). Of Piedmont's 92,768 registered foreign residents, half live in Turin: Moroccans, Albanians and Romanians form the largest communities.

If it weren't for immigration, Piedmont's population would be rapidly shrinking. With nearly a fifth of the population aged over 65, Piedmontese (as with Italians in general) are dying quicker than they're arriving. Every woman would need to bear an average of 2.1 children to keep the population stable – Piedmontese women currently average 1.1 children a head (the national average is 1.2).

ARTS
Literature

Poetry was the main vehicle of expression in early literature, with Asti writer Vittorio Alfieri (1749–1803) adding a tragic element to the whole affair.

Modern Italian literature ushered in Edmondo de Amicis (1846–1908) with his novel, *Cuore* (1886), the tale of a boy's schooldays in Turin.

Palermo-born Natalia Ginzburg (1916–91) spent most of her life in Turin, evoking her adopted city in semi-autobiographical novels such as *Tutti i Nostri Ieri* (All Our Yesterdays; 1952). Capturing the essence of gestures and moments in daily life is her trademark.

Giulio Einaudi (1912–99) opened his publishing house in 1931. The intellectual published dozens of politically inspired books after WWII, including the Communist works written in prison by Antonio Gramsci (p21).

Fascism nurtured a wealth of novelists, including Cesare Pavese (1908–50), whose original manuscripts can be read at the Centro Studi Cesare Pavese in Santo Stefano Belbo (p113), the village where the Langhe writer was born. Pavese spent his literary career in Turin; his greatest novel, *La Luna e Il Falò* (The Moon and the Bonfire; 1950) was published the year he committed suicide in his room at Hotel Roma e Rocca Cavour. Platti (p75) and Tre Galline (p79) were regular Turin haunts of the troubled writer.

PIEDMONTESE PROVERBS

▪ Garlic is the country man's pharmacist – *L'aglio è il farmacista dell'uomo di campagna.*

▪ There's no such thing as a beautiful shoe that doesn't become a slipper – *Non esiste bella scarpa che non diventi ciabatta.*

▪ It's only the mountains that never meet – *Soltanto le montagne non s'incontrano.*

▪ Better a friend than 10 relatives – *Meglio un amico che dieci parenti.*

Like Pavese, Turinese doctor Carlo Levi (1902–75) experienced internal exile in southern Italy under fascism. The result was *Cristo si è Fermato ad Eboli* (Christ Stopped at Eboli; 1945), a moving account of an oppressed world forgotten by Rome.

Turin-born Jew Primo Levi (1919–87) ended up in Auschwitz His poetry collection, *Se Quest'è Un Uomo* (If This is a Man; 1958), is the dignified account of his survival. *Other People's Trades* (1985) includes an account of the Turin apartment at Corso Re Umberto 75, where he committed suicide (by throwing himself down a stairwell in the apartment block).

The treatment of Italy's 48,000-strong Jewish population during WWII is the emotive focus of *Le Strade di Polvere* (The Dust Roads of Monferrato; 1991) by Rosetta Loy (b 1931).

Straight, blunt and bare of rhetoric are the trademarks of Alba writer Beppe Fenoglio (1922–63). Drawing on his experiences as a WWII partisan in the Langhe region, Beppe wrote *I Ventitrè Giorni della Città di Alba* (The Twenty-Three Days of the City of Alba; 1952) and *Il Partigiano Johnny* (Johnny the Partisan; 1968). The life of the Langhe farmer and the remote nature of the land are recurrent themes.

Italian literature in the 1980s was dominated by Alessandria-born intellectual Umberto Eco (b 1932) who shot to popularity with *Il Nome della Rosa* (The Name of the Rose; 1980).

Turin's Alessandro Baricco (b 1958) is one of Italy's boldest contemporary writers. The inventive novelist has scooped literary prizes galore with his strikingly modern prose. *Oceano Mare* (Ocean Sea; 1993), *Seta* (Silk; 1996) and *City* (City; 2001) have all been published in English; Silk has been translated into 27 languages.

Asti-born Bruno Gambarotta (b 1937) writes thrillers from his base in Turin.

Music

No Piedmontese voice is better known than that of Paolo Conte (b 1937; http://paoloconte.warnermusic.it), an Asti-born lawyer, who quit the bar for the stage in the 1970s. Jazz forms the backbone of his gently lyrical songs. In a similar vein is Gianmaria Testa (www.gianmariatesta.com in Italian), a Cuneo voice sufficiently raspy to be deemed sexy.

Mau Mau (www.maumau.it in Italian) and Subsonica steal the show in Turin's dynamic contemporary-music scene. The Mau Mau trio generates an eclectic sound with its innovative use of language (a mix of Italian, French, Spanish and Piedmontese dialect) and acoustics. More world music is contributed by Turin ska band Statuto; Tribà (www.tribafaila.it in Italian); and the Marley-inspired reggae band, Africa Unite (www.africaunite.com in Italian) from Pinerolo.

Turinese production house PiemonteGroove (www.piemontegroove .com) works with electronic dance artists, including funk DJ Roger Rama; experimental DJ Lorenzo LSP; the Nig Nig Nig duo, active in the mid-

---

WHEN IN PIEDMONT DO AS THE PIEDMONTESE DO

■ Shopping in Turin requires etiquette; killer glares from shop assistants will establish if you're doing things right or wrong. Stroking and fondling is frowned upon – ask if you want to try on a garment or inspect it more closely.

■ Sun or no sun, city slickers keen to melt into the Turinese crowd should don dark shades.

■ In rainy weather, umbrellas are allowed no further than the threshold. Most shops, cafés, restaurants and museums sport a soggy-brolly stand at their entrance.

■ Dress modestly in churches – no shorts, short skirts or bare shoulders. Avoid visiting a church during mass or other services.

1990s; and Eiffel 65, a three-man band known for its mix of pop, techno and acid house. The band's DJ element, Turin-born Gabry Ponte (www .gabryponte.com, in Italian), topped the Italian club charts with his first solo single in 2001.

Another strong presence on the Italian dance scene is Feel Good Productions whose album *Funky Farmers* (2003) pays homage to the Langhe farmhouse where the duo started out. DJs Sergio Ricciardone and Giorgio Valletta are the faces behind Xplosiva (www.xplosiva.com), a Turin-based project that fuses funk with break beat, house and techno.

Named after Turin's No 77 bus route, which took them to rehearsals, Linea 77 (www.linea77.com) is a five-piece rock band with a clutch of albums – *Too Much Happiness Makes Kids Paranoid* (2000), *Ketchup Suicide* (2001) and *Numb* (2003) – to its name. Marlene Kuntz, Medusa and Mambassa are other local rock bands to enjoy recognition outside of Piedmont.

Architecture

Piedmont's most notable contribution to European architecture is Turin's baroque collection. As royal architect to the Savoys from 1615, Carlo di Castellamonte (1560–1641) worked on Castello del Valentino (p67), Palazzo Madama (p69) and Piazza San Carlo (p64). The city was further enlarged under Guarino Guarini (1624–83), specialised in chapels and churches. Under Filippo Juvarra (1678–1736), the Savoy capital became an architectural masterpiece: look no further than Palazzo Reale (p62), Palazzo Madama (1718–21; p59), Palazzina di Caccia di Stupinigi (1729; p67) or Basilica di Superga (1715–31; p66) to see why.

In the 19th century Ghemme-born Alessandro Antonelli (1798–1888), from eastern Piedmont, conjured up the most fabulous silhouette on Turin's skyline, the Mole Antonelliana (p66). He also did the 121m-tall baroque cupola atop Novara's Basilica di San Gaudenzio (p134).

A perfect reflection of 20th-century *Stilo Liberty* (Art Nouveau) is Villa Falcini (1902–04) in Domodossola, designed by Turinese architect Annibale Rigotti (1870-1968). Rigotti's later works were influenced by the grandiose style that Mussolini and the Fascist era ushered in. Turin's original FIAT factory in Lingotto (1926) – a five-storey concrete monster (with a roof-top race track) that Le Corbusier hailed as a 'cathedral of technology' – dates to this era. In 1988 Italian architect Renzo Piano started transforming the industrial factory into a hi-tech cultural-centre-cum-shopping-mall, complete with conference room in a blue glass bubble and an art gallery (p67) in a steel 'treasure box'.

Rationalist architect Pier Luigi Nervi (1891–1979) built Turin's exposition hall (1949) and the Palavela (1961), with its innovative sail-shaped roof. Bauhaus inspired the glass facades of the 1950s Olivetti factory buildings in Ivrea, part of a modern architecture museum (p138) today.

Wild child Carlo Mollino (1905–73) was behind Turin's RAI auditorium (1950–53), chamber of commerce (1964) and other civic buildings. In 1959 Mollino scandalously donned the Sala a Ballo Lutrario (dance hall) with neon lights, multicoloured furniture, polychrome tiles, star-spangled curtains and a wacky mosaic floor.

Contemporary architecture has endowed Piedmont with some stunning constructions, and Turin leads the way, thanks partly to its role as 2006 Winter Olympic host (p42 & p63). The university's new Humanities faculty, on the industrial banks of the Dora, was designed by Norman Foster, while Massimiliano Fuksas provided the creative inspiration behind the futuristic glass-towered Palazzo della Regione (2001–04).

Label – essential reading for any contemporary-arts, architecture, fashion, style and culture fiend – is *The Face*, *Wallpaper* and *DazedAndConfused* rolled into one. The Piedmontese avant-garde mag (www.labelmag.com) is published quarterly.

Design

No product better epitomises Italian design than the Vespa (literally 'wasp'), a lightweight scooter designed in Biella in 1946 by Piaggio, a war-wounded Ligurian aircraft manufacturer, who moved operations to eastern Piedmont during the war.

Another Piedmont-born design icon was the Topolino (literally 'little mouse', but also Italian for Mickey Mouse), the first passenger car to be small enough and cheap enough for Joe Bloggs to buy. Developed in 1936 by FIAT, the Topolino was one of dozens of models rolled out by the Turinese car manufacturer; view early models at Turin's Museo dell'Automobile (p67). Many were designed by Nuccio Bertone (1914–97), a car designer who worked with Lancia, Alfa Romeo, Lamborghini and Ferrari from his Grugliasco factory on Turin's outskirts. Italdesign-Giugiaro, founded by Cuneo-born Giogetto Giugiario (b 1938) in 1968, and Pininfarina (founded 1930) are hot-shot design houses driving contemporary car design.

Kitchen and household appliance design was revolutionised by Bialetti and Alessi. Alfonso Bialetti created the Moka Express aluminium coffee-making pot with its distinctive eight-sided shape – a standard in kitchens worldwide today – in Omegna in 1931. Lagostina, founded in the same town in 1901, was the first to design cutlery in stainless steel. Discover more about Omegna's product design industry at the Forum di Omegna (p131), appropriately housed in a converted steel works.

The 1950s ushered in the Olivetti typewriter, manufactured by the Ivrea-based company, founded by Camillo Olivetti (1868–1943) in 1908.

Italian furniture design made its mark in 1972 with an exhibition entitled 'Italy: The New Domestic Landscape' held in New York's Museum of Modern Art. Radical avant-garde works such as *Bocca*, a sultry sofa shaped like a pair of red lips, produced by Turin-based design house Gufram (founded 1966), formed the backbone of the exhibition. The 1980s produced the postmodernist forms of Turin university graduate, Ettore Sottsass (1917–), known for multicoloured works, such as his *Carlton* (1982) set of shelves.

DID YOU KNOW?

An early machine for washing clothes – comprising a lower tub of boiling water with a pipe in the middle through which the soap bubbles were sucked up and slopped around the clothes in the top tub – was the inspiration behind the Bialetti espresso-making pot.

UNESCO WORLD HERITAGE SITES IN PIEDMONT

Among the world's fabulous architectural treasures are:

- The Royal Residences of the House of Savoy (listed in 1997; p12)
- *Sacri Monti* (sacred mountains) of Piedmont and Lombardy (2003; p30)

ALESSI: THE DREAM FACTORY

Borne out of a miniscule copper, brass and nickel silver workshop founded on the shores of Lago d'Orta by sheet-metal worker Nonno (Grandpa) Giovanni in 1921, Alessi is today a world leader in household design. No icon is more instantly recognisable than the little King-Kong man adorning Alessi's leading product line, which has made household design accessible to the masses.

To survive WWII, Alessi made mechanical plane parts, stars for uniforms and later brass ladles for the US army. In the 1950s it scrapped silver for stainless steel and roped in designers from outside (Ron Arad, Philippe Starck, David Chipperfield) to create the fun, innovative and colourfully wacky kitchen products for which the company is known today.

Alessi employs 500-odd people and exports 65% of its annual turnover to 60 countries. Its life, times and designs can be discovered at the **Museo Alessi** (p131), a state-of-the-art museum that doubles as an archive for 20th-century product design. It is inside Alessi's designer headquarters, otherwise called the *fabbrica dei sogni* (dream factory).

Piedmont has made strides on the catwalk, thanks to textile manufacturers such as cashmere king Loro Piana, headquartered since 1924 in Quarona near Vercelli; woollen whizz Ermenegildo Zegna, a family-run business dating to 1910; and Biella-based Cerruti (1881).

Turin-based fashion designer Carlo Pignatelli turns heads with his snappy formal wear designs (p86).

Cinema

Screenings of silent B&W pictures took place in Turin as early as 1896, but it was not until the start of the 20th century that production studios such as F.E.R.T. (Filming with a European Regard in Turin), Ambrosio and Italia Film mushroomed in the city, and peaked at 50 by 1914.

The first Piedmont-made blockbuster was the 123-minute *Cabiria* (1914), a silent epic in which Asti-born film director, Giovanni Pastrone (1882–1959), pioneered techniques such as the dolly and parallel action montage. See snippets of the film at Turin's Museo Nazionale del Cinema (p66).

Italian filmmakers have used Turin as the backdrop for scores of films. It was the steps of Turin's Chiesa della Gran Madre di Dio (p66) that Michael Caine careered down in his Mini Cooper in the cult movie, *The Italian Job* (1968); while it was Turin that horror-movie maker Dario Argento chose for *Profondo Rosso* (Deep Red; 1975) and *Non Ho Sonno* (Sleepless; 2001). *La Donna della Domenica* (The Sunday Woman; 1976) by Luigi Comencini (in which someone is bizarrely bludgeoned to death by a ceramic phallus); Mimmo Calopresti's *La Seconda Volta* (The Second Time; 1995); and *Così Ridevano* (1998), directed by Gianni Amelio are others. The multicultural face of modern Turin is painted in *Tango Story* (2003), a film about an Argentinian immigrant tangoing around the city.

In 2001 Piero Chiambretti, a Turin-based showman and TV personality famed countrywide for his satirical wit, shot parts of his film (in which he plays a TV presenter), *Ogni lasciato è perso* (Everything left is lost) in the city. The same year saw Piedmont's funniest product, Turin-born TV comic Luciana Littizzetto (b 1964), also try her hand at film with the Italian-style Bridget Jones comedy, *Ravanello Pallido* (Pale Radish; 2001).

'Every woman, sooner or later, looks at herself in the mirror and would like to slice her face off with a machete' is one of many witty but true observations on womanhood made by cult comedian Luciana Littizzetto in her confessional bestseller *Sola come un gambo di sedano* (Alone Like a Celery Stalk, 2001).

Environment

THE LAND

Piedmont embraces a brilliant riot of peaks and plains in the northwestern corner of Italy's boot leg: one-third of the region sits above 900m while a soggy third shrugs in sheepishly at 300m or less.

The Western Alps are the sole mountain range. They stretch along Piedmont's western boundary with France and the Valle d'Aosta (another Italian region), and peak in northern Piedmont with Europe's second-highest mountain, Monte Rosa, on the Italian-Swiss border. The Dufour summit (4633m) is one of 22 *punta* (peaks) atop the Rosa massif.

Other giants (from south to north) are Argentera (3297m) in the Maritime Alps (Alpi Marittime; the section of Alps in southern Piedmont); Monviso (3841m) in the Cottian Alps (Alpi Cozie; the middle Alpine stretch from the Colle della Maddalena to Mont Cenis); and Gran Paradiso (4061m) in the Graian Alps (Alpi Graie; the Alpine stretch along the northern part of the Italian, French and Valle d'Aosta border). Monte Rosa and everything north of it falls into the Pennine Alps (Alpi Pennine).

Moving east, Alpine foothills spill into Lago Maggiore, one of Italy's largest lakes, which is split down the middle between northern Piedmont and Lombardy. From the lake's southern foot, the River Ticino snakes south along the regional border, past the flat lands of Novara and Vercelli, into the River Po. The Po – Italy's longest river at 652km – traverses the entire region, flowing west from its Alpine source at the foot of Monviso.

Other notable rivers include the Dora Baltea, Sangone and Stura di Lanzo – all of which meet the Po at Turin.

WILDLIFE

The region's varied landscape makes for a colourful range of flora and fauna.

Animals

In 1856 Victor Emmanuel II turned a chunk of Alpine Piedmont into a royal hunting reserve, thus saving the ibex (mountain goat) from extinction. Today it roams in the Parco Nazionale del Gran Paradiso (home to about 4000), Parco Naturale Alta Valsesia and other high-altitude areas. The marmot, with its shrill whistle of warning, lingers around 2000m to 3000m, while the fox and mouflon (a type of sheep) live below the tree line. Chamois, deer and wolves are other Alpine fauna.

DID YOU KNOW?

The region's name, Piemonte – meaning 'at the foot of the mountain' or 'foothills' – was coined in the 12th century.

Where to Watch Birds in Italy, published by the Italian Bird Protection League (LIPU), highlights over 100 recommendations for species spotting.

Field Guide to Wildflowers of Southern Europe, by Paul Davies and Bob Gibbons, is a pocket-sized identification guide covering around 1200 species.

WHERE TO WATCH WILDLIFE

The two national parks and many of their smaller siblings encourage green-minded visitors to hook up with a naturalistic guide to watch wildlife; details are in the relevant regional chapters. Otherwise, the following observation posts are worth a gander:

- **Migratory birds** at the Centro Studi sulle Migrazione (Migration Study Centre), Fondotoce (p129)
- **Pregnant and newborn deer** at the Osservatorio Faunistico (fauna observatory), Madonna d'Ardua, Parco Alto Valle Pesio e Tanaro
- **White storks and rare ducks** at the Centro Cicogne e Anatidi (White Stork & Anatidae Centre), Racconigi (p116)

DID YOU KNOW?

The white stork flees Piedmont in August, winters in Africa, and returns to nest in March, laying eggs at 36-hour intervals. Some 60% of storks are poached or frazzled to death by overhead electric wires during migration.

The bearded vulture, with its mighty 3m wing span and unsavoury diet of corpse bones, was reintroduced to the Alps in the late 1980s (it disappeared in 1912). Other birds of prey include the golden eagle (17 pairs live in the Parco Nazionale del Gran Paradiso and another seven in the Parco Naturale delle Alpi Marittime), the buzzard, and the kestrel.

The banks of the River Po and the lakeshores of Candia (near Ivrea) and Maggiore (northern Piedmont) lure migratory birdlife. The purple heron, great white egret, bittern and marsh warbler are less-common species. Italy's tiny population of wall lizards inhabits the Po's banks near Saluzzo, while the rare Lanza's black salamander mucks about in the peat bogs at the river's source. The tawny owl, woodpecker and jay are among the 40 species that nest in nature reserves around Asti.

Since the late 1980s the white stork, shot out of Italy's skies by hunters in the 18th century, has been bred at the Centro Cicogne e Anatidi (p116) in Racconigi. The centre, run by the Italian Bird Protection League (LIPU; www.lipu.it in Italian), also breeds threatened duck species.

Plants

Summer grass and winter shrubs, shoots, lichen and conifer needles feed the hungry ibex. The oak and beech tree, dwarf pine, rhododendron, whortleberry and green alder are other species to carpet much of the mountain range, while spruce and silver firs, stone pines and larch trees stud the lower wooded valleys. Botanists can also spot the edelweiss (between 1500m and 3200m) and the exquisite mountain lily.

Log into the official Italian national parks website, www.parks.it, for comprehensive information on Piedmont's parks and reserves, useful publications, details of local wildlife, weather forecasts and educational initiatives.

Southern Piedmont's Parco Naturale delle Alpi Marittime boasts 2600 plant species – more than half of all those found in Italy. The rare *Saxifraga florulenta*, a delicate lilac flower endemic to the Maritime Alps, flowers then dies.

Some of the country's most notable examples of fluvial forest straddle the Po and Ticino. Subtropical flora such as azaleas, magnolias and acacias flourish around Lago Maggiore. Italy's tallest palm trees grow on the fertile island of Madre and several rare and endemic species stud Villa Taranto's lush gardens in Verbania (p129).

ENVIRONMENTAL ISSUES

Air pollution menaces Turin: carbon monoxide emissions create a filthy headache thanks to the city's over-zealous motorists (Italy ranks third in the world after the USA and Australia for the number of cars per capita). In 1999 a token handful of electric cars and buses were introduced in Turin, followed every year since by a series of car-free days in the city centre.

SACRED MOUNTAINS

No mountain has ever been too high for pilgrims who, in the 16th and 17th centuries, scaled great heights to build exquisite sanctuaries in Mother Nature's green heart. Since 2003, these so-called *sacri monti* (sacred mountains) have been Unesco World Heritage sites.

- Sacro Monte Calvario, Domodossola (p133)
- Sacro Monte della Beata Vergine, Oropa
- Sacro Monte della SS Trinità, Ghiffa
- Sacro Monte di Belmonte, Valperga
- Sacro Monte di San Francesco, Orta San Giulio
- Sacro Monte di Santa Maria Assunta, Serralunga di Crea
- Sacro Monte di Varallo, Varallo (p131)

NATIONAL PARKS

Piedmont is protected by two national parks and 56 smaller regional parks and reserves, embracing 1930 sq km (7.6%) of the region. Notable parks include:

Park	Features	Activities	Best time to visit	Page
Parco Naturale delle Alpi Marittime (278 sq km)	Piedmont's largest park; glacial lakes, Alpine meadows, valleys and plus peaks: chamois, golden eagle, wild boar, wolf	botanical trails, climbing, walking	spring & summer	p119
Parco Naturale dell'Alta Valsesia (65 sq km)	Europe's highest protected area at 900–4559m, Walser land bordering Monte Rosa: chamois, deer, golden eagle	glaciological walking trail, Walser house visits	spring & summer	p131
Parchi e Riserve Astigiani (6.5 sq km)	Three protected pockets of woodland and chestnut groves, rich in fossils, around Asti: badger, fox, weasel	cycling, horse-riding, 'green' gymnastics, walking	spring & summer	p105
Parco Nazionale del Gran Paradiso (700 sq km)	Stunning mountain peaks, glaciers and lakes, alpine woods and grasslands (800–4061m); protected since 1922: marmot, ibex (mountain goat), golden eagle, bearded vulture, wolf	bird-watching, botany, climbing, cross-country skiing, horse-riding, snow-shoeing, walking	Jun-Sep (summer activities), Dec-Apr (skiing)	p141
Parco Naturale del Lago di Candia (3.4 sq km)	The most important bird-watching wetland in Piedmont; glacial lake fed by springs; great white egret, purple heron	bird-watching, cycling, lakeside strolling, rowing	spring, summer & autumn	p139
Parco Naturale Orsiera Rocciavrè (112 sq km)	Alpine landscape between Susa, Chisone and Sangone Valleys; glacial lakes and valleys, grassland, four peaks above 2800m: chamois, golden eagle, mouflon	climbing, cross-country skiing, horse-riding, mountain-biking	year-round	p95
Parco Fluviale del Po Torinese (217 sq km)	Riverside reserve (240–3841m) split into three sections, from west of Saluzzo to paddy fields around Alessandria: wild boar, salamander, heron, kite, buzzard	bird-watching, cycling, cross-country skiing, mountain-biking, walking	year-round	p116
Parco Nazionale della Val Grande (146 sq km)	Italy's largest protected wilderness; mountains, valleys, rock engravings and chestnut woods: chamois, deer, shrew, vole, black grouse, golden eagle, viper	bird-watching, guided itineraries, rock-climbing, walking	spring & summer	p133

WWF PIEMONTE

WWF Italia (www.wwf.it), Italy's largest environmental association, safeguards Italy's endangered species and manages five *oasi* (protected areas) in Piedmont.

For information on how to visit and/or work as a volunteer in these protected areas, as well as details of green holidays, nature treks and other nature activities, contact **WWF Piemonte** (☎ 011 473 18 73; Via Peyron 10, 10143 Turin; www.wwfpiemonte.com in Italian).

Litter-conscious visitors will be astounded by the amount of rubbish littered about. In 2002, as part of its Save the Glaciers campaign, cleaning-product manufacturer Lever Fabergé Italy cleaned up the Stelvio glacier on Monte Rosa. The team collected 20,000kg of plastic, cans and glass – some had lurked in the ice for 40 years – while teams in helicopters picked up 18,000kg of construction waste (wood, pylons, ski lifts and the like) from the mountain.

Avalanches, a natural hazard in the Alps, claimed 10 lives during the 2000–01 winter ski season.

Excessive building near rivers and deforestation are key factors in the alarming rise of floods to hit Piedmont. Severe flooding occurred in 1951, 1994 and again in 2000, when flood waters killed 30 people, destroyed 4000 homes and left 40,000 temporarily homeless after the Po burst its banks during torrential rain storms.

Arsonists and irresponsible walkers are further man-made pests to the environment. In 2002, forest fires swept across 35.5 sq km of land (compared to 12.8 sq km the previous year).

Piedmont Outdoors

Blessed with a geography of mountains, hills, lakes and plains, Piedmont is a veritable outdoor playground. In winter, the snow-packed slopes of the Alpine ski resorts attract skiers, boarders, daredevils and poseurs in equal measure; in summer, the same mountains hum with earnest activity as thousands of ramblers, hikers, climbers and cyclists pursue their passions. The wine-rich hills of the Langhe district and the flatlands following the course of the River Po are perfect for days in the saddle, a tasty treat never far away. For those who prefer their thrills in the water, there is a range of sports available, from sedate pootling around on the lakes to wicked white-water tubing in the upper Valsesia.

Tourist offices across the region have bundles of brochures, which they'll happily unload on you, detailing hundreds of itineraries, venues, seasons and organisations.

See www.montagnedoc.it for stacks of information on taking time out in the Olympic mountains.

SKIING

Piedmont's most prestigious ski resorts are to host the 2006 Winter Olympics (p37). Located in the Valle di Susa and Val Chisone, west of Turin, they offer some of the best skiing in the Italian Alps, with nursery slopes for beginners and World Cup black runs for experts.

However, skiing in the region isn't confined to these western reaches. There are popular resorts near the southern city of Cuneo (p120) and in the north, the upper Valsesia (p132) is much frequented. Travellers can even pop up to the pistes of Monte Mottarone (p124) above Lago Maggiore.

The ski season runs from November to April. Prices skyrocket over the New Year holiday, while February is usually the most expensive month. The cost of passes varies hugely, but as a rough guide a six-day pass will cost between €100 and €140 in the low season, €120 to €160 in high season.

Cream of the resort crop is Sestriere (p96), the Agnelli-built resort deep in the heart of the Val Chisone. Along with Sauze d'Oulx (p99), Claviere (p97) and Cesana (p97), it forms the Via Lattea (Milky Way) domain, 400km of interlinked pistes. Nearby the resort of Bardonecchia (p99) has 110km of downhill runs.

Lonely Planet's *Cycling in Italy* has detailed descriptions of cycling routes in the Italian Alps.

Resorts in the south include Limone Piemonte (p120), a weekend favourite, and, in northern Piedmont, Alagna (p132) in the upper Valsesia.

WALKING

Rambling through the summer pastures does it for some people; for others nothing less than a hearty hike over an Alpine peak or two will satisfy. In Piedmont you'll find everything from beautiful riverside walks to extremely tough mountain treks.

TOP FIVE: SPORTING ADVENTURES

- Floodlit skiing by night, Sestriere (p96)
- Golf in Sestriere and Claviere (p97)
- Horse riding in Bardonecchia (p99)
- Mushing in San Sicario (p43)
- Trekking with snow rackets in Bardonecchia (p99)

MOUNTAIN BIKING

Piedmont boasts hundreds of kilometres of bike paths ranging from nice, flat rides in the Po plains, to seriously difficult Alpine climbs that test the pros. Not an expensive sport (it costs from €15 per day to hire a decent bike), there's no specialist equipment required and no particular training is necessary. Clearly a helmet is a wise precaution and in the higher paths, a windproof top is a good idea. For information on hiring a bike, see p69.

The ideal time for cycling is spring, when it's not too hot and the countryside is looking at its best. However if you don't mind a bit of snow and ice, it is also possible in winter. Before setting off you'd do well to arm yourself with a decent route map from the nearest tourist office.

The following are a selection of itineraries ranging from easy to very difficult.

Easy

From Pinerolo in the Val Chisone, this 30km circular route along the Ciclostrada Pinerolese takes in orchards, vineyards and three castles. Setting off from Pinerolo, follow the well-marked route for Stupinigi until Buriasco and its 14th-century castle. From here continue through Macello, complete with castle, to the third castle of the day at Osasco. Returning to Pinerolo takes you past Villa Torrione and its colourful park.

- Nearest town: Pinerolo (p93)
- Information: ☎ 0122 83 03 19
- www.montagnedoc.it

Medium

This 34.5km route, known as the Via dei Saraceni, takes in some spectacular mountain scenery and involves a climb of 1,089m. Departing from Sauze d'Oulx, head toward Monfol and a climb to Monte Genevris. From here continue along the crest, which divides the Valle di Susa from Val Chisone until the peak of Colle Basset. Here you begin your descent, which, by way of Lago Nero and the *rifugio* (mountain refuge) at Pian della Rocca, leads back to your starting point.

- Nearest town: Sauze d'Oulx (p99)
- Information: ☎ 0122 83 03 19
- www.montagnedoc.it

Difficult

Investigate the source of the Po in the Monviso massif with this 60km ride, which takes you up a 1,400m climb. Starting from Saluzzo head for the charming town of Revello in the shade of Monte Bracco. Continue to climb until Paesana, where you can either continue for Piano de Re and the source of the Po at 2,020m or turn off for Staffarda and its famous abbey.

- Nearest town: Saluzzo (p115)
- Information: ☎ 0171 69 02 17
- www.cuneoholiday.com

Very Difficult

A 131km route dedicated to cycling legend Fausto Coppi departs from Tortona and takes you along a circular path through 12 local towns, including Gavi with its wonderful wines, Castagnola, Grondona plus 16th-century towers and Rocchetta Ligure, at 717m the highest point of the ride. To follow the route simply follow the road signs to the next town.

- Nearest town: Alessandria (p107)
- Information: ☎ 0131 28 80 95
- www.alexala.it

The best months for walking in the mountainous areas are late June, July and September. The weather is usually good, although light snowfalls are not unheard of up on the high ground, and it's still light at 9pm. *Rifugi* (mountain huts) usually open their doors from mid-June to late September. In the lower-lying areas it's best to avoid high summer, if possible, as crowds are at their worst, temperatures are often stifling and mosquitoes can be a nuisance, especially around lakes and rivers.

For more detailed information on hiking in the mountains, contact the Club Alpino Italiano on ☎ 01153 79 83 or online at www.caiuget.it (Italian only).

When walking always remember the basic rules of the game: don't throw litter; stay on the paths, especially in the mountains, where it can be dangerous to veer off as well as damaging to the environment; and don't light fires except in appointed areas.

Tourist offices throughout the area can provide maps and walking itineraries.

The big challenge for walkers is the two-week Grande Traversata delle Alpi (GTA), starting near Viozene in southern Piedmont, following a network of Alpine *rifugi* north through the province of Cuneo, Valle di Susa and the Parco Nazionale del Gran Paradiso. It continues across the north of the region before ending on the banks of Lago Maggiore at Cannobio.

Walking is popular everywhere but for the best trails head to the mountain valleys – the Valle del Susa (p98) and Val Chisone (p93), the Monregalese region (p120) in the province of Cuneo and the Valsesia (p132) all offer spectacular walking.

WHITE-WATER SPORTS

The River Sesia (p132) is the place to enjoy some ripping white-water rides. The river, which in 2002 hosted the World Canoe Championships, flows from its source on the slopes of Monte Rosa down through the fantastic scenery of the Valsesia. A mecca for water rats, it's at its best between April and September, when the snows have melted and the warmer weather's kicking in.

Lonely Planet's *Walking in Italy* has extensive details about walks in the Piedmontese Alps.

Sports available include the traditional (canoeing, kayaking, white-water rafting) and the modern: canyoning (descending a river on foot or whatever body part best suits the water conditions); river trekking (similar to canyoning but done at higher altitudes where there's less water); hydrospeed (descending rapids on a floating bob); and tubing (shooting down a river on an inflatable ring).

For all of these sports you'll need to be able to swim and be in reasonably good physical shape. Any specialist equipment that's necessary can usually be provided by local operators. Costs vary, but bank on around €40 for a day's white-water rafting and about €210 for a week's canoeing course.

HORSES & HUSKIES

Horse riding is a much-loved way of exploring the countryside. Predominantly a summer activity, it is also possible to saddle up in the snow in some resorts. A popular approach is to book a place in an *agriturismo* where horse riding is an option. Contact **Agriturismo Piemonte** (☎ 011 224 65 47; www.agriturismopiemonte.it Italian only) for further details. In Bardonecchia (p99), **Silverado** (☎ 333 497 48 51) run a range of equine excursions; an hour's ride costs around €16.

Mushing with the huskies is available in the resort of **San Sicario** (p97). There are lessons for the basic theory, before you head to the snow-packed pine woods to practise; a day-long course (€35) culminates in a 7km run.

TESTING THE WATER

Famed for its sulphurous waters, the spa town of Acqui Terme (p108) is the place to go for a curative course of thermal treatment. At the two major centres you can bathe in the thermal waters, cake yourself in mud or feel your loose ends tightening under the skilled hands of a trained masseur. Mud baths start at €35, massages €49.

For an après-ski sweat there's no better place than Sestriere's plush Fitness Centre (p96). The sauna, Jacuzzis and Turkish bath are just what the doctor ordered.

Further information is available from **Varallo tourist office** (☎ 0163 56 44 04; www.turismovalsesiavercelli.it in Italian) and online at www.accadueo-sesia .it (Italian only).

GOLF

Golf is not a sport that usually springs to mind when thinking of Italy, but Piedmont has more than 40 courses and is at the forefront of the nation's golfing fraternity. Most courses are open year-round although some do close in winter – check with individual clubhouses.

Turin is particularly well supplied with seven courses in the city and environs. For information on special golfing passes see p69. But it's not only the regional capital that likes a good round. In Sestriere you can play on Europe's highest course (p96), while in the Lago Maggiore area some of the views from the smart Des Iles Borromees course are superb (p124).

Green fees depend on the club but expect to pay about €40 for a weekday round and more at the weekend.

The Winter Olympics

For 17 days in 2006, all eyes will be on Piedmont. As host to the XX Winter Olympic Games Turin 2006 (10–26 February 2006) and IX Paralympic Winter Games (10–19 March 2006), the regional capital and its mountainous surrounds will host more than one million spectators, who will come here to watch the world's elite sportsmen and women fight for gold.

THE GAMES: PAST TO PRESENT

The first Winter Olympics sped down the slopes of Chamonix, next-door neighbour to Piedmont, in 1924 – not that the stylish French ski resort knew it was hosting an event that would become one of world sport's hottest dates. The one-off extravaganza, then called International Sports Week, was only rechristened the Olympic Games two years later.

In *Journey of the Olympic Flame: Igniting the Olympic Spirit* Gayle Bodin Petty traces the tremendous travels of the Games' most potent symbol, from Olympia's ancient grove to the globe's furthest-flung corner.

With the exception of a war-torn lull between 1936 and 1948, the Winter Games have been held every four years since, flitting from Switzerland's ritzy glitzy St Moritz (1928, 1948) to California's Squaw Valley (1960), Sapporo in Japan (1972) and socialist Sarajevo (1984) in the former Yugoslavia. Until 1994, the Winter Games fell the same year as the Summer Games; today one or the other happens every two years.

Any country can compete for the gargantuan event by putting forward a candidate city chosen by its national Olympic committee (NOC), the winning city being elected by the International Olympic Committee (IOC). Rules for electing host cities were overhauled after a 1998 scandal revealed some members of the Switzerland-based IOC accepted bribes (cash, diamonds, prostitutes, college scholarships etc) in exchange for 'yes' votes for Salt Lake City, USA, to host the Winter Olympics in 2002.

Politics has always had a role to play on the Olympic stage: spectacular as they were, the 1936 Winter Games in Garmisch-Partenkirchen, Bavaria, were a mere cog in Nazi Germany's great propaganda machine. Four and eight years on, WWII forced the Games to be cancelled, only for Japan and Germany to be banned from fielding athletes in the 1948 Olympics. Cold War politics barred East Germany from the 1952 Games.

In 1956, while several countries pulled out of the Olympics in protest at the Soviet invasion of Hungary, the USSR competed for the first time – and scooped up more medals than any other country. Soviet domination of the Games continued until the superpower's demise in 1991: a US victory over the USSR in ice hockey in 1980 was the only time between 1964 and 1992 that the Soviet squad did not strike gold. The match went down in the Olympic annals as a 'miracle on ice'.

In keeping with the Olympic movement's commitment to nonviolence and equality, South Africa was not allowed to compete between 1960 and 1992. The 1992 Winter Games in Albertville, France, not only saw postapartheid South Africa field its first multiracial delegation of athletes, it also witnessed a unified Germany competing for the first time since 1936, and Croatia, Slovenia, Estonia, Latvia and Lithuania entering as independent nations. Two years on, in the midst of the Balkan conflict (1992–5), the Olympian spirit of peace and solidarity persuaded a Croatian, two Bosnians and a Serb to cast aside their political differences to crew the same four-man bob for Bosnia-Hercegovina.

The Olympics were conceived in ancient Greece in 776 BC as a celebration of peace. French baron Pierre de Coubertin (1863–1937) revived them in 1894.

In 1956 the Olympics were televised for the first time. This, coupled with the advent of satellite broadcasts a decade on, spawned a lucrative deal for the Games. Today's highly commercialised Olympics are funded by the sale of broadcasting rights (TV network NBC has paid €3.5 billion for the rights to broadcast the Turin Olympics into the USA); ticket sales; and a sponsorship programme that sees international corporations showcase their products in exchange for shed-loads of cash.

Piedmont landed the 2006 Olympics in 1999, beating off Helsinki (Finland), Klagenfurt (Austria), Sion (Switzerland), Poprad Tatry (Slovakia) and Zakopane (Poland) to win the host-city contract.

COMPETITORS

Only amateurs were allowed to participate in the earliest Games, 'love of the game' rather than material gain being the driving force. Today anyone can compete, although profiting from Olympic participation remains a cardinal sin: competitors and coaches cannot be paid to enter or take advantage of lucrative advertising deals during the Games.

Olympic athletes form part of a national team. They have to be nationals of the country they are representing and can be any age. Teams vary in size and are selected by the country's national sports federations. National qualifying heats determine team make-up in most sports, although more worldly Olympian principles, such as fair play on the pitch, nonviolence and setting a sporting example, play a part too. Ultimately national teams are fielded by the country's NOC – and accepted (or rejected in the case of apartheid South Africa between 1960 and 1992) by the IOC.

DID YOU KNOW?

Just 13 women (compared to 245 men) competed in the first Winter Games in 1924.

During the Games, athletes eat and sleep in the Olympic Village, built on site by the host country. Catholics, Protestants, Buddhists, Hindus, Muslims, Jews and those belonging to the Orthodox church pray, meditate or worship in specially designated areas, be it a purpose-built church, temple or mosque in the village. A daily newspaper keeps athletes abreast of what is happening (the paper will have an estimated daily circulation of 10,000 during Turin 2006) and there's a multitude of internal TV channels to watch.

Security in the Olympic Village has never been tighter. An attack on Israeli competitors by Palestinian terrorists at the 1972 Summer Games in Munich left 11 dead, while a backpack bomb that exploded during the 1996 Atlanta Games killed one and injured 111. At the 2002 Winter Olympics in Salt Lake City, more than 10,000 security personnel – among them 2000 secret-service and 1000 FBI agents – were on site.

Doping tests are an integral part of Olympic Village life. After every event, urine (and occasionally blood) samples are collected from six athletes (the

THE FLAME

No image better evokes the Olympics than the Olympic flame – a fire that rekindles the sacred fire that burnt on the altar of the pagan god Zeus during the Games in Olympia, ancient Greece.

Two months or so before the Games, thousands of torchbearers carry the flame in relay from Olympia, birthplace of the Olympics in southern Greece, to the host country, where – during a lavish opening ceremony – the Olympic cauldron is lit with the flame. For Piedmont 2006, the torch, sparked from Olympian sun rays with the help of a parabolic mirror and flown by plane to Rome, will kick off its 11,300km journey around Italy in December 2005. Starting in the Italian capital, it will be carried by 10,000 runners around the country, spending Christmas in Palermo and New Year's Eve in Naples. The Italian celebrity who will carry it into the Olympic stadium in Turin is a closely guarded secret.

Every Games has its own torch. Several will be displayed in the Torino Atrium (p63) until 2006, including the minimalist, streamlined torch designed by Philippe Starck for the Albertville Games (1992); Nagano's traditional Japanese torch (1998); and the stalactite-shaped torch that lit up Salt Lake City (2002). Turinese car designer, Pininfarina, will design Piedmont's torch.

first four to finish, plus two others randomly picked) at the doping control station. Samples are tested for illegal, performance-enhancing substances such as steroids, amphetamines, beta-blockers and erythropoietin.

Athletes found guilty of doping are stripped of their medals and sent home. The systematic doping of East German athletes in the 1970s and '80s, which only came to light after the GDR collapsed in 1989, remains the biggest doping scandal ever. Under its state-sponsored doping programme, State Plan 14.25, an estimated 10,000-odd sportsmen and -women were given the power-packed anabolic steroid, Oral Turinabol, helping East Germany to a top-notch ranking in the medal tables.

Olympic medals are at least 60mm in diameter, 3mm thick and – in the case of gold – gilded with 6g of the precious metal. Beyond that, Winter Olympic organisers, unlike their summer counterparts, have carte blanche with medal design. Salt Lake City (2002) rewarded athletes with rustic medals shaped like Utah river rocks, while artists from the Kiso region in Japan created Nagano's lacquered medals in 1998.

TURIN 2006: LEDGER

Sales of broadcasting rights: €4.5 billion

Ticket sales: €70 million

Sponsorship: €3 billion

Source: Toroc

EVENTS

The men's 500m speed skating kicked off the 1924 Winter Olympics, a modest competition attended by 258 athletes. Downhill (Alpine) skiing was not included (it made its Olympic debut in 1936) and there were no separate events for women.

Today athletes vie for gold in almost 100 different skiing (downhill, cross-country and jumping), skating, sledding and snowboarding events.

Ski jumping – one of the most spectacular events – has starred on the Olympic roster since its inception and is one of the few winter sports to remain a male domain. At the 1928 Games in St Moritz (Switzerland), Jacob Tullin Thams of Norway jumped so far (73m) that he jumped right off the hill and ended up 28th. The most memorable (and comical) Olympic jumper was Eddie the Eagle (alias Eddie Edwards), Britain's first and only Olympic ski jumper, who finished 56th out of 57 in the 1988 Games. Ski jumping is also included in Nordic Combined, an Olympic discipline introduced in 1924 that fuses jumping with cross-country skiing.

Equally as heart-stopping to watch is bobsled racing. A foolhardy quest for the ultimate thrill inspired 19th-century spillseekers to sit in two-man sleds and hurtle down semicylindrical tracks made of ice. In 1924 it became an Olympic sport, albeit one sufficiently dangerous to exclude women until 2002.

The 1928 Games dragged the bobsled's ancestor, the skeleton, out of the closet. Named after the skeleton-like metal sleds used in the 1890s, the event required two-person squads to helter-skelter down a bend-laced course – head-first and face down. So perilous was the event that it has only appeared at the Olympics twice since (in 1948 and 2002). Sleds (a scanty fibreglass and steel shell on a pair of steel runners) have no brakes, no steering (they are guided by shifts in bodyweight) and travel at a petrifying 130km/h. Skeleton rider Nino Bibbia gave Italy its first Winter Olympics gold medal in 1948.

The luge, an equally racy affair, became an immediate fixture after joining the Olympic circuit in 1964. Riders bomb down an ice track feet first, on their backs. In doubles, two riders – traditionally men – lay on top of each other, the larger on top to ensure a speedier descent.

The snowboard – a product of 1960s rebel America – whipped down the Olympic slope for the first time in 1998. Enthralling, entertaining and exhilarating to watch with its aerial acrobatics, snowboarding is the maverick of winter sports – making it no great surprise that its first Olympic

Olympic trivia: the brainiest and brawniest, the most brilliant, bizarre and banal are beautifully captured in Floyd Conner's *The Olympics' Most Wanted: The Top 10 Book of Gold Medal Gaffes, Improbable Triumphs and Other Oddities*.

gold medallist, Canadian Ross Rebagliati, tested positive for marijuana and was temporarily stripped of his gold.

Curling, a staid sport by comparison, originates in 16th-century Scotland and made its Olympic debut in 1998. Teams of four take it in turns to bowl eight stones, each weighing 19.1kg (view some in the Torino Atrium; p63), into concentric circles marked on the ice.

Any sport played on ice or snow is eligible for Olympic inclusion. Sports must be approved by the IOC. Proposals for ski mountaineering and ski orienteering to be included in 2006 were rejected on the grounds that the sports were still in their infancy in Europe, scarcely practised elsewhere and difficult for spectators and TV broadcasters to follow.

PIEDMONT'S OLYMPICS

Places on the Piedmont podium will be fought for at seven competition sites in the region, Turin serving as the springboard to a clutch of snow-covered mountain resorts in the Western Alps, where the sporting action will take place.

The fabulous extravaganza kicks off in Turin on 10 February 2006 at Stadio Comunale, host to the Games' opening and closing ceremonies. Watched by an expected audience of 35,000 in the stadium and two billion TV spectators worldwide, the ceremonies will be as much a celebration of Italian culture as of Olympic tradition.

Prior to Italy's head of state opening the Games, as Olympic protocol demands, athletes will parade into the stadium with Greece leading the way and Italy – as Olympic host – coming up at the rear. The Olympic anthem will be sung, the Olympic flag unfurled, and the legendary torch brought into the stadium to light the Olympic cauldron. Inside a semicircle formed by each nation's flag bearer, an Italian athlete will take the Olympic oath on behalf of all competing athletes, swearing to play fair and square, not cheat and stay squeaky clean drug-wise during the 16-day event. One of Turin's 650 judges and umpires involved will likewise promise on behalf of his comrades to judge fairly.

With the opening ceremony formalities done and dusted, the focus will move west to the real business of ripping down snow-packed slopes. Venue hiccups will be scouted out by a series of test events during 2004 and 2005: the Alpine World Ski Championships; the European figure-skating championships; the Six Nations ice-hockey tournament and so on.

Most athletes will fly in and out of Caselle, an airport that will get a €98 million facelift between now and 2006, located 16km northwest of the Turin city centre. During the Games, competitors will live in purpose-built Olympic villages in Turin, Bardonecchia and Sestriere. The 70,000-sq-metre Turin village, built around a 1934 market building in the Lingotto district, will be kitted out with a canteen, shopping mall, recreation areas, medical centre and massage facilities, as well as accommodation for 2500 aspiring medallists. Solar panels are among bio-architectural features destined for the state-of-the-art complex which, after the Games, will become residential

MEN'S SLALOM: LAST ACROSS THE LINE

■ The 1952 Olympics in Oslo saw Antoin Milliordos of Greece fall 18 times as he flew (or rather fell) down the men's slalom. He finished last – with his back to the finishing line.

■ South Korean skier Kyung Soon-Yim learned to ski from books and had never skied on snow before competing in the men's slalom at the 1960 Squaw Valley Games. He finished last.

IN CASE YOU DIDN'T REALISE...

Piedmont's official Olympic logo was inspired by the spire of Turin's Mole Antonelliana. A creation of Milanese design studio Benincasa-Husmann, the logo was picked from 1300 competing designs and features a mountain of blue ice crystals. Beneath it sits the familiar Olympic emblem – the five interlinked rings representing the five continents.

housing and a research centre. Villages in Bardonecchia (a former holiday camp and youth hostel) and Sestriere (the twin-towered Valtur Village complex, built for athletes during the 1997 Alpine World Ski Championships) will accommodate 750 and 1700 competitors respectively.

Piedmont will buzz with 9600 accredited journalists and media operators, based at seven media villages in Turin. At the central Media Centre inside Lingotto Fiere, journalists will file stories and images from working areas in the Main Press Centre (MPC). The MPC will be wired up with 2200 telephones, and technical support for 80 TV stations will be available in the adjoining International Broadcasting Centre (IBC).

On the slopes, the action will be filmed by 400 TV cameras, including James Bond–style microcameras hidden inside competitors' helmets, on bobsleds and so on. The Turin Olympic Broadcasting Organisation (TOBO), with its central control room in the IBC, will mastermind the entire broadcasting operation.

Within the Olympic villages, entertainment for the 39,000-strong Olympic family will be generated by an internal 50-channel satellite network. **Cultural Olympiad** (☎ 800 017 504; ⊠ 10am-1pm & 3-6pm Mon-Fri), an artistic

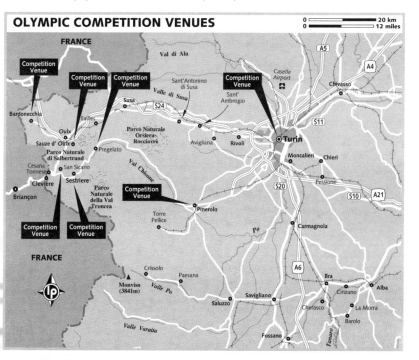

OLYMPIC COMPETITION VENUES

countdown to the Games that's designed to showcase regional culture, will bring a fiesta of festivals to the region. Events, staged both during the Games and before, embrace everything from music, comedy and dance to contemporary art, theatre and film.

Turin

- Ice hockey: men's and women's tournaments
- Figure skating: individual men's and women's; pairs; ice dancing
- Short track: men's and women's 500m, 1000m and 1500m; women's 3000m relay; men's 5000m relay
- Speed skating: men's and women's 500m, 1000m, 1500m, 5000m; men's 10,000m

The Olympic ice-hockey, speed-skating, figure-skating and short-track events will be the hottest events to hit the regional capital since the showing of the Shroud.

Since 2003 builders' bums have hung out up ladders in the Olympic District, an area covering 2 sq km in the Lingotto-ex–Mercati Generali quarter. It will host the Olympic Village, Media Centre and Lingotto Oval, a new speed-skating palace big enough to hold 8200 spectators and four football pitches. After the Games, the €58 million building will become an exhibition space.

Figure- and short-track skaters, including Turin-born world champion Fabio Carta, will compete at the Palavela, a 1960s monster to be revamped by Italian architect Gae Aulenti. Hockey players will battle it out for gold in front of 6000 fans on a temporary rink in Torino Esposizioni and in the Palasport Olimpico, a steely new stadium designed by Tokyo-based architect Arata Isozakj. Next door to the latter is Turin's 1930s Stadio Comunale, a football stadium that's been closed since 1990, but is in line for an Olympic makeover as host to the opening and closing ceremonies.

Bardonecchia

- Snowboard: men's and women's parallel giant slalom, half-pipe, and snowboard cross, a new sport where four boarders race each other along an obstacle course of curves and jumps

Bardonecchia, 90km west of Turin, is sunk in a natural amphitheatre in the Alta Valle di Susa (Upper Susa Valley). One of the rare Alpine resorts

---

TURIN 2006: VITAL STATISTICS

- 2550 athletes from 85 nations will compete.
- There will be 246 medals to be won, spread across 82 events.
- The Games will be wired up with 5000 networked PCs, 14,000 fixed telephones, 8000 mobile phones, 7000 radio sets – and a TV network all of its own.
- A 2000-strong medical team will treat an estimated 12,000 cases during the Games.
- Weathermen predict a 16% chance of rain in Turin on 10 February 2006 (during the opening ceremony) and a 17% chance on 26 February 2006 (closing ceremony). The chance of snow is practically zilch.
- A band of 20,000 to 25,000 volunteers, recruited from NGOs, sports organisations and other walks of life, will help out with tickets sales, information and security and 348 other tasks assigned to the so-called Noi2006 team.

TOP FIVE: HOT SPOTS TO PARTY

Late-night bars, clubs and discos to party and rub shoulders with stars:

▪ Sestriere Café (p97), Sestriere

▪ Piazza Fraitève (p97), Sestriere

▪ Bar Medail (p99), Bardonecchia

▪ Bar Miretti (p99), Bardonecchia

▪ Pub- and bar-lined Via Assietta (p99), Sauze d'Oulx

---

to sport a train station, the border-town ski station lures skiers of all nationalities and abilities. It has dozens of hotels; a clutch of cafés, restaurants and bars; and a shop-clad central street just made for a traditional Italian hand-in-hand *passeggiata* (evening stroll).

Bardonecchia's three downhill ski areas, each named after an Italian skiing great, were among the first in Italy to be kitted out with ski lifts (1939). Aspiring champions can race down Fisi 50, a World Cup run in the Colomion skiing area, or one of two slopes in Melezet, where Italian wild-child Giacomo Kratter and other world-class snowboarders will race in 2006.

Sauze d'Oulx

▪ Freestyle skiing: men's and women's moguls and jumps

The plucky twists, turns and aerial acrobatics of the world's slickest freestyle skiers will draw a crowd of 10,000 to Sauze d'Oulx, a church spire–crowned resort 80km west of Turin, with its fair share of concrete-block hotels in the heart of the Via Lattea (Milky Way).

Seriously big moguls aside, brawny mountains are Sauze's trademark. The Triplex, Bourget and Genevris peaks soar above and around a resort which grew from mountain refuges established by Italy's earliest skiing pioneers. Piero Gros – World Cup winner in 1974 and Olympic slalom gold medallist in 1976 – was born and bred in Sauze d'Oulx.

Cesana Torinese-San Sicario

▪ Alpine (downhill) skiing: women's super-G; freestyle downhill; and freestyle downhill combined
▪ Biathlon: women's 7.5km sprint, 7.5km team, 10km pursuit, 15km individual and 4x6km relay; men's 10km sprint, 10km team, 12.5km pursuit, 15km individual and 4x7.5km relay
▪ Bobsleigh: women's doubles, men's doubles and four-man descent
▪ Luge: men's and women's singles, mixed doubles
▪ Skeleton: men's and women's

When was the first Olympic coin minted? Find the answer on the Olympic Collectors Commission's website at www.collectors.olympic .org, a worldwide meeting point for philatelists, numismatics and Olympic memorabilia geeks.

Roman Cesana Torinese is guarded by the ruins of what was Europe's highest fortress at the confluence of the Dora and Ripa Rivers in the Alta Valle di Susa. From here, snow enthusiasts flock up to San Sicario, a small Via Lattea station linked by ski lift with Cesana, Sestriere and Sauze d'Oulx.

Bob sleds, skeletons and luges will bomb down a 1435m-long Olympic track in Pariol Greniere, a hamlet at 1700m on the road linking Cesana Torinese with San Sicario. Women's Alpine skiing events will speed down the lower slopes of Mont Fraitève (2702m) and Mont Roccia Rotonda (2392m), with competitors zipping through the Soleil Bœuf ski area to cross the finishing line in San Sicario. In February 2005 World Cup athletes

---

TOP FIVE: MOUNTAIN RETREATS WITH CHARM

- Ristorante Biovey (p99), Bardonecchia
- Il Capricorno (p99), Sauze d'Oulx
- Grangia Del Courbaval (p98), Chiomonte
- La Tana degli Orsi (p97), Cesana
- Il Torrione (p93), Pinerolo

---

will test out the Olympic run, reached by the Soleil Bœuf, Roccia Rotunda, Rio Inverso and Fraitève ski lifts.

Sestriere

- Alpine (downhill) skiing: men's super-G, freestyle downhill, freestyle combined downhill, special combined, slalom and giant slalom; women's slalom and giant slalom

Some of the most thrilling Olympic skiing is sure to be seen at Sestriere, the only resort on the Olympic programme that comes even close to being a household name.

Created by Giovanni Agnelli of FIAT fame, Sestriere has lost none of its 1930s sex appeal. The downhill skiing is wild and the nightlife superb, with ample entertainment to keep everyone on their toes, on and off piste.

The first Alpine skiing World Cup blasted down the Kandahar Banchetta run – a notoriously tough and treacherous black run at 2800m in the Via Lattea – in 1967. The same slope pioneered night-time racing in Europe with the 1994 World Cup slalom victory of Italian skiing ace Alberto 'la bomba' Tomba, the only skier to successfully defend an Olympic gold.

In 2006 the drama will unfold on Sestriere's highly technical Sises (men's and women's giant slalom), Kandahar Giovanni Agnelli (slalom) and Kandahar Banchetta (men's downhill and super-G) downhill ski runs.

DID YOU KNOW?

Electronic timing, allowing judges to time Alpine skiers to a hundredth of a second, was used for the first time at the Games in 1964. Instant replay has been in use since 1960.

Pragelato

- Cross-country (Nordic) skiing: men's 15km, 30km and 50km; women's 10km, 15km and 30km; men's and women's 5km combined pursuit; men's and women's 1.5km sprint; men's 4x10km relay; women's 4x5km relay
- Nordic combined: (men only) K95+15km individual; K95+4x5km team; K120+7.5km sprint
- Ski jumping: (men only) K95 & K120 individual; K120 team

With no more than a handful of hotels and places to eat, Pragelato, at the foot of Mont Albergian in the Val Chisone, is quiet.

From the resort, cross-country trails wind through larch and Swiss stone-pine forests, and past Alpine churches. Some venture into the Parco Naturale della Val Troncea, known for its abundance of spring and summer flowers. The Olympic track, on which Italy's Stefania Belmondo will defend her 15km freestyle gold medal in 2006, climbs from 1530m to 1620m.

Ski jumpers will be judged on the best of two almighty big jumps, from a couple of snow-packed hills near the Pragelato hamlet of Rivets.

Between events, punters can ice skate, zip down one of six downhill ski slopes, take a dip in its Pragelato's indoor swimming pool or sip warm wine in one of its two bars.

OLYMPIC MASTERMIND

The mind-boggling task of masterminding the Olympics belongs to the Turin Organising Committee (Toroc). Headquartered in a logo-emblazoned building in Turin, with a 400-strong staff set to hit the 1000 mark by 2006, the committee was formed after Piedmont became Olympic host in 1999.

From mid-2004, enthusiasts hungry for a taste of the Winter Games can tour the **Toroc headquarters** (☎ 011 631 05 11, 011 673 32 22; www.torino2006.org; Corso Novara 96) – otherwise known as the 'Games factory' – and buy the official T-shirt in its shop. Toroc also organises occasional guided visits to Piedmont's seven competition sites. News, views and gossip can be picked up in *Monitor 2006*, Toroc's bimonthly newsletter available free at Turin tourist office, Toroc headquarters and various other distribution points in Turin and other competition towns.

Toroc will die in 2006; the municipal police and a clutch of Turin-based NGOs will inherit its home.

Pinerolo

▪ Curling: men's and women's tournaments

The stunning arena of mountains surrounding it is the most splendid aspect of Pinerolo, a provincial town 40km southwest of Turin in the Cottian Alps where Olympic curlers will slide stones on ice. The hot seat will be the Palaghiaccio, a stadium destined for a €9.5 million revamp.

Sports aside, the fortress town, which was home to the imprisoned 'man in the iron mask' during the reign of French king Louis XIV, sports a small but sweet medieval old town and a sleepy nightlife at best. By 2006, a fast-track motorway will link the resort with Turin.

TICKETS

Tickets will go on sale from November 2004. Prices vary depending on the event, with single-event tickets costing anything from €20 (curling) to €170 (ski jumping). That said, half of the million tickets on sale cost €50 or less. Buy them online through **TicketOne** (www.ticketone.it); in Italy at TicketOne sales points (including FNAC in Turin); and through NOCs in other countries. Tickets will be allocated by lottery 45 days after they go on sale.

FURTHER INFORMATION

Punters seeking more information should make the Turin Organising Committee (Toroc; p45) their first port of call. Olympic-driven urban and social projects in Piedmont can be discovered in the Torino Atrium (p63).

Online, the **Olympic Movement** (www.olympic.org) oozes general information on the Winter Olympics; world peace is championed by the **International Olympic Truce Foundation** (www.olympictruce.org); and research papers and other Games-related academic documentation are filed in the **Olympic Studies Centre** (www.blue.uab.es).

TOP FIVE: SPOTS TO CELEBRATE IN STYLE

▪ Ristorante Biovey (p99), Bardonecchia

▪ Capricorno (p98), Sauze d'Oulx

▪ Fitness Centre (p96), Sestriere

▪ Flipot (p94), Torre Pellice

▪ Grand Hotel Principi di Piemonte (p97), Sestriere

Food & Drink

Delicate and flavoursome, Piedmont cuisine fuses the very best of French and Italian gastronomy. From Alba's intoxicating *tartufo bianco* (white truffle) to Turin's chocolate and coffee houses, the region's world-class products woo the most sophisticated of palates.

Nothing better epitomises the importance placed on food than the early evening *aperitivo* (aperitif), an 18th-century tradition upheld with gusto in the regional capital. Honour the complimentary feast of hors d'œuvres with a Barolo red, Martini dry or glass of sparkling Asti and remind yourself you really are in Piedmont, not paradise.

STAPLES & SPECIALITIES
Savoury

Quintessential dishes like *lumache di bobbio* (wine-stewed snails) and fried *rane* (frogs) testify to the part played by France in the Piedmontese kitchen. Yet the region's predominantly rural nature ensures a simplicity seldom found in French fare.

Risotto – the ubiquitous Italian dish that sees *riso* (rice) slowly cooked in broth to a creamy yet *al dente* consistency – has its roots in eastern Piedmont, where 50% of Italy's rice crop grows. *Risotto alla Piemontese* (white wine and truffle risotto) and *paniscia alla Novarese* (rice with onion, sausage and vegetable soup), from Novara, are local varieties.

Meat forms a fair chunk of the local diet. Feisty specialities include *bollito misto* (seven types of sauce-topped, broth-boiled meat) and *finanziera* (sweetbreads, mushrooms and chicken livers in a creamy sauce). See p47 for some titillating pork options.

One of Piedmont's most respected wines is the secret behind *brasato al Barolo* (braised beef, marinated in aged Barolo wine). Eat it with polenta, a cornmeal porridge traditionally cooked in a copper pot. Polenta is served soft and warm, or cooled then grilled or fried in slices.

Prized for its intense aroma and flavour, the Alba truffle is black *(nero)* or white *(bianco)* and is sniffed out of the ground by dogs. Few can afford to munch through a whole truffle: savour shavings in a lunchtime omelette; atop cheese-, butter- and egg-yolk-fried slices of toast *(fondua)*; or in an *insalata di carne cruda all'Albese* (veal carpaccio seasoned with olive oil, lemon, salt, pepper and garlic, and garnished with truffle shavings). Truffle-infused olive oil makes a great gift for the folks back home.

Several pasta dishes incorporate truffles: *trifulin* is ravioli stuffed with truffle specks and served in a mushroom sauce; *gnocchi alla bava* sees truffle slivers baked with gnocchi, tomato, cream and *fontina* cheese; *tajarin* is thin pasta served with truffles, liver or a meat sauce; and *agnolotti* are meat-filled pasta cushions served with truffles and a tomato or meat sauce. For more truffle details, see p111.

Piedmont has produced cheese since Roman times. Unpasteurised cows' milk from three villages – Castelmagno, Pradleves and Monterosso Grana (p116) – goes into nutty blue-veined Castelmagno, one of six out of 55 Piedmont cheeses to be origin-protected (DOP; *denominazione di origine Protetta*). Raschera (a mild square-shaped, semi-hard cheese from Cuneo), Toma Piemontese (a soft cheese made region-wide), *robiola di roccaverano* (a fresh, slightly sour cheese, made with unpasteurised milk from the Langhe) and murazzano (a fresh sheep's-milk cheese from the Langhe, hand-moulded) are other notable cheeses.

Learn more about regional produce plus where to eat and drink with *The Italian Wine Guide, The Italian Food Guide* and the *Guide alle Città del Tartufo* (Guide to Truffle Cities; in Italian), all published by the Touring Club Italiano (TCI; www.touringclub.it).

Cheese aficionados can eat their way around cheesy Piedmont with the Strade dei Formaggi (Cheese Road) at www .lestradedeiformaggi.it.

Mild Bra, named after the town where it was traditionally stored rather than made, comes in three varieties: hard *(duro)*; soft *(tenero)*; or matured beneath a bed of pressed Nebbolio, Barbera or Dolcetto wine grapes. Fans of the latter should also try *brôs*, an unusual cheese paste made by throwing an aged cheese into a terracotta jar and fermenting it in oil, vinegar, pepper, salt, garlic, herbs, spices and a healthy shot of grappa, for at least a month.

No table is complete without a pot of *grissini Torinesi* – breadsticks, either *stirato* (literally 'straight') or *rubata* (hand rolled).

Sugary Sweet

Turin is *the* Italian city to sample *cioccolato* (chocolate) in all its guises: straight; mixed in a *bicerin* (a Turinese mix of coffee, hot chocolate, milk and whipped cream) or fondue; packed in a *gianduiotto* (pieces of velvety hazelnut chocolate); or spread on toast as Nutella.

Desserts include that old Savoy favourite *panna cotta,* which is not unlike crème caramel; *bonèt,* an egg pudding made with milk, sugar, macaroon, coffee and fortified marsala wine; and *zabaglione,* a sinful calorie-overkill of whipped eggs, marsala and sugar into which sweet almond biscuits *(amaretti)* are dipped.

The Langhe's late-August hazelnut crop *(nocciola del Piemonte)* goes into *biscotti di nocciola* (hazelnut biscuits), *torrone d'Asti* (hazelnut nougat) and *torta di nocciole* (hazelnut cake).

DRINKS
Wine

Southern Piedmont's Barolo and Barbaresco rank among Italy's best reds. Classified as DOCG wines *(denominazione d'origine controllata e garantita;* meaning they can only be produced subject to certain specifications and are quality tested by government inspectors), the two appellations are made from Nebbolio grapes harvested in October in the Langhe region. Red and dry, Barolo is aged for at least two years in chestnut or oak barrels and is best drunk with roast meat, beefy stews and the like. Barbaresco is another meat-dish companion with an intense bouquet and robust taste. Ghemme and Gattinara are full-bodied reds from eastern Piedmont.

Asti's golden whites, drunk at 6°C to 8°C as an aperitif or dessert wine, have been made since medieval times. The sweet pale-yellow Moscato d'Asti

DID YOU KNOW?

Legend says *grissini* (breadsticks) were first cooked up in the royal court of Carlo Emanuele, who told his baker to bake an extra-hardy, well-baked bread to combat the spread of disease in his Savoy kingdom.

PORKY PIEDMONT

No piggy part is wasted in porky Piedmont, where pigs have been bred since Neolithic times. While two-thirds of Piedmont pigs' legs are taken to neighbouring Lombardy and Emilia-Romagna to become San Daniele and Parma hams, the rest of the region's pork invariably ends up in one of the following Piedmontese specialities:

batsoà – pigs' trotters boiled, boned, covered in breadcrumbs and deep-fried.

bundiola – pig bladder stuffed with lard, minced beef and herbs.

fidighin – pork liver, lard and meat sausage.

mustardela – sausage from the Val Pellice, built from blood sausage plus the meat and fat from the pig's head.

preive – literally 'priests'; garlic- and thyme-seasoned pork rind rolled, tied and boiled up with beans and onions to make a thick tummy-filling stew.

sautissa 'd coj – boiled cabbage and pig's fat sausage; traditional peasant food.

salsiccia di riso – boiled rice and pig fat sausage; also called *salame bastardo* (literally 'bastard sausage').

spalot – pork sausage from Biella.

testa in cassetta – literally 'head in a box'; a pig's head boiled, boned, chopped up, seasoned and stuffed into a box.

GRAPPA ETIQUETTE

Pure ecstasy or paint stripper, depending on your taste, grappa has been drunk in Piedmont since the 15th century. This 40%- to 60%-proof mouth-searing type of brandy is made from grape skins and seeds, and can be white, young and pure *(grappa giovane)*; aged and golden *(grappa invecchiata)*; aromatic *(grappa aromatica)*; or flavoured with grass, herbs or fruit *(grappa aromatizzata)*. Drink *grappa giovane* cold and chilled (with or without water and ice), and *grappa invecchiata* at room temperature in a tulip-shaped glass.

Learn more grappa etiquette at the sweetly poetic Distilleria di Romano Levi (p113) or at the five-generation Antica Distilleria di Altavilla (p107). Other great grappa masters include the Distilleria Sibona (www.distilleriasibona.it), home to a century of single-grape grappas in Piobesi d'Alba; and Silvano d'Orba's Distilleria Gualco (www.distilleriagualco.it). The latter distils Grappa Rosina, an aged grappa stored for eight years in acacia barrels and dubbed *la bella Rosina* (the beautiful little Rosa) by grappa lover Vittorio Emanuele II (whose lover was also called Rosa).

---

and its sparkling version, Asti Spumante, are produced from 9500 hectares of Moscato Bianco vineyards around Asti, Alessandria and Cuneo.

The same area also produces the ruby-red Brachetto d'Acqui, a still or sparkling sweet wine. Cortese grapes cultivated in the hillside vineyards around Alessandria are the secret behind Gavi, a dry white that's best when drunk young and with fish.

In addition to Piedmont's seven DOCG wines, Piedmont produces 44 DOC-classified wines *(denominazione di origine controllata;* made to set specifications, quality not guaranteed). Notable appellations include the ruby-red trio, Barbera d'Asti, Barbera d'Alba and Barbera del Monferrato, normally drunk with meals. Dolcetto d'Alba, an older red, is delicious with polenta and matured cheeses; and Cortese dell'Alto Monferrato is a traditional white companion to hors d'œuvres and light meals.

Beer

Local beer is of the crisp, light Pilsner variety. Birra Menabrea (p140), brewed in Biella since 1846, and Peroni, concocted the same year in Vigevano (southeast of Novara; but Rome-based today), are the big boys of the local brands.

In Turin, Biondoppia, Rufus, Clara and Gina are speciality beers made by Birrificio Torino (p81), a microbrewery to find success in recent years. Caffè della Basilica (p81) brews Sangre de Toro (literally 'bulls blood').

Spirits

For an aperitif, take a palate-cleansing Campari bitter (straight), Campari soda (mixed with soda water) or a vermouth (a white wine–based drink with herbs) such as Cinzano or Martini Bianco – all concocted in Piedmont in the late 19th century. Cinzano started out in Turin in 1757 as a humble shop selling 'house' aperitifs concocted from 20 or so herbs, and distils 80% of all its products in the south of the city. Martini & Rossi took root in Turin in 1863, while Campari was created in the 1840s from a secret mix of spices, herbs, tree barks and fruit peels.

After dinner, sink a Barolo Chinato or grappa.

DID YOU KNOW?

During Piedmont's annual September-to-October grape harvest, 450,000 tons of grapes are picked from 55 hectares of vineyards – making 3.3 million hectolitres of wine.

Coffee & Chocolate

Coffee in Italy isn't like anywhere else in the world: it's better. And never more so than in Piedmont, home to coffee tycoon Lavazza (p70) who has roasted beans in Turin since 1895. Throw chocolate into the coffee pot to get a steaming mug of Turinese *bicerin*.

LEXICON

With endless coffee options to choose from, caffeine addicts don't have to go cold turkey in Turin. Everything from an orange-flavoured *cappuccino esotica to* an *espresso autunnalo* (espresso served in a chocolate-lined cup, topped with whipped cream and pureed apple) can be sampled on the spot where Luigi Lavazza opened his first café in 1895 (see p75).

More conventional coffees, available region-wide, include:

bicerin – Turinese mix of coffee, hot chocolate, milk and whipped cream.

caffè americano – large black weak coffee, served watered down or with a jug of hot water.

caffè freddo – long glass of iced, black, sweetened coffee.

caffè freddo amaro – *caffè freddo* minus the sugar.

caffè granita – sweet, strong coffee with whipped cream.

caffè latte – less frothy, milkier version of *cappuccino.*

caffè lungo – diluted *espresso.*

cappuccino or **'cappuccio'** – coffee with hot, frothy milk and dusted with powdered cocoa.

espresso – one mouthful of very strong black coffee, better known as **un caffè**.

latte macchiato – warm milk stained with a spot of coffee.

macchiato – espresso with a dash of milk.

CELEBRATIONS

Food has always played a prime role in Piedmontese parties, the Romans sacrificing a lamb to Jupiter and goating around with wine-drinking games to mark the first grapes of the season.

A day of eating *magro* (lean) precedes a feast day – 12 tummy-filling hours of overindulgence in the main. *Gran fritto alla Piemontese* (a fried banquet of battered brain, sweetbreads, chicken fillets, sausages, liver, heart, courgettes, artichokes, mushrooms and fish as well as pieces of sweet fruit and biscuits) is a typical meal to eat on feasts days and Sundays. In Turin *torta tradizionale valdese alla crema* (a type of cream cake) is a festive cake.

Dozens of festivals are only about food, the most atmospheric being Entracque's Sagra della Patata di Entracque (Entracque Potato Feast) in September, when villagers share a communal feast of homemade gnocchi; Borgo San Dalmazzo's Fiera Fredda della Lumaca (Snail Fair), which has been celebrated for more than 400 years; Alba's white-truffle fair (p112); and Asti's Festival delle Sagre (p105). Pumpkin *(zucca)*, mushroom *(funghi)* and chestnut *(marrone)* fairs abound in autumn. Tourist offices have lists of every last little foodie festival.

WHERE TO EAT & DRINK

In towns, nip into a *tavola calda* (hot table) for prepared meat, pasta and vegetable dishes in a self-service style. Pizza is served in a *pizzeria* and an

BAROLO CHINATO

Served slightly chilled as an aperitif, at room temperature as a digestive, or with a chocolate-inspired dessert, a glass of Barolo Chinato is a must-try.

Cooked up in the 1800s by a chemist (who loved food) from Serralunga d'Alba, the sweet red wine sees an aged Barolo red thrown into an oak barrel for four years with quinine, cane sugar and a clutch of herbs and spices (cinnamon, cloves, ginger and 21 others). The House of Savoy raved about it, serving their favourite tipple at the best of royal banquets.

The recipe remains a closely guarded secret.

osteria is a wine bar serving a small selection of dishes. A *trattoria* is the less-sophisticated sister of a *ristorante* (restaurant). Both impose a cover charge *(coperto)* of up to €2 per person and a service charge *(servizio)* of 10% to 15% of the final bill.

Those seeking authentic food should stick to menu-less *trattorie* that chalk up the day's dishes on a blackboard. The best often accept cash payment only, are only open on weekdays and are heaving by 12.30pm. *Agriturismi* (farmstays) are invariably excellent places to eat as well as sleep.

Quick Eats

Piedmont's pace of eating is far from fast. That said, in towns you'll never be short of somewhere to grab a munch-on-the-move such as *panini* (bread roll) or pizza *al taglio* (by the slice). In Turin, street vendors sell hot roasted chestnuts in paper cones during winter.

VEGETARIANS & VEGANS

In a country where *prosciutto* is not considered meat, vegetarians will encounter the odd tummy rumble.

But all is not lost. Menus feature vegetarian *antipasti* (starters) including Piedmontese *capunet* (a mix of aubergine, courgette, olives, peppers and celery). Nizza Monferrato thistles – delicious boiled, then baked in the oven with butter and cheese – are a more unusual vegetable to look out for.

A couple of regional dishes don't contain meat: *bagna caôda* sees winter diners dip vegetables fondue-style into a hot pot of oil, often spiced up with garlic, red wine and melted anchovies – check what is in the oil before ordering. Rice-stuffed peppers *(peperoni farciti)* are another main-course safe bet. Then, of course, there are truffles and hazelnuts.

Vegans will suffer hunger pangs: dairy products, particularly cheese and butter, are used as a matter of course in cooking.

WHINING & DINING

Dining with kids is pleasurable thanks to kid-friendly Italians who take children out to dinner from a very young age. Children menus are rare, but ordering a *mezzo piatto* (half portion) for pint-sized appetites, or

---

AUTHORS' CHOICE: TOP 10 EATS

Piedmont's 'best' in the conventional sense they might not be, but we followed our stomachs to nose out – several hundreds meals later – this tasty cross-section of taste bud ticklers.

Birreria Menabrea (p140), Biella – brilliant beer and pub grub.

Da Aldo di Castiglione (p105), Asti – the world's best *mousse all'Amaretto* (amaretto mousse).

Antica Trattoria Da Sciolla (p133), Domodossola – excellent-value, top-quality Piedmontese fare.

Osteria della Chiocciola (p118), Cuneo – delicious *carne cruda* (a variety of steak tartare) and a regional wine list longer than a giant's arm.

Biovey (p99), Bardonecchia – original decor, green views and dinky extras to complement high calibre food.

Trattoria Ristorante Monferrato (p139), Ivrea – the antipasto is a winner.

Dai Saletta (p139), Turin – authentic, affordable Piedmontese cuisine at a laid-back pace.

L'Osteria del Teatro (p112), Alba – regional wine and food in a bare brick 'n' bottle atmosphere.

Fratelli La Cozza (p77), Turin – hearty contender for Italy's 'wackiest pizzeria award'.

Combal.Zero (p79), Rivoli – Classy design, amazing views and a dare-to-be-different menu by one of Piedmont's most creative chefs.

WINE TASTING

Wine can be tasted and bought in an *enoteca regionale* (regional winery), of which there are 10 in Piedmont, coordinated by the **Enoteca del Piemonte** (☎ 011 667 76 67; www.enotecaregionaledel piemonte.com; Via Nizza 294, Turin). The latter organises the Turin Wine Fair in November – a grand tasting opportunity for beginners and buffs alike.

There are *enoteche regionali* in Acqui Terme, Barolo, Canale d'Alba, Canelli, Gattinara, Grinzane Cavour, Mango, Roppolo and Vignale Monferrato; see the regional chapters for details. Barbaresco's *enoteca* is in a church, built by villagers in the mid-19th century in thanks for an exceptional grape harvest one year.

---

asking the chef to tailor a dish to meet contrary tastes is acceptable. If all else fails, there's always the bottomless pot of breadsticks for kids to munch their way through.

For more on travelling with children, see p144.

HABITS & CUSTOMS

You'll find city dwellers rarely sit down for *colazione* (breakfast), but rather wash down a *cornetto* (croissant) with a cappuccino at the bar. Bars lay out an astonishing array of complimentary hors d'œuvres from 5pm onwards.

In rural Piedmont, *pranzo* (lunch) is the main meal of the day. For city slickers however, lunch and *cena* (dinner) assume equal importance, the full monty comprising an *antipasto* (starter), *primo piatto* (first course of pasta or *risotto*), *secondo piatto* (second course of meat or fish), followed by *insalata* (salad) or *contorno* (vegetable side dish), fruit or *dolce* (dessert) and a *caffè* (always espresso). Alcohol is routinely drunk with meals. Wine accompanies lunch and dinner, and *digestivi* (liqueurs) are drunk to finish off.

Those with a watch or wallet to watch can opt for a lunchtime *menu del giorno* (menu of the day) – a first and second course, maybe dessert and a 25cL jug of house wine or 50cL bottle of mineral water for a fixed price.

> **DID YOU KNOW?**
>
> Rashchera d'Alpeggio, an Alpine variation of regular Raschera, must be made with milk from cows who've grazed above 900m in nine towns and villages around Mondovì.

COOKING COURSES

Some farmstays (p142) run courses. Otherwise, consider the following:

Enoteca Patrito (☎ 0172 48 96 75; www.enotecapatrito.it, Italian only; Via G Ferraris 6, Cherasco) Wine-tasting school with cheese-tasting sessions too.

Il Melograno (☎ 011 817 31 14; www.cucina-ilmelograno.it, Italian only; Piazza Vittorio Veneto 9, Turin) Three-hour lessons in regional cuisine.

Italian Culinary Institute for Foreigners (ICIF; ☎ 011 991 24 56; www.icif.com; Piazza Vittorio Emanuele 10, Costigliole d'Asti) Courses for chefs in need of a refresher or fresh inspiration.

La Corte Chiusa (☎ 0141 64 46 47; www.lacortechiusa.it; Via Roma 66, Rocchetta Tanaro) Residential courses in an 18th-century Monferrato winery.

SLOWLY DOES IT

Fast food as a concept doesn't sit easily in this neck of the woods, for it was here in 1986 that the first organised, politically active group tackled the issue head-on. Symbolised by a snail, the Bra-based Slow Food movement (www.slowfood.com) has groups in 48 countries and over 77,000 members. The movement promotes good food and wine to be consumed (slowly, of course) in good company, and champions traditional cuisine and sustainable agricultural practices. The volunteer-run groups also organise social programmes of feasting and frivolity.

DOS & DON'TS

- Greet waiters, bar tenders and fellow dining companions with a *buongiorno* or *buonasera*.
- Don't order a cappuccino after noon; Italians only drink it with breakfast and in the morning.
- Dress with style when dining out in Turin. In rural Piedmont, anything goes.
- Generosity at a meal is a sign of hospitality in Piedmontese homes, so refuse at your own peril!
- Eat pasta with a fork. Bite through (rather than slurp) any bits hanging down.

La Fufi (☎ 011 50 02 66; www.lafufi.com, Italian only; Via Marco Polo 37/5, Turin) Three-hour thematic lessons.
Università di Scienza Gastronomiche (University of Gastronomic Sciences; ☎ 0172 45 85 13; www.unisg.it) The world's first university for gastronomes (p103).

EAT YOUR WORDS

Know *batsoà* from *bundiola*? For pronunciation guidelines see p158.

Useful Phrases

DID YOU KNOW?

The trick to making an authentic *bagna caôda* (an oil fondue) is to 'sweeten' the garlic the day before: peel the clove, remove its 'soul' (the green bit) and leave it to soak for 24 hours in milk.

I'd like to reserve a table.	*Vorrei riservare un tavolo.*
vo-*ray* ree-ser-*va*-re oon *ta*-vo-lo	
I'd like the menu, please.	*Vorrei il menù, per favore.*
vo-*ray* eel me-*noo* per fa-*vo*-re	
Do you have a menu in English?	*Avete un menù (scritto) in inglese?*
a-*ve*-te oon me-*noo* (*skree*-to) een een-*gle*-ze	
What would you recommend?	*Cosa mi consiglia?*
ko-za mee kon-*see*-lya	
I'd like a local speciality.	*Vorrei una specialità di questa regione.*
vo-*ray* oo-na spe-cha-lee-*ta* dee *kwe*-sta re-*jo*-ne	
Please bring the bill.	*Mi porta il conto, per favore?*
mee *por*-ta eel *kon*-to per fa-*vo*-re	
I'm a vegetarian / vegan.	*Sono vegetariano/a / Sono vegetaliano/a.*
so-no ve-je-ta-*rya*-no/a / *so*-no ve-je-ta-*lya*-no/a	

Menu Decoder

See www.italianmade.com for recipes, extensive descriptions of regional specialities and booklets that can be downloaded.

bagnet Piemontese – sauce served with boiled meat
bagnet ross – warm sauce with garlic, carrots, onion, tomato, red wine, sugar, salt and chilli
bagnet vert – cold sauce of parsley, garlic, anchovies, breadcrumbs, vinegar and olive oil
coniglio all Canavesana – rabbit in meat stock, with potatoes and spices
fondua – fried 'fondue' mix of milk, melted *fontina* cheese, butter and egg yolks on toast, topped with thin slices of truffle
fonduta – truffle-free version of *fondua*
fontina – fatty, sweet and creamy cheese, similar to Gruyère
lumache al Barbera – fried snails cooked slowly with Barbera, served with ground nuts
lumache alla Piemontese – baked snails with onion, tomato sauce, broth, nuts, anchovies, parsley, salt and pepper
supa barbette – rich stock prepared with chicken, pork, pig's bones, carrots, celery, leek and herbs, served with slices of stale bread and breadsticks
vitello tonnato – veal in a tuna, caper and anchovy sauce
zuppa alla Canavesana – nourishing thick soup prepared with bread, boiled cabbage, broth, meat sauce, lard, onions, garlic and sausage

BRUNCH IN THE AFTERNOON

Merenda sinóira is Piedmontese brunch – except that it is taken in the late afternoon. It typically comprises bread, salami, a choice of local cheeses and *acciughe in salsa verde* (anchovies in a green sauce).

Glossary

breakfast	*prima colazione*	*pree*-ma ko-la-*tsyo*-ne
lunch	*pranzo*	*pran*-dzo
dinner	*cena*	*che*-na
starter/appetiser	*antipasto*	an-tee-*pas*-to
first course	*primo*	*pree*-mo
second course	*secondo*	se-*kon*-do
dessert	*dolce*	dol-che
bill	*conto*	*kon*-to

Turin

CONTENTS

Orientation	56
Information	56
Dangers & Annoyances	57
Sights	59
Activities	69
Walking Tour	69
Courses	70
Turin for Children	70
Quirky Turin	70
Tours	70
Festivals & Events	71
Sleeping	71
Eating	75
Drinking	81
Entertainment	82
Shopping	85
Getting There & Away	87
Getting Around	88

Dynamic and confident, Turin is a city bursting with life. For many years condemned as a grey and smoky industrial centre, Piedmont's capital is today breaking the hold that the production line once held. And as the finishing touches are applied to the Olympic makeover, the feel-good factor rides high.

Touting itself as Europe's capital of baroque, Turin impresses. Visitors who arrive expecting little invariably end up marvelling at the majestic palaces, aristocratic piazzas and grand boulevards. In fact, its royal heritage is stunning, testament to the city's once central status. The Savoy capital from 1563, Turin was also seat of the Italian parliament for a brief period after unification and still today has the air of a capital *manqué*.

Turin's industrial legacy is also evident, most dramatically in the form of the Lingotto Fiere, FIAT's legendary former factory. In its day a model of manufacturing modernism, its renaissance into a shopping complex and cultural centre at the hands of architect Renzo Piano ensures it maintains its emblematic status in the city.

More visible and probably even more photographed is Turin's most famous landmark, the Mole Antonelliana. Itself an example of engineering as art, this remarkable building dominates the cityscape reaching a height of 167m.

But there's more to Turin than extravagant architecture. There's the world famous Holy Shroud of Turin, the linen in which Christ's body was supposedly wrapped after his crucifixion; there's a thriving café culture and vibrant nightlife; and there's chocolate. Lots of it.

HIGHLIGHTS

- **Baroque Beauty**
  Gape at the scale of Piazza Castello (p59)
- **Curiosity**
  Contemplate the Holy Shroud (p63)
- **Museum Mummies**
  Marvel at the Museo Egizio's Egyptian collection (p64)
- **Best View**
  Take the Panoramic Lift up the Mole Antonelliana (p66)
- **Market Mayhem**
  Shop at Europe's largest open-air market, Porta Palazzo (p85)
- **Industrial Icon**
  Visit the former FIAT factory, the Lingotto Fiere (p67)

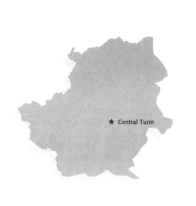

★ Central Turin

| POPULATION: 900,985 | ELEVATION: 240M |

ORIENTATION

Stazione Porta Nuova, the central train station from 1865, is the main point of arrival. Exiting the station, Corso Vittorio Emanuele II, the main tram and bus route, runs southeast–northwest, while Via Roma links the station (southwest) with Piazza Castello (northeast) and the *centro storico* (historic centre). Piazza Carlo Felice, in front of the station, and Via Nizza, which runs southwest through the San Salvario district, are the main axes of Turin's seedier side.

The Mole Antonelliana dominates the horizon to the east, near Via Po (the university area), Piazza Vittorio Veneto and the River Po. Nightlife is centred round the riverside Murazzi del Po and the Quadrilatero Romano, the old-town patch of Turin west of Piazza Castello. Across the water on the river's eastern bank is the quarter of Borgo Po leading up to the hills, home to the city's rich and great.

South of the city centre lie the Savoy hunting lodge at Stupinigi and the royal castle at Moncalieri, the Lingotto Fiere congress centre and much of the city's industrial sprawl.

Maps

The free *Torino mappa turistica* is produced by and distributed through tourist offices throughout the city. It is a decent enough map with an enlarged city centre section and clearly marked major museums, churches and sights of interest.

More detailed city maps can be bought at bookshops throughout town. One of the best is *Minipianta Torino* (1:12,000; €2.32) produced by the Touring Club Italiano (TCI) and sold at the club's bookshop in Via San Francesco D'Assisi.

Otherwise, try *Torino pianta della città* (1:15,000; €5.50), published by Litografia Artistica Cartografica, or the Instituto Geográfico de Agostini's laminated *Torino* map, with a 1:12,000 city-centre spread.

INFORMATION

Bookshops

Libreria Dante Alighieri (Map pp60-1; ☎ 011 53 58 97; www.fogola.com, Italian only; Piazza Carlo Felice 15) Good selection of art books and rare editions.

Libreria Druetto (Map pp60-1; ☎ 011 561 91 66; Via Roma 227) Art, architecture and design books.

Libreria Française (Map pp60-1; ☎ 011 83 67 72; Via Bogino 4) French-language bookshop.

Libreria Luxemburg (Map pp60-1; ☎ 011 561 38 96; Via Battisti 7) Anglo-American bookshop.

Libreria Zanaboni (Map pp60-1; ☎ 011 650 55 16; Corso Vittorio Emanuele II 41) Stocks Lonely Planet in English.

Touring Club Italiano (Map pp60-1; ☎ 011 562 72 07; Via San Francesco d'Assisi 3) Excellent range of maps and assorted guides.

Emergency

Police Station (Questura) (Map pp60-1; ☎ 011 5 58 81; Corso Vinzaglio 10)

Internet Access

1PC4YOU (Map pp60-1; ☎ 011 83 59 08; Via Giuseppe Verdi 20g; per hr €2-6; ⌚ 9am-9pm Mon-Sat, 2-8pm Sun) Hourly rates vary depending on the number of people surfing.

bu.net (Map pp60-1; ☎ 011 440 75 17; www.il-bu.net, Italian only; Via San Quintino 13; before/after 8pm per hr €3.60/4.80; ⌚ 9am-1am Mon-Fri, 4pm-2am Sat) Surf 30 mins free between 6pm and 7pm.

FNAC (Map pp60-1; ☎ 011 551 67 11; Via Roma 56; per 30mins/hr €2/3; ⌚ 9.30am-8pm Mon-Sat, 10am-8pm Sun)

Internet Resources

City Vox (www.cityvox.com) General listings guide.

Comune di Torino (www.comune.torino.it/canaleturismo /en/index.html) Practical information from the city authority.

Extra Torino (www.extratorino.it) Comprehensive, up-to-date listings guide in English.

Torino 2006 (www.torino2006.org) Olympic facts and figures.

Turismo Torino (www.turismotorino.org) Extensive tourist information in English.

Laundry

Lava e Asciuga Via Vanchaglia (Map pp60-1; Via Vanchiglia 10; per 7/16kg load €3.20/6.40; ⌚ 8am-10.30pm); Via Sant'Anselmo (Via Sant'Anselmo 9; per 7/16kg load €3.20/6.40; ⌚ 8am-10.30pm)

Left Luggage

Stazione Porta Nuova (☎ 011 669 04 45; opposite platform No 16; 1st 12/subsequent 12 hrs €3/2; ⌚ 6am-midnight)

Medical Services

Farmacia Boniscontro (Map pp60-1; ☎ 011 53 82 71; Corso Vittorio Emanuele II 66; ⌚ 3-12.30pm) Pharmacy.

Ospedale Mauriziano Umberto I (Map p58; ☎ 011 5 08 01; Largo Turati 62)

Pharmacy (Map pp60-1; ☎ 011 518 64 67; Stazione Porta Nuova; ⌚ 7am-7.30pm) Located inside Stazione Porto Nuovo.

TURIN

Money

Banca CRT (Map pp60-1; Piazza CLN) ATMs and a 24-hour automatic banknote exchange.

Stazione Porta Nuova Bank with an ATM and exchange booth. Further banks line Via Roma and Piazza San Carlo, many of which have ATMs.

Post

Central Post Office (Map pp60-1; ☎ 011 506 02 92; Via Alfieri 10; ☼ 8.30am-7pm Mon-Fri, 8.30am-1pm Sat) Post Restante should be addressed with the receivers name, Fermo Posta and the post office address.

Post Office Branches Via Saachi (Map pp60-1; ☎ 011 5668 42 00; Via Saachi 2b); Via Saluzzo (Map p58; ☎ 011 654 68 32; Via Saluzzo 37)

Telephone

Telecom Booth (Map pp60-1; Via Roma 18; ☼ 8am-10pm) Public pay phones.

Tourist Information

Airport Tourist Office (☎ 011 567 81 24; ☼ 8.30am-10.30pm) In the domestic arrivals area.

City Tourist Office (Map pp60-1; ☎ 011 53 59 01/ 011 53 51 81; www.turismotorino.org, Italian only; Atrium Torino, Piazza Solferino; ☼ 9.30am-7pm Mon-Sat, 9.30am-3pm Sun)

Informacittá (Map pp60-1; ☎ 011 442 28 88; Piazza Palazzo di Cittá 9a; ☼ 8.30am-6pm Mon-Fri, 9am-1pm Sat) City information service.

Stazione Porta Nuova (☎ 011 53 13 27; ☼ 9.30am-7pm Mon-Sat, 9.30am-3pm Sun) A branch of the City Tourist Office.

Travel Agencies

Agenzia Viaggi Passaggi (☎ 011 53 46 63; Stazione Porta Nuova, Via Nizza side) For national and international train tickets, located at the side of the Stazione Porto Nuova.

CTS Viaggi (Map pp60-1; ☎ 011 812 45 34; Via Montebello 2h) Student and youth travel.

DANGERS & ANNOYANCES

Turin is not a dangerous city – you're unlikely to come across violence – but care should be taken to avoid pickpockets who, as in all major Italian cities, are active. Common sense and an under-the-clothes money belt go a long way to reducing the risks. If you don't have a money belt, keep cash in your front pockets and watch out for people who seem to brush close to you.

Bag snatching is not a common occurrence, but it pays to wear the strap of your bag or camera across your body and facing the side away from the road.

As in all cities, there are certain areas that should be avoided at night, particularly for solo travellers of either sex. The streets east and south of Stazione Porta Nuova have an unpleasant reputation and, although not as bad as they once were, should be approached with caution.

Parked cars, particularly those with foreign number plates or rental-company stickers are prime targets for thieves. Never leave valuables in your car.

On the road, city traffic can be dangerous for the unprepared tourist. Many roads that

---

TURIN IN...

Two Days

Start your day with an extravagant *cappuccino all'arancia* (orange cappuccino) at **Café San Tommaso**, the coffee connoisseurs' café. This will set you up for the marvels of **Piazza Castello** including **Palazzo Reale** and **Palazzo Madama**. After a light lunch head to the **Mole Antonelliana** with its amazing panoramic lift and thrilling **Museo Nazionale del Cinema**. Aperitifs in one of the historic cafés will then whet the appetite for an evening in the lively **Piazza Emanuele Filiberto**.

The **Museo Egizio** and **Galleria Sabauda** will keep you busy on your second day, while a visit to the **Cappella della Santa Sindone** is a further must-see.

Four Days

Follow the two-day itinerary, and on the third day relax with some shopping at the **Porta Palazzo** market and a stroll around the cobbled *centro storico*. On the fourth day, head out of town to the Savoy hunting lodge at **Stupinigi**.

One Week

With a week you could relax your pace in the city, adding the **Museo Nazionale del Risorgimento** and **Lingotto Fiere** to your city itinerary. Further afield the Savoy **Castello di Rivoli**, with its excellent modern art gallery, is definitely worth the drive. While you're there treat yourself to dinner at the Michelin-starred **Combal.Zero** restaurant.

GREATER TURIN

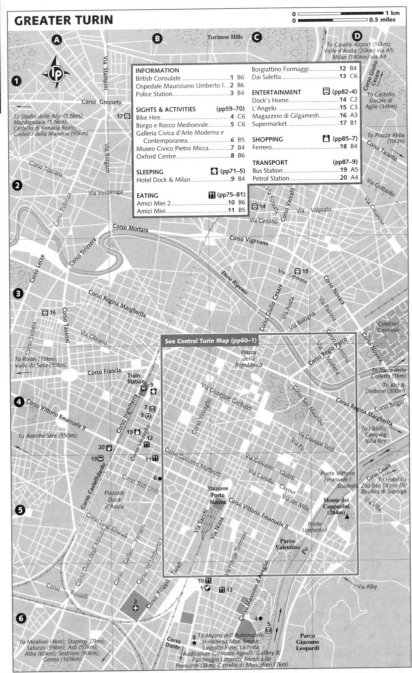

0 — 1 km
0 — 0.5 miles

INFORMATION
British Consulate..........................**1** B6
Ospedale Mauriziano Umberto I...**2** B6
Police Station.............................**3** B4

SIGHTS & ACTIVITIES (pp59–70)
Bike Hire.................................**4** C6
Borgo e Rocco Medioevale............**5** C6
Galleria Civica d'Arte Moderna e
   Contemporanea.....................**6** B5
Museo Civico Pietro Micca............**7** B4
Oxford Centre...........................**8** B6

SLEEPING (pp71–5)
Hotel Dock & Milan.....................**9** B4

EATING (pp75–81)
Amici Miei 2.............................**10** B6
Amici Miei................................**11** B5

Borgiattino Formaggi.................**12** B4
Dai Saletta..............................**13** C6

ENTERTAINMENT (pp82–4)
Dock's Home............................**14** C2
L'Angelo.................................**15** C3
Magazzino di Gilgamesh..............**16** A3
Supermarket.............................**17** B1

SHOPPING (pp85–7)
Ferrero..................................**18** B4

TRANSPORT (pp87–9)
Bus Station.............................**19** A5
Petrol Station...........................**20** A4

See Central Turin Map (pp60–1)

appear to be one-way have lanes for buses travelling in the opposite direction – always look both ways before stepping onto the road.

SIGHTS

Turin city centre is a high-octane mix of baroque extravaganzas, cobbled alleyways and major road arteries. Impressive buildings line the busy streets, elegant piazzas run into one another and round every corner there's yet another 19th-century café lying in wait.

Piazza Castello   Map pp60-1

At the heart of the historic centre, Turin's grandest square is the perfect place to start exploring the city. In fact, you could easily spend a day or two investigating the wealth of museums, theatres and cafés lining its porticoed promenades.

Essentially baroque, the piazza was laid out from the 14th century to serve as the seat of dynastic power for the House of Savoy. Designed to reflect their ambitions for Turin as one of Europe's great capitals, it was steadily transformed by architects such as Filippo Juvarra (1678–1736) into the magnificent space that survives today.

In the northwestern corner of the square is the baroque **Chiesa di San Lorenzo** (☎ 011 436 15 27; Piazza Castello; admission free; ☽ 7.30am-noon & 4-7.30pm Mon-Sat, 9am-1pm, 4-7.30pm & 8.30-10pm Sun), designed by Guarino Guarini, where a richly complex interior compensates for the sparse facade.

PALAZZO MADAMA

This part medieval, part baroque 'castle' (☎ 011 442 99 12; Piazza Castello; admission free; ☽ Tue-Fri & Sun 10am-8pm, Sat 10am-11pm) dominates the square. Built in the 13th century on the site of the old Roman gate, it gained its name as the 17th-century residence of Madama Reale Maria Cristina, the widow of Vittorio Amedeo I. Its rich, baroque facade was added later by Juvarra between 1718 and 1721. Over the centuries it has served as a prison, barracks, royal cellar, senate and court.

Recently re-opened, at least in part, you can now visit Juvarra's **great hall**, the grand **staircase** and the **Voltone room**. Archaeological

---

A CITY OF TWO HEARTS

Turin is a city of magic. Home to the Holy Shroud and, according to legend, of the Holy Grail, it's a sacred town with a diabolical core. Situated on the 45th parallel, it forms one of the three apexes of the so-called white magic triangle with Lyon and Prague and of the black magic triangle with London and San Francisco.

Mysterious and ancient lines of positive and negative energy converge on the city, as do two rivers, the Po and the Dora. The Po is said to represent the sun and the masculine while the Dora symbolises the moon and the feminine. Together they form a protective ring of water around the city.

The black heart of Turin is Piazza Statuto. Located in the west of the city, the Romans believed it to be cursed as its position was unfavourable for the setting of the sun. This, they claimed, was a source of negative energy as sunset symbolised the convergence of good and evil. More prosaically, Piazza Statuto was the site of the city scaffold where thousands met their fate before passing directly through the Gates of Hell, said to lie under the piazza's central flower bed. On the other side of the divide, legend places the Gates of Infinity in Piazza Solferino.

The area around Piazza Statuto is not without its ghosts. Most infamous of all is the Turin Executioner. From his home in the dark and gloomy Via Bonelli he endlessly prowls Piedmont, rigorously dressed in black and carrying a bag containing the macabre tools of his trade.

To combat these sinister forces you should head for Piazza Castello, the centre of the white magic map. In fact, the dividing line between the black and white halves of the city passes through the space between the statues of Castor and Pollux outside the Palazzo Reale.

Believers cite as reasons for the purity of this area the vicinity of the Holy Shroud in the Duomo di San Giovanni Battista, the positive energies emanating from the Museo Egizio and the golden auspices of the cave under Palazzo Madama where the Savoys used to have the master alchemists of the day practise their mysterious arts.

To this cauldron of positivity you can add the beneficial effects of the Holy Grail, which believers claim is buried under the Chiesa della Gran Madre di Dio on the other side of the River Po.

CENTRAL TURIN

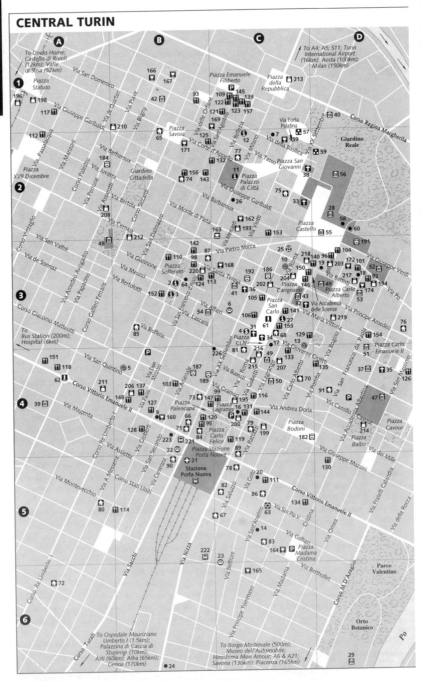

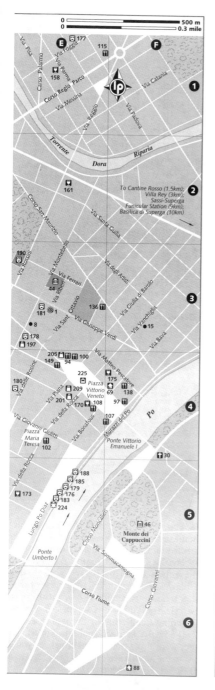

INFORMATION

1PC4YOU	1 E3
Atrium Torino 2006	2 B3
Atrium Torino Città	3 B3
bu.net	4 B4
Banca CRT	5 C3
Central Post Office	6 C3
Circolo Maurice	7 C2
City Tourist Office	(see 2)
Club Alpino Italiano	(see 203)
CTS Viaggi	8 E3
Farmacia Boniscontro	9 B4
Fnac	10 C3
Informacittà	11 C2
Informagay	12 C2
Internet Train	13 C4
Lava e Asciuga	14 C5
Lava e Asciuga	15 F3
Libreria Dante Alighieri	16 C4
Libreria Druetto	17 C3
Libreria Française	18 D3
Libreria Luxemburg	19 D3
Libreria Zanaboni	20 C5
Pharmacy	21 B5
Post Office Branch	22 B4
Post Office Branch	23 C5
Somewhere	24 B6
Telecom Booth	25 C3
Touring Club Italiano Bookshop	26 C2
Vetrina per Torina	27 C3

SIGHTS & ACTIVITIES (pp59–70)

Armeria Reale	28 D2
Biblioteca Reale	(see 28)
Castello del Valentino	29 D6
Chiesa di Gran Madre di Dio	30 F4
Chiesa di San Carlo	31 C3
Chiesa di San Filippo Neri	32 C3
Chiesa di San Lorenzo	33 C2
Chiesa di Santa Cristina	34 C3
Chiesa di Santa Croce Juvarra	35 D4
Chiesa di Santa Teresa	36 C3
Chiesa e Conventa di Santa Maria	(see 46)
Collegio delle Province	37 D4
Duomo di San Giovanni Battista & Cappella della Santa Sindone	38 C2
Galleria Civica d'Arte Moderna e Contemporanea	39 A4
Galleria Sabauda	(see 43)
Mole Antonelliana	(see 44)
Museo Civico d'Arte Antica	(see 55)
Museo d'Antichità	40 D1
Museo della Marionetta	41 C3
Museo della Sindone	42 B1
Museo Egizio	43 C3
Museo Nazionale del Cinema	44 E3
Museo Nazionale del Risorgimento	45 D3
Museo Nazionale della Montagna	46 F5
Museo Regionale di Scienze Naturale	47 D4
Museo Storico Nazionale dell'Artiglieria (Citadel)	48 A3
Palazzo Bricherasio	49 C4
Palazzo Carignano	(see 45)
Palazzo Cavour	50 C4
Palazzo Coardi di Carpeneto	51 D4
Palazzo dell' Accademia delle Scienze	(see 43)
Palazzo dell'Universita	52 D3
Palazzo Granieri	53 D3
Palazzo Lascaris di Ventimiglia	54 B3
Palazzo Madama	55 D2
Palazzo Reale	56 D2
Porta Palatina	57 C2
Prefecture	58 D2
Roman Amphitheatre	59 D2
State Archives	60 D2
Statue of Emanuele Filiberto	61 C3
Statue of Vittorio Emanuele II	62 A4
Synagogue	63 C5
Touring Club Italiano Bookshop	64 B3

SLEEPING	(pp71–75)
Ai Savoia	65 B2
Albergo Astoria	66 B4
Albergo Paradiso	67 C5
Albergo San Carlo	68 C3
Albergo Sila	(see 84)
Casamarga	69 F4
Grand Hotel Sitea	70 C4
Hotel Bologna	71 B4
Hotel Boston	72 A6
Hotel Campo di Marte	73 B4
Hotel Canelli	74 B2
Hotel Chelsea	75 C2
Hotel des Artistes	76 D3
Hotel Dogana Vecchia	77 C2
Hotel Genio	78 C5
Hotel Gran Mogol	79 C4
Hotel Montevecchio	80 A5
Hotel Nazionale Torino	81 C4
Hotel Nizza	82 C5
Hotel Piemontese	83 C5
Hotel Roma e Rocca Cavour	84 B4
Hotel Solferino & Artuá	85 B3
Hotel Versilia	86 C5
Le Petit Hotel	87 B3
Ostello Torino	88 F6
Star Hotel Majestic	89 C4
Turin Palace Hotel	90 B5
Victoria Hotel	91 D4

EATING	(pp75–81)
Abrate	92 D3
Al Bicerin	93 B1
Antonelli	94 E4
Arcadia	(see 203)
Avvignano	95 B4
Baratti & Milano	96 D3
Bokoas Dining Club	97 F4
Brek	98 B3
Brek	99 C4
Caffè Elena	100 E4
Caffè Fiorio & Gelateria Fiorio	101 D3
Caffè Guglielmo Pepe	102 E4
Caffè Miretti	103 B4
Caffè Mulassano	104 D3
Caffè San Carlo	105 C3
Caffè Torino	106 C3
Caffè Flora	107 F4
Café 21	108 E4
Casa Martin	109 C1
Cernaia 3	110 B3
C'era Una Volta	111 C5
Di per Di	112 A2
Di per Di	113 B3
Di per Di	114 B5
Fratelli La Cozza	115 E1
Gatsby's	116 C4
Gennaro Esposito	117 A1
Gerla Chocolate House	118 A4
Giordano Chocolate House	119 C4
GROM	120 B4
Hafa Café	121 C1

I Tre Galli	122 C1
Il Bragatto	123 C1
Il Granaio	124 B3
Il Mercante di Spezie	125 B2
Il Punto Verde	126 D4
Il Vicola	127 B4
Kashmir	128 B4
Kirkuk Kafè	129 C3
L'Agrifoglio	130 D5
La Baita del Formagg & Gertosio	131 C4
La Focacceria Tipica Ligure	132 C2
La Focacceria Tipica Ligure	133 C4
Lucky Nugget Saloon	134 C5
Lunch & Tea	135 D4
Mamma Mia	136 E3
Mamma Mia	137 B4
Mare Nostrum	138 F4
Montagne Viva	139 C1
Mood	140 D3
Neuv Caval 'd Brôns	141 C3
Norman	142 B3
Olsen	143 B2
Pastificio De Filippis	144 C4
Pastis & Free Vélo	145 C1
Pepino	146 C3
Peyrano Chocolate House	(see 211)
Pizzeria Stars & Roses	147 B4
Platti	148 B4
Porto di Savona	149 E4
Ristorante del Cambio	150 C3
Ristorante Emporio Gastronomico	151 A4
Ristorante Vintage 1997	152 B3
San Tommaso 10	153 C2
Société Lutèce	154 D3
Stratta Confectioner	155 C3
Taverna dei Guitti	156 B2
Tre Galline	157 C1

DRINKING	(pp81–82)
Birrificio Torino	158 E1
Caffè della Basilica	159 C2
Caffè Leri	160 B4
Caffè Rossini	161 C2
Cantine Barbaroux	162 C2
Confetteria	163 C2
Damadama Café	164 C5
Diwan Café	165 C6
Enotria	166 B1
Fish	167 B1
Frog	168 C3
KM5	169 C1
La Drogheria	170 E4
Lobelix	171 B2
Roar Roads	172 D3
Suite 29	173 E5
Taberna Libraria	174 D3
Vinicola Al Sorij	175 F4

ENTERTAINMENT	(pp82–84)
Alcatraz	176 E5
Azimut	177 E1
Barrumba	178 E3

Beach	179 E5
Centralino	180 E4
Cinema Massimo	181 E3
Conservatorio Giuseppe Verdi	182 C4
Da Giancarlo	183 E5
Folkclub	184 A2
Jammin'	185 E5
Lux	186 C3
Olimpia	187 B4
Pier 7-9-11	188 E5
Reposi	189 B4
Teatro Carignano	(see 150)
Teatro Gianduja	(see 41)
Teatro Gobetti	190 E3
Teatro Regio Torino & Teatro Piccolo Regio	191 D3
Teatro Stabile Box Office	(see 204)
Theatrò	192 C3

SHOPPING	(pp85–87)
Bottega Fagnola	193 C2
Calzedonia	194 D3
Calzedonia	195 C4
Calzedonia	196 A1
Camden Town	197 E3
Di per Di	198 A1
Fongo Domenico	199 C4
Foresto Borsalino	200 C4
Galleria Cristiani	201 E4
Galleria San Frederico	202 C3
Galleria Subalpina	203 C3
Gucci	204 C3
Icarta	205 C4
La Casa Moderna	206 B4
Lagrange 15	207 C4
Max Mara	(see 204)
Morpholuce	208 A2
Onde	209 E4
P I A N A	210 B1
Parola	211 A4
Pignatelli	212 B2
Porta Palazzo Market	213 C1
Prada	(see 204)
Renni	214 D4
Renni	215 C4
Ricordi Media Store	216 C4
Rock & Folk	217 D3
Rock & Folk	218 C3
Shoeco	(see 154)
Turin Gallery	219 D3
Vini Renato Rabezzana	220 B3

TRANSPORT	(pp87–89)
Bus Stop for Airport	221 B4
Bus Stop	222 B5
Caffè Cervino (Sadem tickets for Airport bus)	223 B4
Imbarco Murazzi	224 E5
Tram Stop to Sassi	225 E4

OTHER	
Regency School	226 C4

excavations can be viewed from the Voltone room.

The **Museo Civico d'Arte Antica** (☎ 011 442 99 12), which is also housed in the Palace, displays paintings and sculptures by Piedmontese artists from the Medieval period to the 17th century. It is due to reopen in time for the winter Olympics in 2006.

PALAZZO REALE

Statues of Roman deities Castor and Pollux guard the entrance to the **Palazzo Reale** (Royal Palace; ☎ 011 436 14 55; Piazza Castello; adult/child €6.50/free; ☑ 9am-7pm Tue-Sun), the Savoy family home until 1865. An austere building, it was erected for Carlo Emanuele II around 1646. Its lavishly decorated rooms, connected to the entrance hall by Juvarra's celebrated *Scala delle Forbici* (literally 'staircase of scissors'), house an assortment of furnishings, porcelain and other bits and priceless bobs, including a collection of Chinese vases.

The Savoys were great collectors of art, but they were also a well-armed bunch, as you'll see in the **Armeria Reale** (Royal Armoury; ☎ 011 518 43 58; Piazza Castello; adult/child €2/free; ☑ 8.30am-2pm

Mon, Wed & Fri, 1.30-7.30pm Thu, Sat & Sun). Hidden under the porticoes just to the right of the palace gates, it contains what some claim to be Europe's best collection of daggers, guns and assorted killing instruments.

In the adjoining **Biblioteca Reale** (Royal Library; ☎ 011 45 38 55; Piazza Castello; admission free; ⏰ 8.35am-6.45pm Mon, Wed & Fri, 8.30am-1.30pm Tue, Thu & Sat) dating to 1831, there are 200,000 volumes, 5000 16th-century books, several thousand manuscripts and a self-portrait scribbled in crayon by Leonardo da Vinci.

The surrounding **Giardini Reali** (Royal Garden; admission free; ⏰ 9am-1hr before sunset), east of the palace, was designed in 1697 by Andrè le Nôtre, creator of the gardens at Versailles.

Under the porticoes in Piazza Castello's northeastern corner you'll find the **State Archives** (Archivio di Stato; ☎ 011 562 46 10; Piazza Castello 209; admission free; ⏰ 9am-5.45pm Mon-Fri, 9am-1.45pm Sat) which, together with a **second State Archives site** (Via Piave 21; admission free), holds documentation from 13 centuries stored on 70km of shelves. The **Prefecture** and the **Teatro Regio & Piccolo Regio** (see p84) adjoin the Archive, forming an 18th-century complex known as the *zona di comando* (the command zone of the Savoys when they ruled their Duchy from Turin) that is linked to the Palazzo Reale by a system of galleries and passageways.

Duomo di San Giovanni Battista
Map pp60-1

Built between 1491 and 1498 on the site of three 14th-century basilicas, Turin's **cathedral** (☎ 011 436 15 40; Piazza San Giovanni; admission free; ⏰ 7am-12.30pm & 3-7pm Mon-Sat, 8am-12.30pm & 3-7pm Sun) is the city's only remaining example of Renaissance architecture. It also happens to be home to Christendom's most controversial cloth – the **Holy Shroud of Turin** (p64), a copy of which is on permanent display in front of the cathedral altar. The **Cappella della Santa Sindone** (1668–94), the rightful home of the shroud since 1694, has

TORINO ATRIUM

Touting itself as the symbol of the new Turin, the **Torino Atrium** (Map pp60-1; ☎ 011 517 81 34; www.atriumtorino.it, Italian only; Piazza Solferino; admission free; ⏰ 9.30am-7pm) is not easy to miss. Designed by Turin-based architect Giorgetto Giugiaro and situated in Piazza Solferino, the two hump-shaped steel-and-glass pavillions act as a striking counterpoint to the architectural rigour of the 19th-century square.

Unsurprisingly, its arrival in early 2004 was widely debated. Many complained that it ruined the elegance of an otherwise classic Turinese piazza while enthusiasts argued that it would add a new and interesting modern element. The deed now done, the debate continues over whether the Atrium should stay or go after the 2006 Olympics.

Divided into two parts, it's been designed to present both the city and the Winter Olympics. The Atrium 2006 (on the right as you approach from Via Alfieri) houses the city's main tourist office (p57) as well as an interesting interactive history of the Winter Olympics and an insight into Turin's preparations for 2006. The Atrium Cittá, on the other side, exhibits the city and the background to the city-wide makeover Turin is currently undergoing.

been closed for restoration since 1997 when it was severely damaged by fire.

The Romanesque **bell tower**, standing alone to the left of the cathedral, was designed by Juvarra and built from 1720 to 1723. Just to the north lie the remains of a 1st-century **Roman amphitheatre** and, a little further to the northwest, **Porta Palatina**, the red-brick remains of a Roman-era gate.

Across the road from these remains is the **Museo di Antichitá** (Museum of Antiquity; ☎ 011 521 11 06; Via XX Settembre 88c; adult/child €4/free; ⏰ 9am-7pm Tue-Sun), a trip down 7000 years of memory lane to the earliest Po valley settlements.

Piazza Carignano & Around
Map pp60-1

Piazza Carignano sits a block south of Piazza Castello. Its western side is flanked by the **Teatro Carignano** (see p84), where Vittorio Alfieri's *Cleopatra* was premiered in 1775, and its southern side is blessed by the **Chiesa** di San Filippo Neri (1714). Vittorio Emanuele II, Italy's first king, was born in the baroque **Palazzo Carignano** (1679–85), on the square's eastern side. It was here that the Chamber of Deputies of the Kingdom of Sardinia met (1848–60) and where Italy's first parliament sat between 1861 and 1864 (until the capital was moved to Florence).

Museo Nazionale del Risorgimento
Map pp60-1

The short-lived parliament forms part of the excellent **Museo Nazionale del Risorgimento** (☎ 011 562 11 47; Via Accademia delle Scienze 5; adult/child €5/3.50; ☯ 9am-7pm Tue-Sun) with extensive displays of arms, paintings and documents tracing the turbulent century from the 1848 revolts to WWII. It's one of the best of this genre in northern Italy but is of limited interest to those who don't speak Italian.

Museo Egizio & Galleria Sabauda
Map pp60-1

Considered to house one of the best collections of ancient Egyptian art outside of London and Cairo, the **Museo Egizio** (☎ 011 561 77 76; www.museoegizio.it, Italian only; Via Accademia delle Scienze 6; adult/child €6.50/free; ☯ 8.30am-7.30pm Tue-Sun) is absolutely compelling. Based in the imposing **Palazzo dell'Accademia delle Scienze** since 1824, the museum's mammoth collection grew out of a bunch of antiquities Carlo Felice of Savoy purchased from a French consul in Egypt in 1824. Among its wealth of recreated tombs is that of pharaoh architect Kha and wife Merit; the contents displayed (unearthed in 1906) were buried with them and are believed to date to 1400BC.

Allow at least two hours to do the museum justice.

In the same building, the **Galleria Sabauda** (☎ 011 547 440; adult/child €4/free; ☯ 8.30am-7.30pm Tue-Sat mid-Sep–May, 8.30am-7.30pm Tue-Fri, 8.30am-11pm Sat Jun–mid-Sep) houses the Savoy collection of art. On display since 1865, it's a showcase of 14th- to 19th-century Piedmontese, Italian and Flemish masters.

A combination ticket for admission to both museums costs €8 for adults (children free).

Piazza San Carlo & Around
Map pp60-1

Known as Turin's elegant drawing room, **Piazza San Carlo** (1637–60) acts as something of an aperitif for the banquet that is Piazza Castello. In fact, aperitifs are central to life

---

THE HOLY SHROUD

The *Sindone* (Holy Shroud) is Christianity's greatest icon of faith and object of devotion, luring millions of pilgrims to Turin when it is publicly displayed every 25 years (next in 2025).

For centuries experts and fanatics have argued over the authenticity of the shroud, said to be the burial cloth in which Jesus' body was wrapped after the crucifixion. Tests in 1981 uncovered traces of human blood and pollen from plants known to exist only around Jerusalem. Many guessed the shroud as being from AD 1260 to 1390; carbon dating carried out in 1988 seemed to confirm this, tying it to the 13th century and making it far from sacred. Most agree that the white cloth – 4.37m long and 1.10m wide – was woven in the Middle East.

How the image of a human body – with fractured nose, bruised right cheek, lance wound on chest, scourge marks on back, thorn wounds on forehead and nail wounds on both wrists and feet – was formed on the cloth remains the biggest mystery. Anti-shroudies claim it's neither the blood of Christ nor a medieval fake but, rather, the first ever attempt at photography (using a camera obscura) by Leonardo da Vinci.

Crusaders first brought the shroud to Europe. It belonged to Louis of Savoy from 1453 who folded the cloth into squares and stashed it in a silver treasure trove in Chambéry in France. The tie dye–style brown patterns visible on it today were caused by a fire in 1532 that saw a drop of hot silver fall into the casket and through the folded layers. Safeguarded in Turin since 1578, the shroud is laid out flat today in a vacuum-sealed box, which in turn is stored in a controlled atmosphere.

Shroud fiends shouldn't overlook the **Museo della Sindone** (☎ 011 436 58 32; Via San Domenico 28; adult/child €5.50/2.50; ☯ 9am-noon & 3-7pm), which, despite its informative displays and unexpected shroud paraphernalia, does little to unravel the major unanswered questions. Guided tours are in Italian only; ask for a free English-language audio guide.

DETOUR

Modern art enthusiasts should make their way to the **Galleria Civica d'Arte Moderna e Contemporanea** (Map pp60-1; GAM; ☎ 011 562 99 11; www.gamtorino.it; Via Magenta 31; adult/child €5.50/free; 9am-7pm Tue-Sun), dedicated to 19th- and 20th-century artists, including Renoir, Courbet, Klee and Chagall. With around 15,000 works to admire, the Philippe Starck chairs provide welcome relief.

To get to the gallery from Via Lagrange, head south to Stazione Porta Nuova, then turn right down Corso Vittorio Emanuele II. When you reach the statue of Vittorio Emanuele, turn left and you'll find the museum on the corner of Via Magenta and Corso Galileo Ferraris.

on the square, with several historic cafés to be found in its characteristic porticoes (of which central Turin has 18km).

Traffic revolves around an equestrian **statue of Emanuele Filiberto** (1838), the Savoy duke who made Turin the capital of his duchy, while twin baroque churches, **Chiesa di San Carlo** (1619) and **Chiesa di Santa Cristina** (1715–18) overlook the square's southern entrance.

A confirmed fan of Turin's café culture, Count Camillo Benso di Cavour, the architect of Italian unification, was born, and died, just south of the piazza in **Palazzo Cavour** (☎ 011 53 06 90; www.palazzocavour.it, Italian only; Via Camillo Cavour 8; adult/child €6.50/free; 10am-7.30pm Tue-Sun), a baroque palace dating to 1724. It can be visited during temporary exhibitions held in its grandiose interior.

What Cavour would have made of the exhibitions held at the 17th-century **Palazzo Bricherasio** (☎ 011 571 18 11; www.palazzobricherasio.it; Via Lagrange 20; adult/child €6.50/free, audio guide 1/2 people €3.50/5; 2.30-7.30pm Mon, 9am-8pm Tue, Wed & Sun, 9am-11pm Thu-Sat) is anybody's guess. The modern-art gallery has hosted surrealist Dali and been 'wrapped' by Christo and Jeanne-Claude in its time.

Many a deal has been wrapped up in Turin's austere banking district west of Piazza San Carlo. **Palazzo Lascaris di Ventimiglia** (1663–5), home to the Consiglio Regionale del Piemonte (Piedmont Regional Council) at Via Alfieri 19, has a lavish courtyard worth a peek, although the interior of the building is not open to the public.

Those game for a laugh should walk a block north to the **Museo della Marionetta** (Marionette Museum; ☎ 011 53 02 38; Via Santa Teresa 5; adult/group €2.60/2.07; by appointment only) adjoining **Chiesa di Santa Teresa** (1642). The museum houses a vast collection of period puppets, costumes and props, as well as a puppet theatre, the **Teatro Gianduja** (see p84).

Via Giuseppe Garibaldi & Around
Map pp60-1

Turin's medieval and largely traffic-free *centro storico*, immediately west of Piazza Castello, is a lovely area to get lost in. Fortified until the 17th century, its main thoroughfare is **Via Giuseppe Garibaldi**, lined today with affordable shops, cafés and pavement terraces. A chessboard of narrow pedestrian streets borders it to the north and south: **Via Mercanti**, **Piazza delle Consolata** and **Via delle Orfane**, named after the 16th-century orphanage at No 11 on the street, are all inviting.

With the liberation of Turin from the French in 1563, Emanuele Filiberto graced his ducal capital with a mighty star-shaped **citadel** (1564–8). Its flamboyant history is told in Turin's oldest museum, the **Museo Storico Nazionale dell'Artiglieria** (☎ 011 562 92 23; Corso Galileo Ferraris 0; study visits by appointment only) inside the keep (all that remains of the citadel). Scholars can study the unique collection of 14th- to 20th-century artillery.

Museo Civico Pietro Micca
Map p58

The might of Turin's citadel was tested in 1706 when the French besieged the Savoy capital, the drama of which is vividly captured in the **Museo Civico Pietro Micca** (☎ 011 54 63 17; Via Guicciardini 7; adult/child €3/2; 9am-7pm Tue-Sun), a fascinating museum named after the hero of the four-month siege. Detailed captions in English outline French attacks on other fortresses in the Duchy of Savoy and there's a scale model of Turin before the Battle of Turin (1706). The highlight is a guided tour by torchlight of a 300m section of the defensive tunnels running beneath the city.

Via Po & Around
Map pp60-1

Turin's hip scene, revolving around the city's university, can be found around Via Po, the street connecting Piazza Castello with Piazza Vittorio Veneto and the river. Known as one of Europe's widest and most beautiful streets in the 18th century, it became home to the royal university, **Palazzo dell'Università**, under Vittorio Alberto II.

Turin's single most remarkable sight is the **Mole Antonelliana** (Via Montebello 20), a couple of blocks north of Via Po. Intended as a synagogue when it was started in 1863, this extraordinary structure – 167m tall – is awe-inspiring when you first see it from the surrounding narrow streets. Capped by an aluminium spire, it is engineering as art form and quite a spectral sight when lit at night.

MUSEO NAZIONALE DEL CINEMA

Since 2000, the Mole has housed the equally riveting **Museo Nazionale del Cinema** (☎ 011 812 56 58; www.museonazionaledelcinema.org; adult/child €5.20/free; 🕑 9am-8pm Tue-Fri & Sun, 9am-11pm Sat). Split across five floors, it leads visitors on a fascinating interactive tour of Italian cinematic history – from its birth in Turin to the present day. Love, death, horror and Turin are among the themes illustrated with movie clips in 10 chapels in the Temple Hall; in the 'love' chapel you lie on a bed of red heart-shaped cushions to watch the movies, and in the 'humour' one you walk through an American fridge and sit on a toilet.

If all that doesn't satisfy you, and even if it does, you won't want to miss the breathtaking **Panoramic Lift** (adult/child €3.62/2.60, lift & museum ticket €8/2.60), which silently whisks you up to the Mole's roof terrace in 59 seconds. The view from the top is breathtaking.

Borgo Po   Map pp60-1

The most visible landmark in this area across the **Ponte Vittorio Emanuele I** (1810–15) is the lumbering dome of the **Chiesa della Gran Madre di Dio** (☎ 011 819 35 72; Piazza Gran Madre di Dio 4), built between 1818 and 1831 to commemorate the return of Vittorio Emanuele I from exile. It's worth a look. The steps leading up to the church were the ones Michael Caine famously careered down in the cult film, *The Italian Job*, while some mystics would have you believe that the Holy Grail is actually buried under the church.

From Piazza Gran Madre di Dio, a road spirals up **Monte dei Cappuccini** (284m), used as a defensive outpost since Roman times. Carlo Emanuele I destroyed its previous fortification in 1583 to build the **Chiesa e Convento di Santa Maria**. From the front terrace there's sweeping views of Turin and the Alps.

One wing of the 17th-century convent now shelters the **Museo Nazionale della Montagna** (☎ 011 660 41 04; www.museomontagna.org; Via Giardino 39; adult/child €5/free; 🕑 9am-7pm), founded by the Club Alpino Italiano (CAI) in 1877. Exhibits focus on Alpine flora and fauna, as well as man's meddling with mountains and his attempts to scale the world's peaks.

Slightly further north and set into a wooded hill, the 17th-century **Villa della Regina** (Strada Santa Margherita 40) was chosen by Queen Anne d'Orleans, the wife of Vittorio Amedeo, as her hillside residence. Currently closed for restoration, it's on the UNESCO World Heritage List. Renovations are slated for completion in 2005, although a reopening date is not known at the time of writing.

Basilica di Superga

In 1706, Vittorio Amedeo II pledged to build a basilica to honour the Virgin Mary if Turin was saved from besieging French and Spanish armies. The city was saved, and architect Filippo Juvarra built the **Basilica di Superga** (☎ 011 898 00 83; Strada della Basilica di Superga 73; admission to the dome €3/2, to the Savoy tombs €3/2) on a hill about 10km northeast of Piazza Castello. It is the final resting place of the Savoys, whose lavish tombs make interesting viewing. In 1949, a plane carrying the Turin football team crashed into the basilica in thick fog, these tombs lie to the rear of the church.

To get there, take tram No 15 from Piazza Vittorio Veneto to the Sassi-Superga stop on Corso Casale, then walk 20m to **Stazione Sassi** (☎ 800 01 91 52; Strada Communale di Superga 4; adult/child Mon-Fri €3.10/1.55, Sat-Sun & hols €4.15/2.60; 🕑 9am-noon & 2-8pm Mon & Wed-Fri, 7am-midnight Tue, 9am-8pm Sat), the cable-car station from where an original tram dating to 1934 rattles the 3.1km up the hillside (18 minutes, hourly).

Piazza Carlo Emanuele II & Around   Map pp60-1

Back on the left bank, a short stroll west along Via Giovanni Giolitti takes you past the bench-clad squares of Piazza Maria Teresa and Piazza Cavour to the **Museo Regionale di Scienze Naturali** (Natural Science Museum; ☎ 011 432 30 80; Via Giovanni Giolitti 36; adult/child €5/2.50; 🕑 10am-7pm Wed-Mon). An Alaskan brown bear personally welcomes visitors to this animal-stuffed museum inside the eastern wing of a monumental 17th-century hospital with four inner courtyards and a chapel.

A block north is **Piazza Carlo Emanuele II**, a square laid out with noble palaces and churches between 1675 and 1684. Daughters of the aristocracy studied at the convent and **Chiesa di Santa Croce Juvarra** (1718–30) on the square's southern side, and the brightest of the poor attended the **Collegio delle Province** (1737) next door but one. Someone filthy rich resided at **Palazzo Coardi di Carpeneto** (1680), a palace at No 17 with a heavily embellished 18th-century stuccoed facade and ornate interior courtyard.

South along the Po

Walking southwest along the River Po, you come to the 17th-century **Castello del Valentino** (Map pp60-1; ☎ 011 669 45 92; Corso Massimo d'Azeglio), a mock French-style chateau where Maria Cristina and Vittorio Amedeo I held their courtly frolics. Technically, it's closed to the public, but as it houses the architectural faculty of Turin polytechnic, you can surreptitiously wander around.

The carefully designed French-style **Parco Valentino** around it opened in 1856 and is one of the most celebrated parks in Italy – particularly by rollerbladers, cyclists and smooching young romancers. Equally admired are the **Orto Botanico** (Map pp60-1; ☎ 011 661 24 47; Viale P Mattioli 25; adult/child €3/1.50; ☒ 9am-1pm & 3-7pm Sat & Sun, by appointment only Mon-Fri Apr-Sep), botanical gardens dating to 1729 and tended by green-fingered university profs.

Continuing a little further south you find the decidedly strange, Disney-style medieval **Rocca** (Map p58; Castle; Viale Virgilio 107; adult/child €3/2; ☒ 9am-7pm Oct-Mar, 9am-8pm Apr-Sep) and **village** (admission free), collectively known as **Borgo Medievale**. They were built for the Italian General Exhibition in 1884.

For a dose of modern art with a metallic sheen, head for the **Museo dell'Automobile** (☎ 011 67 76 66; www.museoauto.org, Italian only; Corso Unità d'Italia 40; adult/child €5.50/4; ☒ 10am-6.30pm Tue-Sat, 10am-8.30pm Sun). Among its 400 masterpieces is one of the first ever FIATs, and the Isotta Fraschini driven by Gloria Swanson in the film *Sunset Boulevard*. Take bus No 34 from beside Stazione Porta Nuova.

Via Nizza & Around

Via Nizza and the surrounding area is worth exploring but can be dodgy at night. If you do happen to be wandering around here, admire the Oriental strangeness of the 19th-century **synagogue** (Piazzetta Primo Levi) before continuing south to the hulking **Lingotto Fiere** (Via Nizza 280), Turin's congress centre and exhibition hall. Until 1982 FIAT cars were manufactured in this former factory, constructed in 1912-23 and transformed into the architectural icon it is today by architect Renzo Piano. The distinctive ball of blue glass sheltering a conference room at the top of the building was Piano's creation, although Lingotto's crowning glory remains the rooftop **track** (admission free; ☒ 8.30am-7.30pm) on which FIAT tested its cars.

The Lingotto is also home to the **Pinacoteca Giovanni e Marella Agnelli** (☎ 011 006 27 13; www.pinacoteca-agnelli.it; Via Nizza 230; adult/child €4/2.50; ☒ 9am-7pm Tue-Sun), an art gallery featuring, among its 18th- to 20th-century works, a series of early sketches made for FIAT advertisements. Known as the *Scrigno* (jewel case), it was here that Giovanni Agnelli's coffin was placed before his funeral (see p68).

Royal Castles

LA PALAZZINA DI CACCIA DI STUPINIGI

A visit to the Savoys' sprawling hunting lodge, in manicured grounds beyond Mirafiori, is a must. The Juvarra creation, a rococo delight, was designed for Vittorio Amedeo II in 1729. Many parts of the building are in their original condition and the rest is slowly being restored with FIAT money. Pieces of art and furniture from Savoy palaces are displayed in the **Museo di Arte e Ammobiliamento** (☎ 011 358 12 20; pstorico@mauriziano.it; adult/child €6.20/5.20; ☒ 10am-6pm Tue-Sun Apr-Oct, 9am-5pm Tue-Sun Nov-Mar).

Take bus No 4 south from Via San Secondo or along its southbound route from Piazza della Repubblica to Piazza Caio Mario, then bus No 41 to the palace.

CASTELLO DI RIVOLI

The preferred residence of the Savoy family from the 14th century onwards lies 13km to the west of central Turin in Rivoli. The 17th-century **castle** (☎ 011 956 52 22; www.castellodirivoli .org; Piazza Mafalda di Savoia; adult/child €6.20/free; ☒ 10am-5pm Tue-Fri, 10am-7pm Sat & Sun, 10am-10pm every 1st & 3rd Sat of the month) now houses a stunning contemporary art gallery known as the Museo d'Arte Contemporanea, as well as a Michelin-starred restaurant (p80).

TURIN

L'AVVOCATO

Cars and Turin evoke different images. To Brits of a certain age, they mean Michael Caine and a group of likely lads racing through the city sewers in a brace of souped-up Minis. To Italians, and most of the rest of the world, they mean FIAT. And, for more than 30 years, FIAT meant Giovanni Agnelli.

Turin was Agnelli's city, but when news of his death hit the ether on 24 January 2003, the whole of Italy fell into a state of shock. At the age of 81 he had finally succumbed to prostate cancer. Two days later queues of 20,000 waited in the freezing cold to pay their respects to a man who had come to symbolise Italian style and *savoir faire*.

Friend to many of the 20th century's great and powerful – both Kissinger and Khrushchev spoke to him before the Italian government of the day – he was an enthusiastic member of the European jet set as a young man. Rita Heyworth and Anita Ekberg were former lovers and to the end of his days he remained passionate about fast cars, football and FIAT. He was a regular at the Stadio delle Alpi to watch Juventus, the family team, and at grand prix to watch his beloved red Ferrari.

But it was FIAT that played the central role in his and modern Turin's life. In 1963, L'Avvocato, as Agnelli was known to one and all (Agnelli was a qualified lawyer, hence his nickname: the Advocate), became managing director of the firm his grandfather had set up in 1899. Three years later he took over as chairman and steered the company through the good times and the bad. In the 1970s, labour unrest and militancy – resulting in the birth of the Red Brigade – were creating a series of crippling strikes at the company's massive Mirafiori complex. In 1979, events came to a head when Agnelli laid off 23,000 workers and the factories remained closed for 35 days before resuming production.

The 1980s proved good years for the company. Driven by boss Cesare Romiti, sales held up well and by the early 1990s, 50% of all Italian drivers owned a FIAT. However, it was not to last and today FIAT's fate is once again in the balance. Ironically, Agnelli's death could pave the way for the selling off of the group's loss-making car arm, something he fought tooth and nail to avoid in his lifetime.

Take GTT bus No 36 from Piazza Statuto to Rivoli bus station, then bus No 36n (or any No 36 marked 'Castello') up the hill. Journey time is about one hour (€1.25).

REGGIA VENARIA REALE

Known as the Versailles of Italy, this massive **castle** (☎ 011 459 36 75; www.reggiavenariareale.it; Piazza della Repubblica 4; adult/child €5/3; ✆ 9-11.30am & 2.30-5.30pm Tue, Thu, Sat & Sun, by appointment only Mon, Wed & Fri) is in Venaria Reale, about 4.5km northwest of Turin. Commissioned by Carlo Emanuele II in 1658, it was originally designed by Amedeo Castellamante and later worked on by Filippo Juvarra. His *Galleria di Diana* and *Cappella di Sant'Uberto* are celebrated highlights.

To get to Veneria, there are regular trains from Stazione Dora. The ten-minute journey costs €1.60.

CASTELLO DE LA MANDRIA

The Savoys used to graze their horses on the land surrounding this royal retreat in Venaria. Standing at the heart of the 6,500-hectare estate, the 18th-century **castle** (☎ 011 499 33 22; Viale Carlo Emanuele II 256, Venaria Reale; admission €5.15; ✆ by appointment only) was

restored in the mid-19th century as a country hideaway for Vittorio Emanuele II and his lover, the bella Rosina. Today, you can visit the royal apartments as well as enjoy the vast park, the largest wooded area in the Po Valley where wild deer and boars roam freely.

There are regular trains to Venaria from Stazione Dora station (€1.60; 10 minutes).

CASTELLO DI MONCALIERI

As a setting for police barracks, this imposing **castle** (☎ 011 64 13 03; Piazza Baden Baden, Moncalieri; admission €2; ✆ 9.30am-12.30pm & 2.15-6pm Thu, Sat & Sun) takes some beating. Dating to the 12th century, it was given an extensive makeover in the mid-17th century by Castellamonte, Juvarra and Alfieri. This imposing castle today houses a Carabinieri barracks, as well as a number of royal apartments open to the public; look for the *Salotto Reale* (royal drawing room), the *Salotto degli Specchi* (mirror room) and the regal lavatories of Queen Maria Adelaide, wife of Vittorio Emanuele II.

Moncalieri is 7km southwest of Turin, or a 20-minute ride by train from Lingotto station (€1.25).

ACTIVITIES

The surrounding mountains are Turin's biggest playground, where Turinese dash at weekends to walk, ski, climb, mountain bike and mush. See the Valle di Susa & Val Chisone chapter (p90) for further details. However, within the city limits there are plenty of opportunities to stretch your legs.

Cycling

Cycling is a popular pastime in Turin. Before donning your helmet and pedalling off ask at a tourist office for the excellent *Carta dei percorsi ciclabili di Torino* (1:17,500), which maps all of the city's 40km of cycle paths.

Turin's local cycle club **Bici & Dintorni** (☎ 011 88 89 91; www.biciedintorni.org, Italian only; Via Andorno 35b) organises group rides ranging from family outings of 20km to serious marathons of up to 250km.

Bikes are available for hire from the **Parco Valentino** (Viale Ceppi; ☺ 3-7pm Mon-Fri 10am-1pm & 3-7pm Sat-Sun Mar, Apr & Oct, 3-10pm Mon-Fri 9am-10pm Sat-Sun May-Sep), **Parco della Colletta** (Via Carcano; ☺ 3-7pm Mon-Fri 10am-1pm & 3-7pm Sat-Sun Mar, Apr & Oct, 3-10pm Mon-Fri 9am-10pm Sat-Sun May-Sep) and out of town at the **Parco della Mandria** (☎ 011 499 33 33; Corso Vittorio Emanuele II 256, Venaria; ☺ 3-7pm Mon-Fri 10am-1pm & 3-7pm Sat-Sun Mar, Apr & Oct, 3-10pm Mon-Fri 9am-10pm Sat-Sun May-Sep). Expect to pay €1/7.80/10.35 (one hour/24 hours/weekend).

Walking

Walkers for whom pounding the city streets is not challenging enough might want to contact the **Club Alpino Italiano** (Map pp60-1; ☎ 01153 79 83; www.caiuget.it, Italian only; Galleria Subalpina 30; ☺ 10am-1pm & 4-7pm Mon-Wed & Fri, 10am-1pm & 8-10pm Thu, 10am-1pm Sat), which has masses of information on guided hikes and *rifugi* (mountain huts) in the surrounding mountains.

Golf

There are seven courses within easy reach of town, four of which offer free rounds to holders of the **Torino Golf Pass**. The pass comes in two forms: the €25 version covers green fees and hire of clubs for any 24-hour period between Monday and Friday, while the €60 pass pays for 72 hours from Monday to Friday with a small extra necessary for weekend play. Details are available from tourist offices.

WALKING TOUR

To take in Turin's entire baroque splendour would require a determination and stamina beyond most enthusiasts. This itinerary, which is by no means exhaustive, gives a taste of what the busy baroque architects left in their wake.

Starting from Piazza Castello, where you'll find the **Palazzo Reale** (**1**; p62) and the **Chiesa di San Lorenzo** (**2**; p59), take Via Palazzo di Città until Via XX Settembre. Go right and you'll find the Duomo di San Giovanni and the **Cappella della Santa Sindone** (**3**; p63). Returning to the square, head for **Palazzo Madama** (**4**; p59) and, continuing down Via Po, **Palazzo dell'Università** (**5**; p66). From here Via Bogino heads southwards past **Palazzo Granieri** (**6**; Via Bogino 9) to Via Maria Vittoria. Go left at Via Maria Vittoria for Piazza Carlo Emanuele II and its three baroque beauties: **Palazzo Coardi**

> **WALK FACTS**
>
> Start/Finish: Piazza Castello
> Distance: 4.2km
> Duration: 3.5 hours

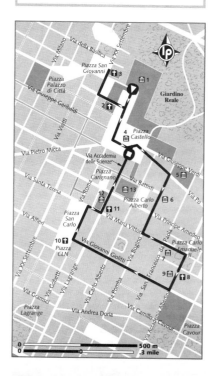

di Carpeneto (**7**; p67), the **Chiesa di Santa Croce Ju-varra** (**8**; p67) and the **Collegio delle Province** (**9**; p67). Via Accademia Albertina leads to Via Giovanni Giolitti, which you turn right into and head down until Piazza San Carlo. Here the **Chiesa di Santa Cristina** (**10**; p65) will sustain you for the last leg down Via Accademia della Scienze. Before you plunge down this imposing road, take a peek at **Chiesa di San Filippo Neri** (**11**; pp63-4), before passing the **Accademia delle Scienze** (**12**; p64) on your left, and finally **Palazzo Carignano** (**13**; p64) further down on your right.

COURSES

Turin offers various possibilities for courses, particularly language learning and cookery.

Language

The centrally located **Regency School** (Map pp60-1; ☎ 011 562 74 56; www.regency.it; Via Arcivescovado 7) is a well-known school offering a series of language courses. To learn Italian expect to pay €740 (plus €64 for materials) for a block of 20 individual lessons, or €550 (materials included) for lessons in groups of up to 10 students.

The **Oxford Centre** (Map p58; ☎ 011 66 315 33; Corso Dante 64) has seven schools in Turin. Italian lessons cost €350 for 36 hours in classes of six to eight students, or €1050 for one-on-one lessons.

FACTORY TOURS

Turin, for good and bad, is synonymous with industry. Its factories led Italy's post-war economic boom and today the city's industrial sector still sets standards of innovation and efficiency. To show how it's done, some companies have opened their doors, offering guided factory tours. Two of the biggest are FIAT and Lavazza.

Lavazza (☎ 011 239 85 00; Strada Settimo 410; admission free; ☒ 9.30-11.30am & 3.30-4.30pm Sep-Jun) offers two-hour guided tours to groups of no more than 30 people. Mirafiori is the massive (three-million-sq-metre) FIAT factory complex to the south of the city centre. For information on guided tours of the car plant, contact **FIAT** (☎ 06 003 42 69; Corso Giovanni Agnelli 200; admission free; by request only) directly. Both places can arrange English tours.

Cooking

For details of cookery courses, see Food & Drink pp51-2.

TURIN FOR CHILDREN

A boat trip along the **River Po** (p67), a funicular chug uphill to **Superga** (p66) or a rooftop ride in a slick glass lift at the **Museo Nazionale del Cinema** (p66) will please the biggest of fidgeters in the regional capital. Watching cartoons on a toilet seat at the cinema museum is another guaranteed winner, as is a puppet show at the **Museo dela Marionetta** (p65) or in the **Borgo Medievale** (p67). Older children visiting Turin will enjoy exploring the underground tunnels at the **Museo Civico Pietro Micca** (p65), tripping back to medieval Piedmont at the Disney-style **Borgo e Rocco Medioevale** (p67) and ogling at big fast cars in the **Museo Nazionale dell'Automobile** (p67).

QUIRKY TURIN

To see Turin in a completely new light, sign up for one of the unusual tours organised by the agency **Somewhere** (Map pp60-1; ☎ 011 668 05 80; www.somewhere.it; Via Nizza 32). To explore the city's underbelly, including bomb shelters and tunnels built by secretive Savoys, book yourself onto the **Torino Sotterranea tour** (€25). Lasting three hours, it descends into the depths underneath Piazza Vittorio Veneto every Wednesday and Friday.

However, if the city's magical myths prick your curiosity, the **Torino Magica tour** (€20) is for you. It departs from the city's heart of darkness, Piazza Statuto, every Thursday and Saturday and lasts 2½ hours. Tours are available in English on request, although you'll need to book about 10 days in advance.

For more on Turin's magical nature, see A City of Two Hearts, p59.

TOURS

An effective way of covering the city sights is to jump aboard the **Turismo Bus Torino** (☎ 011 53 51 81; 1-day ticket adult/child €5/3; ☒ 10am-6pm daily Jul-Sep & late-Dec–early-Jan, weekends & holidays at other times). A hop-on hop-off bus service run by public transport company GTT, it has an on-board hostess and serves 14 different points around central Turin. Buy tickets on board.

GTT also operates two boats on the River Po under the banner **Navigazione sul Po** (☎ 011 74 48 92; adult return €3.10; 6 trips daily Tue-Sun mid-Jun–Sep, 6 trips Sat-Sun only May–mid-June; 3 trips Sun & holidays only Oct-Apr). Boats for the 15-minute trip to the Borgo Medievale in Parco Valentino depart from Imbarco Murazzi (Murazzi del Po 65).

FESTIVALS & EVENTS

The city's calendar bursts with cultural events ranging from colourful traditional celebrations with a religious and/or historical flavour through to festivals of the performing arts, including opera, music and theatre.

January

Linguaggi Jazz (www.centrojazztorino.it, Italian only) Jazz swings into town with concerts and themed films.

March

CioccolaTò (www.cioccola-to.com, Italian only) For further details see the boxed text Chocolate p76.
Automotor International exhibition concerning everything to do with cars, held at the Lingotto Fiere.
Turin Marathon (www.turinmarathon.it) Twenty-six miles of Turin.
International Women's Cinema Festival (http://utenti.tripod.it/festivalcinemadonne) Eight days of films, shorts and documentaries by, with and for women.

April

Turin International Gay & Lesbian Film Festival (www.turinglfilmfestival.com) Judy Garland was the icon of the 2003 edition of this five-day gay and lesbian film fest.
BIG Torino (www.bigtorino.net) Biennial of Emerging Art provides a showcase for young artists. The next edition is due in 2006.
International Turin Roller Marathon (www.custorino.it, Italian only) Check out the blades in Parco Valentino.
Il Gioco del Teatro (www.teatrodellangolo.it) Plays by young performers and theatre workshops.

May

Salone Internazionale del Libro (www.fieralibro.it, Italian only) Italy's biggest book fair at the Lingotto Fiere.
Interplay (☎ 011 54 06 75; www.juvarramultiteatro.it; www.mosaicodanza.it; Via Juvarra 15; 22-29 May) Experimental dance at the Teatro Juvarra

June

Festival delle Colline Torinesi (Turin Hills Festival; 14 Jun-13 Jul) Theatre takes to the Turinese hills.
Festività Patronale di San Giovanni Battista (24 Jun) Feast of St John the Baptist (Turin's patron saint) sees celebrations fill the streets.
Momenti Estate (Jun-Sep) Street dances, open-air concerts and historical processions on the banks of the River Po.

July

Torino Extra Festival (www.extrafestival.com) Rock, pop, techno and acid jazz as performed by the Chemical Brothers, Lou Reed, St Germain et al.
Burattini Al Borgo (www.marionettegrilli.com, Italian only; Jul-Sep) Puppet theatre for all the family in the Borgo Medievale.

September & October

Torino Settembre Musica (www.comune.torino.it/settembremusica; Sep) Two concerts of music daily for 36 days.
Feminine Blues (www.centrojazztorino.it/blues.html, Italian only; Oct-Dec) Blues for the ladies.
Salone del Gusto (www.slowfood.it; late Oct) Gastronomic celebration of food.
Cinemambiente (www.cinemambiente.it; Oct) Italy's top environmental film festival.

November

Turin Film Festival (www.torinofilmfest.org; Nov) After Venice, Italy's most prestigious film festival.
Sottodiciotto Film Festival (www.aiacetorino.it, Italian only) Films for the younger generation.
Musica 90 (www.musica90.net, Italian only; autumn & spring) Ranging from ethnic sounds to jazz and pop, this eclectic music fair is held in Lingotto Fiere.

December

Luci d'Artista (mid-Nov–mid-Jan) Art illuminates Turin's central streets.

SLEEPING

Accommodation in Turin is largely geared towards the business market and tends to the mid- and upper-price brackets. Budget options do exist but you'll find fewer of them than in other big cities.

Securing a bed for the night is generally not a problem, particularly at weekends when the business folk head home and many upmarket hotels offer discounts of 10 to 15%. Arrive midweek, however, and you could find your choices limited.

Many of the cheaper sleeps are located in the not-so-beautiful area around Stazione Porta Nuova. The streets southeast of the station (to the east of Via Nizza) can be unpleasant and are best avoided by solo women. However, all the hotels we list are clean, safe and reliable.

To enjoy the more edifying pleasures of the *centro storico*, head for the streets that surround the two central squares, Piazza San Carlo and Piazza Castello. Prices here are correspondingly higher but you'll be right in the heart of things and within easy walking distance of most of the sights.

The tourist offices all carry extensive accommodation lists for the city and its environs.

Unless otherwise stated, the prices listed are for rooms with a bathroom.

Budget
HOSTELS

Ostello Torino (Map pp60-1; ☎ 011 660 29 39; hostelto@tin.it; Via Alby 1; dm B&B €14, dm in family room B&B €13-17; ☒ mid-Jan–mid-Dec) Turin's 76-bed hostel, about 2km from the train station, can be reached by bus No 52 (No 64 on Sunday) from Stazione Porta Nuova. Family rooms have their own bathroom and dormitories sleep three to eight. A nightly heating charge of €1 is charged between October and April. Non HI-card holders can buy a one-night stamp or annual card on arrival.

HOTELS – AROUND STAZIONE PORTA NUOVA

Hotel Bologna (Map pp60-1; ☎ 011 562 01 91; www .hotelbolognasrl.it, Italian only; Corso Vittorio Emanuele II 60; s/d €60/85; ☒) More luxurious than many three-star hotels, the two-star Bologna is an excellent choice. Just across the road from Stazione Porta Nuova, it is a friendly and smiling place with large, comfortable rooms. However, its charms are well known and it can be tricky to bag a room.

Hotel Nizza (Map pp60-1; ☎ 011 669 05 16; Via Nizza 9; s/d €45/70; ☐) A good bet in an area little known for its charms. Recently restored, it boasts good-sized rooms which, although a little anonymous, are bright and comfortable. Breakfast is an additional €6.

Hotel Versilia (Map pp60-1; ☎ /fax 011 65 76 78; Via Sant'Anselmo 4; d with/without bathroom €55/45) Vases of fresh flowers provide a fragrant welcome at this modest hotel. Standing opposite a synagogue, it has clean and comfortable rooms. Italian breakfast (coffee and croissant) is included in the price.

Hotel Montevecchio (Map pp60-1; ☎ 011 562 00 23; www.hotelmontevecchio.com, Italian only; Via Montevecchio 13; s/d €68/88, low season €58/75; ☐ ☒) Hovering between budget and mid-range, this bright, family-run place in a quiet residential area is hard to beat for a sound night's sleep.

Albergo Sila (Map pp60-1; ☎ 011 54 40 86; Piazza Carlo Felice 80; s/d with shower €43/55, s/d with shower & toilet €55/68) Albergo Sila looks down on the busy Piazza Carlo Felice from the third floor of its porticoed building. Fortunately, there is a lift to carry you to its decent and maniacally clean rooms.

Albergo Paradiso (Map pp60-1; ☎ 011 669 86 78; paradisalb@tiscali.it; Via Berthollet 3; s/d with/without bathroom €42/29) One of Turin's cheapest hotels, the homely Paradise extends a warm welcome. Rooms are simple, clean and free of most mod cons although they do come with a TV and basin.

Hotel Campo di Marte (Map pp60-1; ☎ 011 54 53 61; fax 011 513 27 77; Via XX Settembre 7; s/d €40/50) On the first floor up a rather dank staircase, this bargain joint offers the bare essentials and little else. The 10 rooms are all clean but come with absolutely no frills.

HOTELS – AROUND PIAZZA CASTELLO

Albergo San Carlo (Map pp60-1; ☎ 011 562 78 46; www .albergosancarlo.it; Piazza San Carlo 197; s/d €55/75; ☐) You can't get more central than this modest

Central Turin (p59)

View over Saluzzo (p115)

Battle of Oranges, Ivrea Carnival (p138)

MARTIN MOOS

Street lanterns in Casale Monferrato (p106)

Piedmont is the host city of the 2006 Winter Olympics (p37)

GRANT SOMERS

Torre Troyana o dell'Orologio, Asti (p104)

MART

hideaway overlooking Piazza San Carlo. The style is old world and the rooms, although modest, are decent value for money.

Hotel Canelli (Map pp60-1; ☎ 011 54 60 78; Via San Dalmazzo 5b; s/d €24/32) Not much motorised traffic passes by this ageing place on the fringe of cobbled Turin. Tatty and yellowing corridors lead to bare but serviceable rooms. Staff speak Italian only.

CAMPING

Villa Rey (☎ /fax 011 819 01 17; Strada Val San Martino Superiore 27; person/tent/car €5/4/1.10; ☺ Mar-Oct) Take bus No 61 from Piazza Stazione Porta Nuova to the last stop, then bus No 54 from the corner of Corso Casale and Corso Gabetti to get to this camp site east of the River Po.

Mid-Range
B&BS

Casamarga (Map pp60-1; ☎ 011 88 38 92/339 437 10 86; Via Bava 1bis; s/d €40/60) A make-yourself-at-home informality is the order of the day at this friendly B&B near Piazza Vittorio Veneto. There is only one split-level bedroom for use either as a single or double, adjacent to a large kitchen where breakfast is served. The owner welcomes guests with animals and has a dog herself.

Ai Savoia (Map pp60-1; ☎ 339 125 77 11; Via del Carmine 1/B; rooms €77) Located in an 18th-century townhouse, Ai Savoia offers three classically styled rooms, two of which retain their original wood-beamed ceilings. The gilt-laden breakfast room overlooks Piazza Savoia. All rooms sleep at least 2 people.

HOTELS – AROUND STAZIONE PORTA NUOVA

Hotel Boston (Map pp60-1; ☎ 01150 03 59; www.hotelbostontorino.it; Via Massena 70; s/d from €118/150, at weekends €83/105) Every room is different at this funky, eccentric hotel. The decor ranges from brothel chic to ethnic with a touch of Dali thrown in for good measure. Fun and comfortable, it's certain to make an impression.

Hotel Roma e Rocca Cavour (Map pp60-1; ☎ 011 561 27 72; www.romarocca.it; Piazza Carlo Felice 60; s/d from €69.50/87.50; P ⊠ ⊠ ⊠) Piedmont novelist Cesare Pavese is said to have spent some of his last days at this historic hotel before committing suicide in 1950. Rooms are individually decorated, some with antique furniture and parquet but all with an eye to style.

Victoria Hotel (Map pp60-1; ☎ 011 561 19 09; www.hotelvictoria-torino.com; Via Nino Costo 4; s/d from €107/154; ⊠ ⊠ ⊡) Marble-clad walls, floral sofas and wood panelling add to the charm of this English country–style hotel. Placed on a lane, it even boasts a small garden.

Albergo Astoria (Map pp60-1; ☎ 011 562 06 53; www.astoriahotel.it; Via XX Settembre 4; s/d €95/116; ⊠ ⊡) Imposing marble columns lend an air of grandeur to this elegant three-star hotel, offering functional and modern rooms. Discounts are available for weekend stays.

Hotel Genio (Map pp60-1; ☎ 011 650 57 71; www.hotelgenio.it; Corso Vittorio Emanuele II 47; s/d €135/190; P ⊠ ⊠ ⊡) Tucked beneath the arcades on one of the city's major thoroughfares, Hotel Genio is slick and efficient. Rooms are comfortable and decked out with the regular three-star trappings in a style that could be conservatively termed floral.

Hotel Gran Mogol (Map pp60-1; ☎ 011 561 21 20; www.hotelgranmogol.it; Via Guarini 2; s/d €135/190; P ⊠ ⊡) A sister hotel of the Genio, this place is comfortable, convenient and corporate, although somewhat lacking in character. Rates include a buffet breakfast.

Hotel Piemontese (Map pp60-1; ☎ 011 669 81 01; www.hotelpiemontese.it; Via Berthollet 21; s/d €129/181; P ⊠ ⊠) Brandishing three stars, you really can't go wrong at this lovely Liberty-style hotel, which languishes inside a late-19th-century townhouse. Pricier rooms with spa bath and hydromassage are available. Rates drop at weekends and include breakfast.

HOTELS – AROUND PIAZZA CASTELLO

Hotel Dogana Vecchia (Map pp60-1; ☎ 011 436 67 52; www.hoteldoganavecchia.com; Via Corte d'Appello 4; s/d €88/105; P ⊠) Mozart and Verdi were among the more distinguished guests to stay at this 17th-century inn. Now a charming three-star pad, it offers warm hospitality in elegant surroundings. For drivers the parking is also a big plus.

Hotel Chelsea (Map pp60-1; ☎ 011 436 01 00; www.hotelchelsea.it; Via XX Settembre 79; s/d €85/110; P ⊡) The family-run Chelsea is ideal for those with a serious sight-seeing agenda, as it's situated within a stone's throw of Piazza Castello. The flower-filled restaurant (dinner €25–30) is a fragrant bonus, especially as it allows parents to dine while children sleep upstairs with a baby monitor.

Le Petit Hotel (Map pp60-1; ☎ 011 561 26 26; www.lepetithotel.it; Via San Francesco d'Assisi 21; s/d €90/132;

Standing on the fringes of the *centro storico*, the Petit is a friendly place with modern rooms spread over three floors. Rooms overlooking the internal courtyard tend to be quieter than those fronting the street. Weekend discounts are available.

Hotel Solferino & Artuá (Map pp60-1; ☎ 011 517 53 01; www.hotelartua.it; Via Brofferio 1; s/d €100/125; P □ ✗) Just off the grand and leafy Corso Re Umberto I, Hotel Artuá resides in a grandiose old townhouse. Ride the fantastic old wooden lift with glass doors to the 4th floor. A laptop is available at reception for guests to surf in their room.

Hotel des Artistes (Map pp60-1; ☎ 011 812 44 16; www.desartisteshotel.it; Via Principe Amedeo 21; s/d €130/180; P ✗ ✗) A reassuring choice with no surprises up its sleeve, Hotel des Artistes offers excellent accommodation. The rooms are bright and decorated in an uncluttered modern style with soundproofing keeping out much of the city centre noise. Rates fluctuate (watch for 'special offers' on its website) and drop by 20% on nonholiday weekends.

Hotel Dock & Milano (Map p58; ☎ 011 562 26 22; www.dockmilano.com; Via Cernaia 46; s/d €105/125; ✗ □) A grand Liberty staircase leads up to rooms which are spacious and elegantly decorated. Parquet and natural light add a

sense of warmth to the simple furnishings. The hotel is near Stazione Porta Susa.

Hotel Lo Scudiero (☎ 011 839 93 52; www .hotelloscudiero.it; Corso Casale 89; s/d/t/q €62/80/93/113.60; ✗ □) Just across the river from the Mole Antonelliana, this decent enough three-star is ideal for late-night revellers as its open 24 hours. Breakfast is included in the room rates.

Hotel Nazionale Torino (Map pp60-1; ☎ 011 561 12 80; www.hotelnazionale.com; Piazza CLN 254; s/d €103/135; ✗ □) Fans of the horror flick *Profondo Rosso* will recognise the square in front of this none-too-beautiful concrete block. Inside, the decor is little better, with rooms warranting neither complaint nor exultation. Popular with school parties, it offers weekend discounts.

Top End

Le Meridien Art + Tech (☎ 011 664 20 00; www .lemeridien-lingotto.it; d €282; Via Nizza 262; ✗ ✗ □) Comfort combines with industrial chic at this slick four-star hotel in the Lingotto. Renovated by architect Renzo Piano, Le Meridien retains the factory's original full-length windows letting light flood into the fashionably designed rooms. Guests can also enjoy Turin's largest fully equipped gym.

CONSTRUCTION FEVER

Turin's builders have never had it so good as the city prepares for the 2006 Winter Olympics. New five-star hotels are going up, a slick metro system is in the pipeline and the city's rail network is being thoroughly overhauled.

Turin's hotel market has traditionally served the needs of its predominantly business clientele with plenty of three- and four-star hotels, but precious few top-of-the-line models. However, two major developments are hoping to buck the trend.

Joining the ranks of banks and corporate headquarters that surround Via Arcivescovado, Turin Hotel International's latest project will add 315 five-star beds to the city's accommodation directory. Situated in the former Toro Assicurazioni building at No 16, the as-yet-unnamed hotel represents an investment of more than €27.8 million for the city-based chain, with €4.2 million being contributed by the Piedmont region. Proposed features include a gym and fitness centre, two restaurants and a conference centre.

Farther south in Via Bisalta, the new Hotel Torino Lingotto will offer 174 beds in a project costing investors and the region €13.5 million.

Dive underground and the activity is equally feverish. Tunnellers are tirelessly working on the city's new metro system (p89), desperate to meet their Olympic deadlines. Scheduled to open in 2006, the big question remains, will it be ready in time?

Overground tracks are also being laid as part of the massive Crossrail project to upgrade the city's integrated rail network. The project involves, among other things, the construction of four new stations and the upgrading of three existing stations, the creation of a major new road and numerous urban reclamation schemes.

TURIN

Star Hotel Majestic (Map pp60-1; ☎ 011 53 91 53; www.starhotels.com; Corso Vittorio Emanuele II 54; s/d €209/369; ❊ ▯) Geared for the international conference circuit, this slick four-star offers considerable discounts for weekend breaks.

Turin Palace Hotel (Map pp60-1; ☎ 011 562 55 11; www.thi.it; Via Sacchi 8; s/d €225/277; ℗ ❊ ❊ ▯) A hotel since 1872, this is Turin's last word in late-19th-century luxury, with tastefully decorated rooms that effortlessly incorporate modern gadgetry into the classic decor. Significant reductions apply at weekends.

Grand Hotel Sitea (Map pp60-1; ☎ 011 517 01 71; www.thi.it; Via Carlo Alberto 35; s/d €190/255, low season 116/155; ℗ ❊ ❊) This top-notch oasis of calm and sophistication is apparently where the Juventus football team is put up when in town. Rooms are decorated in an upmarket corporate style.

EATING

With a gourmet culture as well defined as Piedmont's it should come as no surprise that eating in the region's capital is taken very seriously. Michelin-starred chefs compete with family-run trattorias and pizzerias vie with ethnic eateries to satisfy the demands of a highly discerning public.

Snacking is also a big time activity, particularly in early evening when the historic cafés swell with locals and tourists alike. For many, the sumptuous hors d'oeuvres laid out to accompany the aperitif constitute a meal themselves; for others they simply serve to whet the appetite.

Turin's cosmopolitan population means that the city serves some of the best ethnic food in Italy. Especially popular is north African and Middle Eastern fare, although most major world cuisines are represented.

For self-caterers, the city's delicatessens stock a bewildering array of cured meats and cheeses. Ideal for picnic purchases – simply add fresh bread and a bottle of red wine. They often stock beautifully packaged local produce, perfect to take home as a tasty gift.

All price ranges are catered to but expect to pay around €20 a head for a sit-down meal in a mid-range trattoria or restaurant. Drinking wine by the bottle will up this by at least €10.

Turin's cafés are centred around the central piazzas, while the city's 800-odd restaurants are fairly dotted around the place.

Cafés

Partly due to Turin's legacy of French and Austrian involvement, the city has a flourishing café scene. Many of the historic cafés date to the 19th century, when Risorgimento heroes, intellectuals and town gadabouts would flock to their ornate bars.

San Tommaso, 10 (Map pp60-1; ☎ 011 53 42 01; Via San Tommaso 10) Coffee connoisseurs crowd the narrow bar at this fabled address, mulling over a menu which includes orange cappuccino and tiramisu espresso. The cappuccino, which tastes like the most natural combination in the world, is a winner. Luigi Lavazza, father of the eponymous coffee brand, first began roasting beans here in the 1890s.

Al Bicerin (Map pp60-1; ☎ 011 436 93 25; Piazza della Consolata 5) Cavour, Dumas et al came here to drink *bicerin* (€4), a hot mix of coffee, chocolate, milk and cream. Other chocolate goodies cooked up at this café dating to 1763 include chocolate on toast and hot chocolate with ice cream. Its terrace at the foot of a 14th-century church bell tower is one of Turin's most peaceful.

Caffè San Carlo (Map pp60-1; ☎ 011 53 25 86; Piazza San Carlo 156; 1st/2nd courses from €5.50/7) Said to have been the first Italian café to introduce gas lighting, the sumptuous San Carlo was host to a gaggle of Risorgimento nationalists and intellectuals in the 1840s. Dating to 1822, it's now where suited folk meet to network. It offers cocktails, toasted snacks and 28 types of coffee.

Caffè Mulassano (Map pp60-1; ☎ 011 54 79 90; Piazza Castello 15) An Art Nouveau gem (built 1907–9) lined with a marble floor, mirrored walls, a coffered ceiling and even four tables (no mean feat considering the size of the place). As in days gone by, the theatre mob from nearby Teatro Regio adores this relic. It was here that the *tramezzino* (small sandwich) was invented.

Baratti & Milano (Map pp60-1; ☎ 011 561 30 60; Piazza Castello 27; menu from €10) Situated at the entrance to the Galleria Subalpina, Baratti & Milano has been serving coffee, cakes and light lunches since 1873. Crowds flock here on Sunday to buy cakes, sweets and biscuits (boxed and ribbon-wrapped) from its old-fashioned shop counter.

Platti (Map pp60-1; ☎ 011 506 90 56; platti1875@tin .it; Corso Vittorio Emanuele II 72; lunch menu €15.50) The

TURIN

CHOCOLATE

Turin's relationship with chocolate has deep historical roots. It was Duke Emanuele Filiberto, a Savoy general in the 16th-century Spanish armies, who first introduced choc to the city. Returning from South America in 1587, he presented the family with this rather good cocoa drink that the Aztecs seemed to swear by. Being experts in the finer things in life, the Savoys approved and chocolate had arrived in Piedmont.

But it was in the late 18th and 19th-centuries that Turin's fame as the centre of the choc world was established. In 1867, confectioner Michel Prochet came up with the idea for what was to become the symbol of Turin's sweet heart, *gianduja*. A mix of hazelnuts from the Langhe hills and cocoa paste, it was a hit from the beginning and is still today produced in reassuringly large quantities.

To experience these sticky treats, feasting your way around Turin's fiesta of old-fashioned sweet shops and chocolate makers is the sweetest way to tour the city.

Peyrano (Map pp60-1; ☎ 011 53 87 65; www.cioccolato-peyrano.it; Corso Vittorio Emanuele II 76), creator of *Dolci Momenti a Torino* (Sweet Moments in Turin) and *grappini* (chocolates filled with grappa), is Turin's most-famous chocolate house. Others include **Gerla** (Map pp60-1; ☎ 011 54 54 22; Corso Vittorio Emanuele II 88) and **Giordano** (Map pp60-1; ☎ 011 54 71 21; Piazza Carlo Felice 69).

Turin's best-known confectioner, **Leone** (www.pastiglie-leone.com), has been making sweets since 1857. Favourites include fruity bonbons inscribed with the word *allegria* (meaning 'happiness') on the outer wrapper; old-fashioned 'matchboxes' filled with tiny *pastiglie* (lozenges) in mint, mandarin and myriad other flavours; and its gold-wrapped *gianduja*. Historic shops selling Leone bonbons, chocolates and jellied fruits include **Stratta** (Map pp60-1; ☎ 011 54 79 20; Piazza San Carlo 191), founded in 1836; **Abrate** (Map pp60-1; Via Po 12a), with its lovely 1920s shop; and **Avvignano** (Map pp60-1; Piazza Carlo Felice 50), founded in 1883 and known for its *sorrisi di Torino* (literally, 'smiles from Turin').

For true chocoholics, nothing can beat **CioccolaTò** (www.cioccola-to.com), the city's grand homage to chocolate. A three-week festival in March, its opening fair in Piazza Castello draws huge crowds who flock to taste, point, nibble and marvel at the huge array of chocolate curiosities on display.

A city-wide initiative, it encompasses chocolate workshops, sculptures and films while many restaurants participate by offering chocolate-based menus. These include Casa Martin, La Montagne in Vetrina, Tre Galli and C'era Una Volta. To save a few euros (if not a few pounds), buy a special chocopass (€10), which pays for 10 tastings in a 24-hour period.

To recreate the taste of Turin at home, try brewing up your own *bicerin*. For four people, you'll need one litre of milk, 70 grammes of plain chocolate and 200 grammes of sugar. Add the milk and sugar gradually to the chocolate as you stir over a low heat. Once the mixture is thick and gloopy pour it into a glass, add a hot espresso and serve with whipped cream on top.

favourite café of author Cesare Pavese and editor Giulio Einaudi, the original Art Nouveau interior (1870) remains intact at this sweet-laden coffee, cake and liquor shop. Skip the noisy terrace and lunch beneath gold leaf inside.

Caffè Torino (Map pp60-1; ☎ 011 54 51 18; Piazza San Carlo 204; 1st/2nd courses from €10.50/12.50) Torino has served coffee beneath its chandelier-lit, frescoed ceiling since 1903. Stand with the Turinese at the bar or pay a fortune for silver service (a glass of wine costs €6.80). When leaving, rub your shoe across the brass bull in the pavement for good luck.

Confetteria (map pp60-1; Via San Francesco d'Assisi 17) Sporting an original mosaic facade, this historic café is a must for chocoholics. Each espresso comes with a spoon of chocolate to dip into the coffee and lick.

Caffè Elena (Map pp60-1; ☎ 011 812 33 41; Piazza Vittorio Veneto 5; ☒ Thu-Tue) The trendiest of Turin's historic bunch, Elena lures a chic set with its wood-panelled interior and Starck-designed chairs on a terrace overlooking one of the city's most vivacious squares. It also boasts a wine list of more than 700 labels.

Neuv Caval 'd Brôns (Map pp60-1; ☎ 011 54 53 54; Piazza San Carlo 157; ☒ Thu-Tue) With a lavish vaulted trompe l'oeil ceiling, this place doubles as a sophisticated café and a purveyor of tasty little cakes and delicate pastries.

The following is a selection of more contemporary cafés where you can pass pleasant hours idling away your time with a coffee and cake. Come early evening, they're the place for an aperitif in relaxed company.

Olsen (Map pp60-1; ☎ 011 436 15 73; Via Sant' Agostino 4b; lunch menus from €5) Strudels, muffins, banoffee pie (banana, toffee and cream pie) and cherry *clafoutis* (French baked-custard pastries) are baked at this down-to-earth, jam-packed lunchtime spot. Look for the cherry-topped fairy cake outside.

Pastis (Map pp60-1; ☎ 011 521 10 85; Piazza Emanuele Filiberto 9; ☺ 9am-3.30pm & 6pm-2am) Food design is what this boldly painted café-cum-bar prides itself on. Pop here any time of day for any type of drink, to be downed between geometric patterns inside or beneath trees outside. French-inspired Free Vèlo next door lures a similar clientele.

Mood (Map pp60-1; ☎ 011 566 08 09; Via Battisti 3e; ☺ 8am-9pm Mon-Sat)At this modern reading café, flick through design and art books while sipping cappuccinos or munching brunch.

Antonelli (Map pp60-1; ☎ 011 817 25 44; Piazza Vittorio Veneto 1) A fashionable choice for a super-gloopy hot chocolate or an *aperitivo della casa*. As you sup, soak up the sun's late afternoon rays on the spacious terrace.

Caffè Flora (Map pp60-1; ☎ 011 817 15 30; Piazza Vittorio Veneto 24) A pre-dinner cocktail slips down a treat at this Po-side café. Alternatively, come a little earlier to pass a lazy afternoon with an English newspaper, waiting for the early evening nibbles to come out.

Norman (Map pp60-1; ☎ 011 54 08 54; Via Pietro Micca 22) On the fringes of the *centro storico*, this chandelier-lit café is a good bet for a lunchtime plate of pasta (from €5). In summer, tables spill out beneath the arcade.

Café 21 (Map pp60-1; ☎ 011 812 22 09; Piazza Vittorio Veneto 21) Turin's trendsetters have welcomed Café 21 to the early evening aperitif circuit, appreciating the house specialities: cocktails based on absinthe.

Restaurants
BUDGET
Fratelli La Cozza (Map pp60-1; ☎ 011 85 99 00; Corso Regio Parco 39; pizzas from €5) A Turin institution, this legendary pizzeria is worth the hike just to have a look at the wacky interior. Resembling a bizarre Tarantino film set, it incorporates gigantic red plastic peppers, glass chandeliers and delicious Neopolitan pizzas. Its owner – Turinese comic Piero Chiambretti – is himself something of a cult figure.

Pizzeria Stars & Roses (Map pp60-1; ☎ 011 516 20 52; Piazza Paleocapa 2D; pizzas/pasta €8/9) Newcomer Stars & Roses is a colourful place to eat. Downstairs pizzas are served in the sunny orange room, while upstairs stylish greys and blacks dominate. The menu ranges from the classic to the outrageous – pizzas with salmon and whisky and caviar and vodka are radical departures for Italian cuisine.

Taverna dei Guitti (Map pp60-1; ☎ 011 53 31 64; Via San Dalmazzo 1; 1st/2nd courses €6/7) A lovely place to lunch, this welcoming tavern offers a range of excellent-value pastas and salads, cheeses and cured meats. In the evening you can often catch a jazz performance as you munch.

Gennaro Esposito (Map pp60-1; ☎ 011 53 59 05; Via Passalacqua 1g; pizzas from €5; ☺ 12.15-2.30pm & 7.15pm-midnight Mon-Sat) Ideal for late eaters, this bright and cheerful joint may well be the best pizzeria in town – certainly the numbers waiting to get in would suggest so. When you eventually get to your table choose from one of the 26 varieties of pizza. Reservations are essential.

Mamma Mia (Map pp60-1; ☎ 011 88 83 09; Corso San Maurizio 32; pizzas/pasta from €4.50/5) Hugely popular Mamma Mia is a Turin favourite. The cheerful atmosphere and extensive menu – some 45 varieties of pizza are dished up on large wooden boards – make for a winning combination. There is also a **branch** (Map pp60-1; ☎ 011 54 10 20; Via Parini 7) a short stroll from Stazione Porta Nuova.

Amici Miei (Map p58; ☎ 011 506 99 61; Corso Vittorio Emanuele II 94; pizzas from €5) At midday, tables at Amici Miei are fought over by the office crowd, while in the evening the casual diners move in. Connoisseurs swear by the wood-fired pizzas, while the sweet-toothed rave about the *zeppole di San Giuseppe* (fried doughnuts). There's an **Amici Miei 2** (Map p58; ☎ 011 650 28 51; Via Calusa Valperga 5) south of Stazione Porta Nuova.

Cernaia 3 (Map pp60-1; ☎ 011 54 90 81; Via Cernaia 3; pizzas €4-8) Join the Turinese who lunch at this busy city-centre pizzeria. Spacious and split across two floors, it offers more than 68 pizzas, both deep pan and thin crust, all crisped to perfection in the wood oven.

Société Lutéce (Map pp60-1; ☎ 011 88 76 44; Piazza Carlo Emanuele II 21; main/menu €5/10) Mix with the glam crowd at this trendy bistro complete with retro furnishings, weekend brunch and a fab pavement terrace. The atmosphere is laid back and the square-side setting elegant.

Il Granaio (Map pp60-1; ☎ 011 562 10 03; Via San Francesco d'Assisi 27; mains around €5; ☒ noon-2.30pm Mon-Sat) Walk through the *pastifico* (pasta shop) to uncover this cheap self-service restaurant packed with Turinese. Predictably, the pasta dishes are superb, as is its Tuscan *castagnaccio* (chestnut-flour cake topped with pine kernels and rosemary).

Il Vicola (Map pp60-1; ☎ 011 53 52 33; Via Gioberti 3; crêpes/risotto from €5.50/7.75; ☒ Mon-Fri & Sat evening) A sweet and savoury pancake house, Il Vicolo also rustles up a pretty decent risotto. To round off your meal, you could do worse than the crêpe smothered in Nutella (€5.50).

MID-RANGE
Dai Saletta (Map p58; ☎ 011 668 78 67; Via Belfiore 37; 1st/2nd courses from €7/8; ☒ Mon-Sat) A hugely popular trattoria, Dai Saletta is a modest family-run place that takes considerable pride in its cooking. The menu offers regional classics such as *brasato al Barolo* (mouth-melting tender beef braised in Barolo wine), while the wine list is dominated by Piedmontese reds. A great place to sample excellent value-for-money local cuisine, but book ahead.

Kirkuk Kafè (Map pp60-1; ☎ 011 53 06 57; Via Carlo Alberto 16bis; mains €4.50-6.50; ☒ 6.30pm-midnight Mon & Tue, noon-3pm & 6.30pm-midnight Wed-Sat) Sit cross-legged on the silk cushions and tuck into the Kurdish, Turkish, Iraqi and Iranian fare served up at this perennially popular eatery. The food is good, the service informal, and for the stiffer-limbed there are traditional tables and chairs. You'll need to book.

Il Punto Verde (Map pp60-1; ☎ 011 88 55 43; Via San Massimo 17; lunch menu/degustazione menu €8.50/25;

PIZZA PARTY
To taste Turin's top pizzas head for:

- **Gennaro Esposito** p77 Classical pizzas served in a bubbly atmosphere.
- **Fratelli La Cozza** p77 Lunatic decor that's more colourful than your pizza.
- **Mamma Mia** p77 A Turin tradition.
- **Pizzeria Stars & Roses** p77 Caviar and vodka, tandoori chicken – toppings to shock.
- **Amici Miei** p77 A fave for trendy pizza lovers.

☒ Mon-Sat) One of the few vegetarian restaurants in Turin. There are various menu options to choose from as well as a selection of *monopiatti* (single dishes) for €6.

Ristorante Emporio Gastronomico (Map pp60-1; ☎ 011 562 90 26; Corso Vittorio Emanuele II 88; 1st/2nd courses €6/10) There are few surprises to be had here, rather, simple Italian staples are prepared without fuss and served in healthy portions. The marinated fish makes for an excellent starter, while the fillet steak is large, succulent and grilled to perfection.

I Birilli (☎ 011 819 05 67; Strada Val San Martino 6; mains €8; ☒ Mon-Sat) Frequented by actors and football players, I Birilli is another of local comic Piero Chiambretti's city restaurants. A member of *Le Tavole di Sapore* (Tables of Taste), an organisation set up by the city tourist authority, it offers a good-value set menu at lunch and dinner.

Kashmir (Map pp60-1; ☎ 011 562 73 91; Via Gioberti 4; meal from €15) A modest and unassuming Indian and Pakistani place, Kashmir makes no attempt to venture into unexplored culinary ground, instead sticking to the old favourites: samosa, tikka masala, chicken korma. The food is nothing amazing, but it's not bad either.

Lucky Nugget Saloon (Map pp60-1; ☎ 011 669 50 58; Corso Vittorio Emanuele II 21; mains around €8; ☒ Tue-Sun) Difficult to miss, this vast music restaurant-cum-bar is the place for your Tex-Mex fix. There are all the usual staples on the menu, the atmosphere is cheerful and the tacos are tasty.

In the fashionable Quadrilatero Romano quarter west of Piazza Castello are some fine spots to eat and drink. The area is particularly popular in the summer when many restaurants spill over onto the narrow streets and atmospheric piazzas.

Il Mercante di Spezie (Map pp60-1; ☎ 011 521 73 56; Via Sant'Agostino 15; mains €12; ☒ Tue-Sun evenings) Enjoy a trip down the world's spice trail at this fascinating restaurant-cum-tearoom. Chef Maurizio Tiani and his team of international cooks have created a stylishly Arabian atmosphere in which diners select from a spicy menu of international dishes. Credit cards are not accepted.

Casa Martin (Map pp60-1; ☎ 011 436 22 09; Via Sant'Agostino 23/m; 1st/2nd courses from €6.50/12; ☒ Tue-Sun) Deep in the heart of the vibrant quarter, Casa Martin serves Piedmontese fare to a predominantly young clientele. In summer the candlelit tables in the internal courtyard add an air of romance to the friendly atmosphere.

I Tre Galli (Map pp60-1; ☎ 011 521 60 27; Via Sant' Agostino 25; mains €8; ⏰ Mon-Sun) Known as much for its 1,200-label wine list as its hearty Piedmontese food, I Tre Galli is spacious, rustic and full of light. It serves food until 12.30am, although its fantastic array of aperitif snacks served on the buzzing pavement terrace is enough to ensure it's often full.

Il Bagatto (Map pp60-1; ☎ 011 436 88 87; Via Sant' Agostino 30a; 1st/2nd courses from €4/6; ⏰ 5pm-2am or 3am Tue-Sun) Another late opener, this wine bar serves a spoilt-for-choice range of vintages to accompany the decent food. Ochre-washed walls add a warm touch.

Hafa Café (Map pp60-1; ☎ 011 436 70 91; Via Sant'Agostino 23c; mains from €6; ⏰ 11-2am Tue-Sat, 12-7.30pm Sun) Named after a café frequented by the beat generation in Tangier, here's the place to eat spicy couscous and grilled meats or sip mint tea. Alternatively, spend a Saturday afternoon learning how to paint your hand with henna.

Montagne Viva (Map pp60-1; ☎ 011 521 78 82; Piazza Emanuele Filiberto 3a; mains €10; ⏰ Mon-Sat) Traditionalists will enjoy the Piedmontese fare at this classic *agriturismo* restaurant, run by the regional consortium for agricultural products. Strictly local ingredients (honey, meats, wine) are used in a variety of dishes.

The lively Piazza Vittorio Veneto is another area rich in eating options. Overlooking the River Po, the square is a vibrant pocket of after-dark activity. It's ideal for clubbers who want to eat before heading to the nearby Murazzi district.

Porto di Savona (Map pp60-1; ☎ 011 817 35 00; Piazza Vittorio Veneto 2; 1st/2nd courses from €5.50/10; ⏰ Tue-Sun) A lovely authentic trattoria, this laid-back eatery serves refreshingly large portions of classic Piedmontese dishes. Staples include risottos, sausage with polenta and gooey chocolate pudding. The bread sticks are also delicious. A different speciality is served each day of the week.

Bokaos Dining Club (Map pp60-1; ☎ 011 812 89 31; Piazza Vittorio Veneto 23; 1st/2nd courses from €9/11; ⏰ 8pm-3.30am Tue-Sun) Minimalism is the hallmark of this fashionable London-style restaurant bar. Attracting a sleek moneyed crowd, it's a place where looks count and the well dressed come to look. Enter from Piazza Vittorio Veneto or via the riverside entrance.

PIEDMONT ON A PLATE

For wonderful regional cooking, reserve a table at:

- **Dai Saletta** p78
- **Ristorante Vintage 1997** p79
- **L'Agrifoglio** p79
- **Porto di Savona** p79
- **Montagne Viva** p79

Caffè Guglielmo Pepe (Map pp60-1; ☎ 011 812 97 87; Via della Rocca 19; pasta from €4.50, meat dishes €6-9) Aiming to recreate its halcyon days as one of the top aperitif spots in town, this café-cum-wine-and-music bar is a great place for a bite to eat or an early evening drink. Dine on frogs' legs on Piazza Maria Teresa or enjoy a late tipple in the Art Nouveau interior.

TOP END

Ristorante Vintage 1997 (Map pp60-1; ☎ 011 53 59 48; Piazza Solferino 13; menu degustazione €45; ⏰ Mon-Fri & Sat evening) A relative newcomer, this gold-and-gilt-laden Michelin-starred restaurant has quickly established itself in the upper echelons of Turin's dining circles. The menu is Piedmontese, the wine list is extensive and, according to fans, the food is sensational.

L'Agrifoglio (Map pp60-1; ☎ 011 83 70 64; Via Accademia Albertina 38d; mains from €12; ⏰ Tue-Sat evenings) Finding a table at L'Agrifoglio without a reservation is no easy task, so popular is this much-lauded little restaurant. Dishes successfully add modern takes to traditional recipes and are much appreciated by the discerning clientele. Wine buffs can select from the 250-label list.

Antiche Sere (☎ 011 385 43 47; Via Cenischia 9; mains from €12; ⏰ Mon-Sat evening only) Much loved as an example of a traditional trattoria, this is where the Turinese take friends and guests when in town. Meat dishes predominate, although vegetarians might go for the vegetable quiche. You'll need to reserve a table.

Tre Galline (Map pp60-1; ☎ 011 436 65 53; Via Bellezia 37d; mains from €13; ⏰ Mon-Sat) Cesare Pavese was a regular at this well-known and well-loved restaurant. Now run by the same folk as the nearby I Tre Galli, it serves new takes on Piedmontese classics. The *fritto misto alla piemontese* (mixed-fry, Piedmontese style) is something of a signature dish.

Mare Nostrum (Map pp60-1; ☎ 011 839 45 43; Via Matteo Pescatore 16; mains around €18; ⊙ evenings) Appropriately enough, Turin's top fish restaurant sits on a street meaning 'fisherman'. Mare Nostrum is an upmarket lip-licking choice which uses only the freshest of ingredients in its carefully thought-out menu.

Restaurant del Cambio (Map pp60-1; ☎ 011 54 37 60; Piazza Carignano 2; mains from €21, menu degustazione €66; ⊙ Mon-Sat) The grand old master of Turin fine dining peers out at Palazzo Carignano from its snug position next to Teatro Carignano. The decor is stucco and antiques, the waiters are liveried and the cuisine classic (as favoured by former regular Count Cavour). Advance reservations and smart dress are recommended.

C'era Una Volta (Map pp60-1; ☎ 011 65 54 98; Corso Vittorio Emanuele II 41; 1st/2nd courses from €6.50/8.50; ⊙ Mon-Sat evenings) Located on the 2nd-floor of an townhouse, C'era Una Volta serves classic Piedmontese fare. The boiled meats are excellent and on Fridays (or on reservation) the *fritto misto* (mixed fry) is popular. Good value is the €25 menu *degustazione*. Buzz to enter through hefty wooden doors.

Arcadia (Map pp60-1; ☎ 011 561 38 98; Galleria Subalpina 16; sushi from €12) Turin's only sushi bar is a large and bright affair set inside one of Turin's glass-topped galleries off Piazza Castello. Tuck into a plate of octopus or opt for a menu *giapponese* (Japanese menu) rigorously prepared by the Japanese chef.

La Pista (Map p58; ☎ 011 631 35 23; Via Nizza 262; mains about €20) An ultra-stylish combination of industrial chic and innovative cuisine, La Pista is the restaurant of the moment. Overlooking the legendary race track on the roof of the Lingotto Fiere, it's location is as memorable as the food. New takes on Piedmont classics are the hallmark of chef Massimo Guzzone's beautifully presented dishes. Advance booking is essential.

In Rivoli, 13km west of Turin central, lies one of Piedmont's top restaurants.

Combal.Zero (☎ 011 956 52 25; Piazza Mafalda di Savoia, Rivoli; 1st/2nd courses from €18/25; ⊙ Wed-Sun) Slickly incorporated into the Castello di Rivoli, it offers a mix of haute cuisine and minimalist design. The stark Japanese-style place settings contrast with the complexities of chef Davide Scabin's combinations. Quail eggs, peanut butter and sea lettuce combine to form one of his innovative starters.

Quick Eats

La Focacceria Tipica Ligure (Map pp60-1; ☎ 011 53 01 85; Via Sant'Agostina 6 & Via Giovanni Gioliiti 4) Bite into a slice of *farinata* (€1.05, a traditional Ligurian focaccia) with one of 13 different toppings, or a pizza (€0.75 per slice) at this munch-on-the-move option.

Brek (Piazza Carlo Felice; Map pp60-1; ☎ 011 53 45 56; Piazza Carlo Felice 10; meals around €8; ⊙ 11.30am-3pm & 6.30-10.30pm; Via Santa Teresa; ☎ 011 54 54 24; meals around €8; ⊙ 11.30am-3pm & 6.30-10.30pm) Italy's very luxurious version of fast food is a quick stumble from the train station and heaves

---

ICE-CREAM LEGENDS

The Turinese have bestowed legend status on four of its many *gelaterie* (ice-cream parlours).

Caffè Fiorio & Gelateria Fiorio (Map pp60-1; ☎ 011 817 32 25; Via Po 8; ⊙ Tue-Sun) A nationalist haunt favoured by professional gourmet and sometime politician Count Cavour and other pro-unification patriots, Fiorio first opened its doors in 1780. Since then it has never looked back as the place in Turin to wrap your tongue around a ball of creamy pistachio or pesky peach.

Pepino (Map pp60-1; ☎ 011 54 20 09; Piazza Carignano 8) Dating from 1884, Pepino is among Turin's oldest *gelaterie*. Try the *pinguino* (penguin) ice cream covered in chocolate at the outside terrace.

Caffè Miretti (Map pp60-1; ☎ 011 53 36 87; Corso Giacomo Matteotti 5; ⊙ 7.30-1.30am Tue-Sun) Flavours here include yogurt, peach, nougat, chestnut, zabaglione with amaretti, and minty After Eight – licked on the move or on its sunny pavement terrace. Some claim the orange cream flavour is the pick of the bunch.

Gatsby's (Map pp60-1; ☎ 011 562 25 45; Via Soleri 2; ⊙ 8am-midnight Mon-Sat) Turin's swish modern spot to go suck ice. Come dark, feast on a vanilla and strawberry ice cream doused in champagne.

GROM (Map pp60-1; ☎ 011 511 90 67; Piazza Paleocapa 1D; ⊙ noon-11pm) A new kid on the ice-cream block winning rave reviews for its ice-cream made from original ingredients, such as pistachio nuts from Sicily and cocoa from Guatemala. The going rate for a typically generous cup/cone is between €1.50 and €1.70, and for a kilogram is from €17 to €19.

at lunch time. Its interior courtyard beats many of the better restaurants' outside dining areas in the charm stakes.

Lunch & Tea (Map pp60-1; ☎ 011 562 93 16; Via Giovanni Giolitti 16; panino & drink €4.50) For a quick lunchtime pause, Lunch & Tea fits the bill. A fairly unremarkable self-service place offering a cheap, munchable menu and a decent selection of panini.

Self-Catering

La Baita del Formagg (Map pp60-1; ☎ 011 562 32 24; Via Lagrange 36) A well-stocked delicatessen selling sausages, Castelmagno (the king of Piedmont cheeses), unusual meats and fats (such as lard laden in aromatic herbs), jars of white truffles, truffle butter and other conserved delicacies.

Gertosio (Map pp60-1; ☎ 011 562 19 42; Via Lagrange 34) Before you dive into La Baita del Formagg, pop in here first to stock up on bread (savoury, fruit or sugar-topped). Your sliced meats will then make the perfect sandwich fillers. If you're interested, they also sell 50 different types of praline here.

Pastificio De Filippis (Map pp60-1; ☎ 011 542 21 37; Via Lagrange 39) A gastronomic delight, De Filippis sells every type of pasta under the Italian sun. House specialities include tortellini stuffed with unexpected fillings such as spinach, salmon and *fonduta* (a type of melted cheese from Valle d'Aosta); artichokes, asparagus, eggplant and mushrooms; or ham, walnuts and gorgonzola cheese.

Borgiattino Formaggi (Map p58; ☎ 011 55 38 37; Corso Vinzaglio 29) Buy a smelly slice of gorgonzola to take home from this authentic *formaggeria* (cheese shop), run by the Borgiattino family since 1927.

Di per Di (Map pp60-1; Via Passalacqua 3, Via Santa Teresa 19, Via Gioberti 32 and Piazza Savoie 2; ☉ 8.30am-7.30pm Mon-Sat 8.30am-noon Wed) Most Italian supermarkets have fairly well-stocked delicatessen counters and often sell lovely fresh bread.

DRINKING

The drinking scene in Turin is lively and fun. New bars are constantly opening and there is no shortage of pubs and cafés to serve your tipple of choice, be it an elegant aperitif or a pint of the amber stuff.

Adding to the very considerable pleasure of drinking in Turin is the hugely civilised habit of serving delicious bar snacks.

> **TOP FIVE APERITIFS**
>
> For a sundowner and snack:
>
> ▪ **Lobelix** p81
> ▪ **La Drogheria** p82
> ▪ **Caffè 21** p77
> ▪ **Société Lutéce** p77
> ▪ **Caffe Elena** p76

In some cases these constitute a meal in themselves, although the Turinese tend to nibble elegantly rather than scoff hungrily. The choice of snacks ranges enormously, but staples include bite-sized pizzas and tarts, small sandwiches, salads of various hues, cheese and cured meats. Many bars and cafés will add to these with their own house specialities.

There are two established pockets where thirsty Turinese flock – the riverside area around Piazza Vittoria Veneto and the so-called Quadrilatero Romano district east of Piazza Savoia. However, in recent years a number of trendy and well-frequented places have opened in the San Salvario area to the south and east of Stazione Porta Nuova.

In the Quadrilatero try the following.

Lobelix (Map pp60-1; ☎ 011 436 72 06; Via Corte d'Appello 15f; ☉ Mon-Sat) The leafy terrace beneath trees on Piazza Savoia is a favourite with the 'in' crowd for *aperitivi* (aperitifs; €6); its banquet of snacks laid out from 6pm is one of Turin's most extravagant.

Cantine Barbaroux (Map pp60-1; Via Barbaroux 13f; ☉ 6pm-2am) One of the oldest cellars in the city, this rustic *cantina con cucina* (wine cellar with kitchen) has its entrance on pedestrian Via Mercanti. The place to sip wine in the traditional style (its red-brick, checkered-tiled cellar is original), it also features a menu of hearty fare such as Tuscan bean soup (€4.50).

Frog (Map pp60-1; ☎ 011 440 77 36; Via Mercanti 19; ☉ Tue-Sun) The Frog is a large music bar and restaurant with a typical pub-style interior: dark wooden panelling, table lamps and heavy curtains.

Caffè della Basilica (Map pp60-1; ☎ 011 433 86 35; Via della Basilica 3; ☉ Tue-Sat & Sun evening) Despite a decent wine list, the major attraction here is the beer brewed in-house. For those preferring something light there is Santa Maria, while heavyweights will want to try a pint of Sangre de Toro (bull's blood) or Motor Oil. Not recommended is looking down into the ancient *ghiacciaia* (ice cellar) after too much of the bull's blood. The downstairs seating area is no smoking.

KM5 (Map pp60-1; ☎ 011 431 00 25; Via San Domenico 14/16; ☽ 6pm-3am Tue-Sat) The formula at KM5 is a winner: loud music, dim lights, free-flowing drinks and a young out-for-fun crowd. In summer, tables spill on to the street.

Enotria (Map pp60-1; ☎ 011 436 66 78; Via Bligny 8; ☽ 10am-2am Mon-Sat) Unique for a Turin wine bar, Enotria specialises in *vino* from the south of the country. Friendly and often full, this is an excellent place for a glass of something different in an atmospheric internal courtyard.

Fish (Map pp60-1; ☎ 011 521 79 33; Via Valerio 5/B; 1st/2nd courses €6/12; ☽ 7pm-3am Tue-Sun) Check out the Dali–inspired living room as you enter. A laid-back brick vault of a place, you can enjoy a late dinner, or on Thursday to Saturday nights, the DJ-spun music.

The area around Piazza Vittorio Veneto conceals a number of trendy drinking spots. Attracting an elegant and well-to-do crowd, this is the place for a fashionable cocktail rather than an evening of drinking games.

La Drogheria (Map pp60-1; ☎ 011 812 24 14; Piazza Vittorio Veneto 18; ☽ 8-2am) As comfy as a living room and laid-back to the point of being a statement, La Drogheria continues to pull in the punters. Aperitif junkies will find snacks laid out on the early evening bar.

Vinicola Al Sorij (Map pp60-1; ☎ 011 83 56 67; Via Matteo Pescatore 10c; ☽ 6pm-2am Mon-Sat) Another wine bar hot on the trail of Turin's more moneyed crowd, this tiny spot just behind Piazza Vittorio Veneto has a cellar of more than 500 different wines.

Suite 29 (Map pp60-1; ☎ 011 1971 49 02; Via della Rocca 29/a; ☽ Tue-Sat) A current favourite with fashionable 30-somethings, Suite 29 is a magazine spread waiting to appear. Each of the rooms in this renovated townhouse is decorated in a different style, so you might end up lounging on Oriental cushions or draping yourself over a *fin-de-siecle* chaise lounge.

Taberna Libraria (Map pp60-1; ☎ 011 83 65 05; Via Bogino 5; ☽ 10am-9pm) The mainstay of this *enolibreria* (wine bookshop) is its excellent array of wines to taste and buy. A definite highlight for wineophiles at that favourite Turinese time of day: aperitif hour!

Near Stazione Porta Nuova, in the area to the east of Via Nizza, a couple of fashionable drinking dens have sprung up.

Diwan Café (Map pp60-1; ☎ 011 669 80 49; Via Baretti 15/c) Literary types can discuss contemporary novels over a cool beer at the Diwan, a relaxed book-and-sofa-style place. Many of the books on display are for sale.

Damadama Café (Map pp60-1; ☎ 011 65 57 11; Piazza Madama Cristina 6; ☽ 6pm-1am Tue-Sat, noon-1am Sun) Spread over three floors, there's something for everyone here – provided you like wine, music and tapas. Try the tapas on the ground floor, head upstairs for the DJ, or plunge down into the basement and internal courtyard.

Further afield, there are various places dotted around the city.

Roar Roads (Map pp60-1 ☎ 011 812 01 71; Via Carlo Alberto 3; mains around €5) A good spot for a very un-Italian selection of beers, served on an odd wooden contraption, and pub grub.

Birrificio Torino (Map pp60-1; ☎ 011 287 65 62; Via Parma 30) Located in a former biscuit factory, Birrificio Torino is a hulking monster of a pub. Clara, Rufus, Gina and Biondoppia, brewed on site and piped direct from the giant copper urns behind the bar, are guaranteed to charm. The cutely named beers are served at wooden tables that fade into the distance on the huge drinking floor.

Caffè Rossini (Map pp60-1; ☎ 011 521 41 05; Corso Regina Margherita 80a; ☽ 10.30am-3.30am) Another historic venue much loved by the city young, the Rossini is a safe bet for a lively atmosphere. Open seven days a week, it's particularly popular for a late night drink.

ENTERTAINMENT

Turin buzzes after dark. The pub scene (see above) is lively, often serving to whet the appetite for clubbers out on a night; cinemas and theatres abound; and concert halls echo to the sounds of classical orchestras or cutting-edge techno. Sports fans can of course enjoy the city's football talent.

Entertainment listings are included in *Torino Sette*, the Friday insert of newspaper *La Stampa* (www.lastampa.it, Italian only); cinema, theatre and exhibition listings are also included in its daily *Spettacoli Cronaca* section. Also worth picking up at the tourist office and in many bars is the free 80-page *News Spettacolo* (www.newspettacolo.com, Italian only), a weekly booklet listing several hundred entertainment venues, ranging from straight to gay to innocent to downright naughty. Many venues have their own web sites listing upcoming events.

Tickets for rock concerts are sold at the **Ricordi Media Store** (Map pp60-1; ☎ 011 562 11 56; Piazza CLN 251). **Vetrina per Torino** (Map pp60-1; ☎ 800 01 54 75; www.torinocultura.it, Italian only; Piazza San Carlo 159; ⏰ 11am-7pm Mon-Sat) has cultural information and a ticketing service.

Nightclubs

Turin's nightlife is among Italy's best. Most clubs offer a mix of tunes spun by resident DJs and late-night, live-music gigs. Although the action rarely heats up before midnight, many clubs open their doors earlier for cocktails and nibbles. Entry is usually free, but for a concert in an established venue, expect to pay up to €15 to €20.

In the centre of town, things get particularly heated on Murazzi del Po (also called Lungo Po Murazzi), the arcaded riverside area stretching between Ponte Vittorio Emanuele I and Ponte Umberto I.

Pier 7-9-11 (Map pp60-1; ☎ 011 83 53 56; Murazzi del Po 7-11; ⏰ Mon-Sat) Named after its original address, this is a trendy disco where dancers sweat to mainly commercial sounds. In summer, everything spills over to the outdoor dance floor. Thursday night is particularly popular with the city's young, moneyed set.

Beach (Map pp60-1; Murazzi del Po 18-22) The sexy steel-and-glass decor and cool young crowd ensure that the dance floor is heaving. Expect to queue to get in.

Jammin' (Map pp60-1; ☎ 011 88 28 69; Murazzi del Po 17-19) A late starter, Jammin' doesn't open for business until midnight. But that's not a problem as it's a disco for serious dancers who are happy to see in the dawn.

Alcatraz (Map pp60-1; ☎ 011 83 69 00; Murazzi del Po 37) Known for its bars, Alcatraz is a hugely popular den of dance. The decor pays homage to the notorious prison, while the music is rock and house.

Da Giancarlo (Map pp60-1; ☎ 011 521 41 05; Via Murazzi del Po 49) Young and old happily drink together at Giancarlo's, a riverside institution. Still going strong, the future looks bright, as the presence of young rockers Subsonica ensures a following.

Elsewhere, there's plenty going on across the city.

Theatrò (Map pp60-1; ☎ 011 518 71 07; Via Santa Teresa 10) Still going strong, Theatrò is an old Turin favourite. A music restaurant in an old cinema, it regularly features a clutch of young DJs who mix tunes from 11pm.

Zoo Bar (☎ 011 819 43 47; Corso Casale 127; ⏰ Tue-Sat) Over the river, Zoo is an industrial bar hosting bands, DJs and cabarets. Friday and Saturday nights are strictly dance music.

Barrumba (Map pp60-1; ☎ 011 819 43 47; Via San Massimo 1; ⏰ Tue-Sat) An indie-rock club, this is one of the best places to catch a big-name act. The music doesn't start until midnight as the club is under a cinema.

Docks Home (Map p58; ☎ 011 28 02 51; Via Valprato 68) The real star of Turin's music scene is set in a converted 1912 warehouse complex. Top DJs regularly highlight, with the emphasis on house music. The complex also hosts shows and exhibitions.

Hiroshima Mon Amour (☎ 011 317 66 36; Via Bossoli 83) The other big name in the dance and music circuit, HMA plays everything from folk to tango, techno, rock and ska.

Magazzino di Gilgamesh (Map p58; ☎ 011 749 28 01; Piazza Monceniso 13b) Something of a musical hothouse, di Gilgamesh is well known as a venue for live blues, jazz and rock, although you can also catch Latino tunes and world music here.

Supermarket (Map p58; ☎ 011 25 94 50; Via Madonna di Campagna 1; ⏰ Mon-Sat) Housed in an old cinema, Supermarket is a big disco attracting big crowds and big-name European DJs.

Azimut (Map pp60-1; ☎ 011 23 24 58; Via Modena 55; ⏰ Wed-Sat) Well-known on the clubbing circuit, Azimut also exhibits work by young local artists and stages book presentations.

L'Angelo (Map p58; ☎ 011 28 43 59; Via Cremona 2) A thumping discopub, L'Angelo pumps out R'n'B music in a friendly atmosphere.

Live Music

Turin's musical calendar is comprehensive and eclectic. Big name artists, both Italian and international, regularly perform in the city and one of Italy's most prestigious orchestras, the Orchestra Sinfonica Nazionale della RAI is based in town.

Comprehensive information is available from Vetrina per Torino (p83) or from the website www.torinocultura.it (Italian only) which lists all major upcoming concerts.

Music buffs in town for a while should consider buying a Nessun Dorma, a carnet of six tickets (€66) valid for an assortment of classical music concerts held at the venues mentioned here; Vetrina per Torino sells the carnet.

Auditorium Giovanni Agnelli (☎ 011 664 04 58; Via Nizza 280) In the giant Lingotto complex, this is home to the Orchestra Sinfonica Nazionale della RAI (www.orchestras infonica.rai.it) while its regular base, the Auditorium Rai (Via Verdi 31), is closed for restoration.

Conservatorio Giuseppe Verdi (Map pp60-1; ☎ 011 436 06 91; Piazza Bodoni) Seat of the Orchestra Filarmonica di Torino (www.oft .it, Italian only), the Conservatorio hosts a seasonal calendar of symphonic and chamber music.

Mazdapalace (☎ 011 455 90 90; www.mazdapalace .it, Italian only; Corso Ferrara 30) Formerly known as the Palastampa, this is Turin's premier pop arena. To get here, take bus No 9, 3, 40 or 62 from the city centre.

Folkclub (Map pp60-1; ☎ 011 53 76 36; www .folkclub.it, Italian only; Via Perrone 3b) World music and jazz feature strongly in the calendar proposed by this modern music club. International artists often appear.

Concerts are also held in many nightclubs, while the Teatro Regio (p84) holds a season of symphonic concerts.

Cinemas

Turin's relationship with the big screen is a historic affair and cinema going continues to be a popular pastime, particularly on Monday nights. The city is well served with cinemas, some of which screen films in their original language. On average, expect to pay about €7 for a ticket.

Massimo (Map pp60-1; ☎ 011 812 56 58; Via Montebello 8) Near the Mole Antonelliana, the Massimo offers an eclectic mix of films, mainly in English or with subtitles. One of its three screens is run by the Museo Nazionale del Cinema (p66), and only screens classic films from its huge film library.

Lux (Map pp60-1; ☎ 011 54 12 83; Galleria San Frederico) With a capacity of more than 1000, Lux is worth a visit for its fabulous location, if nothing else, inside Galleria San Federico (see Shopping p85) off Via Roma.

Other cinemas screening films in their original language include **Reposi** (Map pp60-1; ☎ 011 53 14 00; Via XX Settembre 15) and **Olimpia** (Map pp60-1; ☎ 011 53 24 48; Via Arsenale 3).

Theatre

Whether experimental dance or more traditional theatrical fare is your thing, there's usually something to tickle your fancy.

Teatro Regio Torino (Map pp60-1; ☎ 011 881 52 41; www.teatroregio.torino.it, Italian only; Piazza Castello 215; ☒ ticket office 10.30am-6pm Tue-Fri, 10.30am-4pm Sat & 1hr before performances) More an opera house than a traditional theatre, the Regio dates back to 1740. However, little of the original interior remains after a fire gutted the theatre in 1936. Tickets for performances start at €17 and rise rapidly.

Sold-out shows can sometimes be watched for free on TV in the adjoining **Teatro Piccolo Regio** (Map pp60-1; ☎ 011 881 52 41), where Puccini premiered La Bohéme in 1896.

Teatro Stabile (☎ 011 517 62 46; www.teatrosta biletorino.it; Via Roma 49) A historic name in Turinese theatrical circles, the Stabile is a company without a home. Performances are staged at the **Teatro Carignano** (Map pp60-1; ☎ 011 516 94 11, box office ☎ 011 517 62 46; Piazza Carignano 6) and the **Teatro Gobetti** (Map pp60-1; ☎ 011 566 94 11, box office ☎ 011 815 91 32; Via Rossini 8).

Teatro Gianduja (Map pp60-1; ☎ 011 53 02 38; Via Santa Teresa 5) Housed in the Museo della Marionetta (p65), this is a theatre with a difference: all the actors are string puppets. A winner for parents with children.

Sport

'La Vecchia Signora' (The Grand Old Lady) is the nickname given to **Juventus** (☎ 011 6 56 31; www.juventus.it; Corso Galileo Ferraris 32), the more successful of the city's two football teams. City rival **Torino** (☎ 011 571 22 11; www.toro.it, Italian only; Via del Carmine 29) attracts fervent support from the Turinese, but can't compete with the riches that continued success and ownership by the Agnelli dynasty bring to Juve.

Both teams play in the spectacular **Stadio delle Alpi** (☎ 011 966 59 93; Strada Altessano 131) in the city's outer reaches. To get to the stadium, take bus No 12, 62, 72, 75, or on match days, 9b. The Stadio Comunale, renamed the Nuovo Comunale (Corso Galileo Ferraris 294), is scheduled to re-open in December 2004. Torino football club are due to move back to the stadium where they played all their home matches until 1990 when they moved into the Stadio delle Alpi.

Tickets for matches start at around €20 and are found at Ricordi Media Store (p86) and various tobacconists in the city.

SHOPPING

Like all Italians, the Turinese enjoy a good shop. Clothes shopping, in particular, is a national pastime, with designer gear hotly sought after and labels worn to be seen. Clothes shoppers in Turin are well served, with all the major designer names represented and a host of funky street-style shops catering to grungier tastes.

Fashionable design also counts in the Italian home and there are a number of homeware shops where the emphasis is very much on style. Look out for Alessi kitchenware, a much sought after Piedmontese design.

It would be a shame to leave the city without picking up a box or two of beautifully packaged chocs (p75), or a bottle (even a case) of locally produced wine (p87). Delicatessens also abound (p81), stuffed to the brim with gourmet delights.

Turin's most prestigious shopping street is **Via Roma**, which, on Saturday and Sunday afternoons, throngs with weekend strollers parading beneath its porticoes and peering at its expensive window displays. Unlike most other shops in Turin, these boutiques open from 3pm to 7 pm on Sunday. Designer stores also stud parallel **Via Lagrange**.

The elegance of another age is captured in the glass-topped malls of **Galleria Subalpina** (Map pp60-1; 1873), linking Piazza Castello with Via Battisti, and Versace-clad **Galleria San Frederico** (Map pp60-1), which runs in a T-shape between Via Roma, Via Bertola and Via Santa Teresa. Expensive art, antiques and bookshops linger in these covered shopping malls.

Porticoed **Via Po**, with its pavement cafés and alternative fashion shops, attracts a younger crowd. In Turin's medieval quarter, **Via Mercanti**, with its traditional bookbinders and candlestick makers, is the street to stroll for handmade crafts and unusual souvenirs.

Design

Sexy lighting, sleek kitchenware, cheeky retro furniture – there's something for the interior designer in everybody.

Ferrero (Map p58; ☎ 011 54 32 98; Corso Matteotti 15) An interior design shop for those in the know. Outstanding are the Panton chairs and remakes of other design legends.

La Casa Moderna (Map pp60-1; Corso Re Umberto I 14) Among the brands sold at this 'modern house' is the slinky Alessi kitchenware range: funky steel cafetieres, dinky salt shakers and the like.

BARGAINS GALORE

Markets are a fundamental part of any shopping experience in Italy, where you'll see the bare-knuckle bargain hunters on their home turf. Generations of Italian cooks have spurned the supermarkets for the colourful fresh food markets where quality is the norm and prices are low. But it's not just food that you'll find in Turin's great markets – traders cheerfully push everything from antiques to postcards, second-hand books to kitchenware and jewellery. And even if you're not on the lookout for anything in particular, the markets are fantastic places for aimless people watching.

Turin's major markets are:

Porta Palazzo (Map pp60-1; Piazza della Republica; ☼ 8.30am-1.30pm Mon-Fri, 8.30am-6.30pm Sat) Europe's biggest open-air market boasts 685 food and clothes stalls and low prices.

Balôn (Via Borga Dora; www.balon.it, Italian only; ☼ Sat) Heaven for antique bargain hunters.

Gran Balôn (Via Borga Dora; ☼ 2nd Sun of the month) Antique dealers come from far and wide to do their business.

Antico in Musica (Piazza G.C. Abba; ☼ 4th Sun of the month Feb-July, Sep-Dec) As befits the address, a music and antique market.

Donne in Campo (Piazza Carignano; ☼ last Sun of the month Feb-Jun, Sep-Dec) Piedmontese women display their handicrafts.

Mercatino delle Erbe (Piazza Palazzo di Cittá; ☼ 1st Sun of the month Mar-Jun, Sep-Dec) For regional wines and produce (since Medieval times).

Mercatino della Crocetta (Via Marco Polo & Largo Cassini; ☼ 8.30am-1pm Mon-Fri, 8.30am-6.30pm Sat) A chic boutique in the open.

Naturalmente (Piazza Statuto; ☼ 1st Sun of the month & Corso Cairoli; ☼ 4th Sat of the month) A bonanza of natural, biological and environmentally friendly products.

A MAN FOR ALL SEASONS

When it comes to dressing for the happiest day of your life, you could do worse than put yourself in the clothes of Carlo Pignatelli.

Famed for his wedding wear, this highly acclaimed Turinese designer is in great demand. Official stylist to Juventus football club, in his time he has also dressed English football team Watford, Italian pop star Renato Zero and a host of TV celebrities.

Pignatelli's hallmark is classical formal wear (suits are a speciality) for ladies and gents who favour elegant understatement over glitzy glamour.

Carlo Pignatelli's Turin **showroom** (Map pp60-1; ☎ 011 53 36 32; Via Cernaia 17g) is west of Piazza Castello.

Morpholuce (Map pp60-1; ☎ 011 54 12 13; Via Ottavio Assarotti) Lighting becomes art as contemporary designs by Starck, Castiglioni and Pagani illuminate this smart lamp shop.

Galleria Cristiani (Map pp60-1; ☎ 011 83 59 03; Via Maria Vittoria 41) One of a number of fashionable art-cum-design shops that peppers the area west of Piazza Vittorio Veneto. This modern art gallery exhibits works by 20th-century Italian designers.

Fashion

Turin, like most Italian cities, is fantastically well supplied with clothes shops. Whether your tastes run to Armani suits or secondhand army fatigues, rest assured you'll find something to take home.

The place to head for if you want to give your wallet a serious workout is Via Roma. Most of the big-name Italian designers have a boutique here, including:

Gucci (Map pp60-1; ☎ 011 51 14 11; Via Roma 49)
Prada (Map pp60-1; ☎ 011 51 14 11; Via Roma 49)
Salvatore Ferragamo (☎ 011 562 59 40; Via Roma 108)
Giorgio Armani (☎ 011 518 71 82; Via Roma 145)
Max Mara (☎ 011 56 21 05; Via Roma 49)
Marina Rinaldi (☎ 011 518 70 50; Via Roma 314)

There is also a string of more affordable shops on Via Roma such as **Benetton** (Via Roma 48) and **Stefanel** (☎ 011 538 569; Via Roma 287).

Bolder dressers should strut down to the Via Po area.

Renni (Map pp60-1; Via Cavour 2) For the fun-at-heart there are funky shoes, boots, bags and cutting-edge items to (kind of) cover the body. There's a second shop at Via Madama Cristina 141a.

Camden Town (Map pp60-1; ☎ 011 812 25 07; Via San Massimo 5) An ode to Alexander McQueen, this hip fashion/music store is full of tartan trousers, glitter shirts with fur cuffs and the latest in London street fashion. It's a good place to ask about 'in' clubs, bars and happening events.

Shoeco (Map pp60-1; ☎ 011 88 32 53; Piazza Carlo Emanuele II 19) The military look is catered for here, with heavy-duty footwear and recycled army jackets filling the racks.

Calzedonia (Map pp60-1; Via Po ☎ 011 817 49 39; Via Po 10a; Via Roma, Via Roma 372; Piazza Statuto, Piazza Statuto 5) Stockings and tights for wild and sexy pins can be purchased at this cheery chain store.

Foresto Borsalino (Map pp60-1; ☎ 011 53 04 89; Piazza Carlo Felice 9) This is the place to go for a natty piece of classical headwear. A traditional gentleman's hatter, this shop bears the name of Giuseppe Borsalino, the father of the famous hat bearing his name.

Music

Ricordi Media Store (Map pp60-1; ☎ 011 562 11 56; Piazza CLN 251) The mainstream choice for CDs of all genres: rock, pop, classical, Italian, international and more . It also sells tickets for concerts (see Live Music p83).

Rock & Folk (Map pp60-1; ☎ 011 839 45 42; Via Bogino, Via Bogino 4; Via Battisti, Via Battisti 19) Its staff are young, fun and know exactly what bands are playing where.

Onde (Map pp60-1; ☎ 011 88 23 72; Via Plana 1/M) Just off Piazza Vittorio Veneto, this small shop is a meeting point for aficionados

AUTHOR'S CHOICE

Turin Gallery (Map pp60-1; ☎ 011 812 30 83; Via Maria Vittoria 19) Worth a visit even if you're not buying, this veritable Aladdin's cave of 20th-century design classics is fit to burst with wacky furniture, colourful glassware and *objets d'art*. Styles range from the sublime to the avant-garde, from the elegant to the barmy. A highlight is a pouf shaped like an upturned bowler hat filled with an apple entitled 'Homage to Magritte' designed by Dino Gavina.

and fans of world music. The selection of contemporary music is eclectic and features releases by many independent labels.

Wine

Turin's proximity to the great wine-producing areas ensures a readily available selection of some of Italy's most sought-after vintages. For further details on Piedmont's prodigious wine industry, contact the **Enoteca del Piemonte** (Map pp60–1; ☎ 011 667 76 67; www.enotecaregionaledelpiemonte.com; Via Nizza 294), the central office representing the 10 regional wine cellars.

Vini Renato Rabezzana (Map pp60–1; ☎ 011 54 30 70; Via San Francesco d'Assisi 23/c) The friendly and knowledgeable owner of this well-known *enoteca* (wine shop cum bar) will happily share her wisdom with you, helping you choose from the predominantly Piedmontese cellar. The Rabezzana family also produce and sell their own wine.

Parola (Map pp60–1; ☎ 011 54 49 39; Corso Vittorio Emanuele II 76) Near Stazione Porta Nuova, Parola is a first-rate wine cellar, which stocks regional vintages from the last 100 years.

Fongo Domenico (Map pp60–1; ☎ 011 54 13 37; Via Giuseppe Mazzini 3) Fill up your own bottle with cheap red wine or choose from a selection of world drinks, everything from grappa to Moscovskaya vodka. The shop also runs a little bar where you can whet your whistle with a quick shot or two.

P.I.A.N.A (Map pp60–1; Via Giuseppe Garibaldi 38) Stocks several hangovers' worth of wine, spirits and liqueurs.

SHOPPING CENTRES

Despite the predominance of small, family-run shops and designer boutiques, Italy has not been spared the spread of the shopping centre. Two centres that might be of interest:

Lagrange 15 (Map pp60–1; ☎ 011 517 00 75; Via Lagrange 15) Spread over several floors, it includes chain store La Rinascente.

8 Gallery (☎ 011 67 32 27; Via Nizza 262) In the Lingotto, this vast commercial centre incorporates a shopping centre and an 11-screen cinema multiplex.

GOURMET BUYS

Piedmont bursts with tempting tastes. To take home a little edible something, you won't go far wrong at one of the following shops:

Vini Renato Rabezzana Piedmont's classic wines (p87)

La Baita del Formagg White truffles, cured meats and cheese (p81)

Borgiattino Formaggi Cheese has never smelt so good (p81)

Pastificio De Filippis Pasta in every shape imaginable (p81)

Peyrano Chocolate as only the Turinese make it (p76)

Paper

The traditional arts of book binding and paper production are alive and well in modern Turin. Both these shops are ideal for picking up an imaginative gift.

Bottega Fagnola (Map pp60–1; ☎ 011 54 42 66; Via Mercanti 9a) This artisan shop binds and restores antique books and makes handcrafted paper. A set of five sheets of cotton writing paper with real flowers costs €5.

Icarta (Map pp60–1; ☎ 011 81 23 685; Piazza Vittorio Veneto 1) In a similar vein, Icarta sells books of paper embedded with dried flower petals and pretty little notebooks.

GETTING THERE & AWAY
Air

Turin airport (TRN; ☎ 011 567 63 61; www.turin-airport .com) is 16km northwest of the city centre in Caselle. International destinations include London Stansted, Birmingham, Frankfurt, Brussels, Lisbon, Madrid and Paris; national flights serve Rome, Naples, Palermo, Bari, Cagliari, Catania and Pescara.

Turin is also linked directly by bus to Milan's international **Malpensa Airport** (☎ 02 7485 22 00; www.malpensa.com, Italian only), 100km to the northeast.

Bus

Turin is very well connected with buses serving international, national and regional destinations. Most, though not all, services terminate at the **bus station** (Map p58; ☎ 011 433 25 25; Corso Castelfidardo; ✆ ticket office 6.30am-1.25pm &

2-8.30pm Mon-Sat, 6.30am-1.15pm & 2-8.30pm Sun; international ticket office 9am-12.30pm & 3-7pm Mon-Fri, 9am-12.30pm Sat).

For destinations in the Valle di Susa and Val Chisone, **Sapav** (☎ 0121 32 20 32; www .sapav.it, Italian only) operates frequent services from the bus station to Pinerolo (€2.65; 45 minutes) and Sestriere (€5.10; 2¾ hours). To head north and east, **SADEM** (☎ 011 300 06 11; www.sadem.it, Italian only) runs regular buses from the bus station to Ivrea (€3.50; 1 hour) and Novara (€5.47; 1 hour 25 minutes), while for the south **Satti** (☎ 011 576 41; www .satti.it, Italian only) serves Alba (€3.70; 1 hour 20 minutes) and the surrounding towns. These buses depart from Largo Marconi 3, 600m south of Stazione Porta Nuova down Via Nizza.

International operator **Eurolines** (☎ 055 35 71 10; www.eurolines.it) departs from the bus station for a number of European destinations, including London (€87), Paris (€54) and Barcelona (€100).

Car & Motorcycle

Turin lies at the centre of Piedmont's extensive road network, and is also a major staging post on the overland route to France. The major motorways serving Turin are the A4, which traverses the north of Italy passing by Milan on the way to Venice; the A5 for Ivrea and Aosta; the A6 for Savona and the Ligurian coast; the A21 for Asti and Alessandria; and the A32 for the Valle di Susa ski resorts and the Fréjus tunnel into France.

Main roads include the SS11 running east to Venice, the SS20 for Cuneo and the south and the SS23 for Sestriere.

Train

There are four train stations in Turin, although the majority of trains terminate at the main station, **Stazione Porta Nuova** (Piazza Carlo Felice). Regular daily trains connect Turin with Milan (€14.57, one hour 45 minutes) and Rome (€40.44, seven hours). Within Piedmont there are frequent trains for Alessandria (€10.54, one hour), Arona (€6.25, two hours), Cuneo (€4.70, one hour 20 minutes) and Novara (€3.85, one hour 15 minutes).

Turin's other train stations are **Stazione Porta Susa** (Corso Inghilterra), **Lingotto** (Via Panunzio 1) and **Stazione Dora** (Piazza Baldissera).

GETTING AROUND
To/From the Airport

SADEM (☎ 011 300 01 66; www.sadem.it, Italian only) runs buses to the airport from Stazione Porta Nuova (40 minutes), stopping also at Stazione Porta Susa (30 minutes). Buses depart every 30 minutes between 5.15am and 10.30pm (6.30am and 11.30pm from the airport).

Single tickets (€5) are sold at Porta Nuova at **Caffè Cervino** (Corso Vittorio Emanuele II 57). Buses use the stop on the corner of Corso Vittorio Emanuele II and Via Sacchi. At Stazione Porta Susa, **Bar Milleluci** (Piazza XVIII Dicembre 5) sells tickets.

At the airport, you can buy tickets at the tourist office in the Arrivals (domestic/EU flights) hall, from the automatic ticket machine inside the main entrance, or for an extra €0.50 on the bus. Buses arrive and depart from the stop in front of the arrivals hall (domestic flights exit).

From Stazione Dora, trains leave for the airport every 30 minutes between 5.15am and 7.45pm. Tickets for the 20-minute journey cost €3.

By taxi, the journey to the airport from Stazione Porta Nuova takes about 30 minutes and costs anything between €26 and €42.

SADEM runs three daily services to and from Milan's Malpensa airport. Buses leave from the main bus station and a ticket for the two-hour journey costs €17.50. Alternatively, you can pay €118 and take Alitalia's twice-daily Volobus service from Stazione Porta Nuova to Malpensa. The service is free for Alitalia passengers, who can even check in their luggage at the **Club Eurostar office** (☎ 011 669 02 46) on the Via Nizza side of the station. Tickets must be booked when you buy your air ticket.

Car & Motorcycle

Driving in Turin is either fun or hair-raising depending on your nerves. What is not fun, however, is parking in the city centre. Thankfully, the Turinese don't give a damn who parks where, meaning it's quite acceptable to abandon your vehicle in the middle of certain streets (literally) or on the pavement. Street parking (in the official blue spaces) costs anything from €0.50 to €2 per hour. Tickets are available from meters, tobacconists and newsagents.

To leave your car in an authorised car park costs from €0.40 to €1.30 per hour.

The major city car parks are:

Parcheggio Valdo Fusi (Between Via Giolitti, Via San Francesco da Paola, Via Cavour and Via Accademi Albertina) 480 spaces.

Parcheggio Madama Cristina (Piazza Madama Cristina) 259 spaces.

Parcheggio Emanuele Filiberto (Piazza Emanuele Filiberto) 100 metres from Piazza della Repubblica, 110 spaces.

Parcheggio Roma (Piazza Carlo Felice) In front of Stazione Porta Nuova, 348 spaces.

Parcheggio Re Umberto (Corso Re Umberto) 128 spaces.

Parcheggio Lingotto (Via Nizza 294) 4000 spaces.

Driving is limited, and in some parts prohibited, in much of the *centro storico*. In particular, the area between Piazza Statuto and Piazza Castello, comprising Via Garibaldi and several adjacent streets, is off-limits to traffic.

There are 24-hour petrol stations on the corner of Corso Vittorio Emanuele II and Corso Massimo d'Azeglio; and on Piazza Borromini on the other side of the river.

Public Transport

The city boasts a dense network of buses, trams and a cable car run by **Gruppo Torinese Trasporti** (GTT; toll-free ☎ 800 01 91 52; www .comune.torino.it/atm, Italian only), which has an **information office** (🕓 7am-9pm) at Stazione Porta Nuova.

Buses and trams run from about 5am to midnight and tickets cost €0.90 for 70 minutes unlimited travel (€1.80 for four hours between 9am and 8pm and €3 for a one-day pass). Tickets are sold at tobacconists, the automatic ticket dispensers at train stations, and larger bus and tram stops. To validate your ticket, punch it in the orange machines on board buses, trams and the cable car.

In 2006 the first section of Turin's brand new **metro** is set to open. The principal line of the €975 million project, Line 1, is due to connect Collegno in the west of the city with Stazione Porta Nuova, while a second line is to run from Stazione Porta Nuova to Lingotto Fiere. The 8.4km of Line 1 will be accessed by 15 stations, with a further six being constructed for the shorter 3.9km second line. For further information, refer to www.metrotorino.it.

Taxi

Hailing a cab, as in whistling and waving your arm, doesn't work in Turin. Telephone for one or wait at a taxi rank.

Reliable operators include **Centrale Radio** (☎ 011 57 37) and **Radio Taxi** (☎ 011 57 30/ 011 33 99). **GTT** (☎ 011 818 32) operates a service for disabled people.

If you phone for a taxi, the driver will turn on the meter immediately and you'll pay the cost of travel from wherever the driver receives the call.

Taxis are metered, so always make sure the meter is switched on. To avoid unfortunate misunderstandings, always go with the meter fare rather than a pre-arranged price.

Valle di Susa & Val Chisone

CONTENTS

Val Chisone   **93**
Pinerolo   93
Forte di Fenestrelle   95
Pragelato   95
Sestriere   96
Cesana   97
Clavière   97
Valle di Susa   **98**
Sacra di San Michele   98
Susa   98
Chiomonte   98
Oulx & Sauze d'Oulx   98
Bardonecchia   99

Dazzling snow-packed slopes and stunning Alpine scenery are the hallmarks of these two parallel valleys immediately west of Turin. Slick resorts cater to the skiing fraternity, while the well-trodden summer trails reveal proud traditions and unexpected rewards.

It is to the legendary Via Lattea (Milky Way) that the Turinese flock in winter for some of the best skiing in the country. Undisputed king of the resorts is Sestriere, the sophisticated resort founded by the Agnelli dynasty as an Italian competitor to the plush venues of Austria and Switzerland.

Challenging for the title of 'young gun of the pistes' is Bardonecchia, the trendy well-to-do's resort of choice. It is conveniently situated on the valley's main motorway, at Valle di Susa's most westerly point.

Guarding the head of the Valle di Susa is one of Piedmont's most photographed features, Sacra di San Michele. A solemn and awe-inducing spectacle, it rises up from its perch above the valley floor to afford some incredible views.

Head off the beaten path and you're rewarded with some unexpected finds. Europe's biggest talc mine is hidden away in the Val Germanasca, a southern branch of the Val Chisone; the dynamite museum at Avigliana is an improbable lesson in local history; and the forts at Exilles and Fenestrelle take you back to a time when the valleys were regularly routed by marauding invaders.

VALLE DI SUSA & VAL CHISONE

HIGHLIGHTS

▪ **Awesome Abbey**
Climb to the brooding Sacra di San Michele (p98)

▪ **On the Piste**
Roar down the slopes of the legendary Via Lattea (Milky Way; p96)

▪ **Top Tees**
Putt round Europe's highest golf course in Sestriere (p97)

▪ **Dogs Away**
Learn the art of mushing in San Sicario (p97)

▪ **Military Might**
Stop by the massive Forte di Fenestrelle (p95)

★ San Sicario ★ Fortezza di Fenerstrelle
★ Sestriere ★ Sacra di San Michele

VALLE DI SUSA & VAL CHISONE

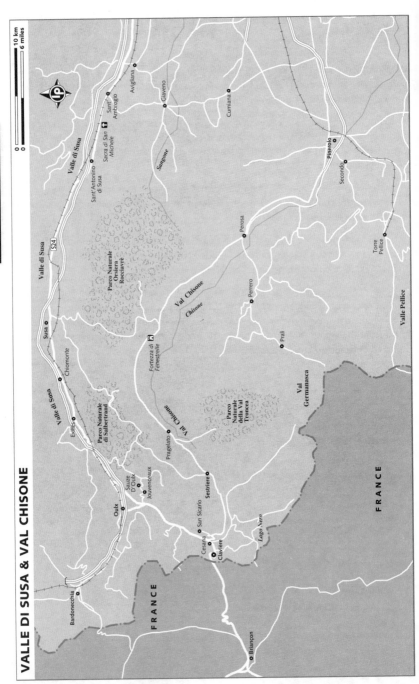

VAL CHISONE

PINEROLO

pop 35,112 / elevation 376m

Beloved by 19th-century author Edmondo de Amicis, for whom it was the 'Nice of Piedmont', thanks to its mild climate and beauty, Pinerolo is a somewhat sprawling place redeemed by a charming *centro storico* (historic centre). Not a place to idle at for long, it makes a good base for exploring the nearby valleys, Val Chisone and its offshoot, Val Germanasca, and Val Pellice.

Orientation & Information

Corso Torino, which becomes Stradale Fenestrelle west of Piazza Cavour, is the main thoroughfare, with the major sights to the north. Coming in by train you'll arrive in Piazza Garibaldi, from where it's a short walk west to the *centro storico*.

The **tourist office** (☎ 0121 79 40 03; www.montagnedoc.it; Viale Giolitti 7-9; ⊙ 9am-12.30pm & 3-6pm Mon-Fri, 10am-1pm & 2-5pm Sat & Sun) is east of the town centre.

On the main drag, the **Banca di Roma** (☎ 0121 37 63 24; Corso Torino 90; ⊙ 8.30am-1.30pm & 3.30-4.30pm Mon-Fri) has an ATM, while public phones can be found at the **Telecom Phone Centre** (Corso Torino 94; ⊙ 8am-8pm).

The **Biblioteca Comunale** (Council Library; ☎ 0121 769 44; Via Battisti 11; ⊙ 8.30am-12.30pm & 2-4.30pm Mon-Fri) offers free Internet use on the first floor. You must book by signing the reservations book.

Sights & Activities

There are few outstanding sights but the **Museo Nazionale dell'Arma di Cavalleria** (☎ 0121 37 63 44; Viale Giolitti 5; admission free; ⊙ 9-11.30am & 2-4pm Tue-Thu, 9-11.30am Sat & Sun) is worth an hour or two. Spread over three floors, this cavalry museum displays uniforms, flags, regimental paraphernalia and a comprehensive collection of weapons. Pinerolo's cavalry connection dates back to 1849, when the Military Cavalry School was inaugurated in the building, which now houses the museum.

Almost directly behind this is the **Civico Museo Etnografico e Museo del Legno** (Municipal Museum of Local Customs and Traditions and Museum of Wood; ☎ 0121 79 43 82; Via Brignone 3; admission free; ⊙ 10.30am-noon & 3.30-6pm), which tells the story of life in the Val Chisone, Val Pellice and Val Germanasca.

In the *centro storico* the 10th-century **Duomo di San Donato** (Piazza San Donato; admission free; ⊙ 7am-noon & 2.30-7pm) is worth a look while, up the hill, the gothic **Chiesa di San Maurizio** (Piazzale San Maurizio; admission free; ⊙ 7am-noon & 2.30-7pm) displays a peculiar, one-handed clock.

For the more sporty-minded the **Ciclostrada Pinerolese** (bike path) runs along the fruit-rich flatlands from Turin to Pinerolo by way of the Palazzina di Caccia di Stupinigi (see p67).

Festivals & Events

For much of June, July and August the town centre becomes a hive of cultural activity. As part of the **Arcipelago Estate** season of summer festivals, films are screened in the piazzas and puppet theatres entertain kids and parents alike. Most famous of all is the **Vincoli Sonori Klezmer and Gypsy Music Festival**, which fiddles into town in mid-July.

Sleeping & Eating

Short of an Olympic-sized event, you're unlikely to have problems bagging a room in Pinerolo.

Villa San Maurizio (☎ 0121 32 14 15; Via de Amicis 3; s/d €47/62; P) Up the hill from the centre, this charming two-star hotel is a lovely place to stay. Grand on the outside but less so inside, rooms are nevertheless comfortable, bright and airy and the staff friendly and helpful. Breakfast is an additional €4.

Il Torrione (☎ 0121 32 26 16; www.iltorrione.com in Italian; Via Galoppatoio; s/d €53/106) Family home to the Marquess Doria Lamba, the 17th-century Villa Torrione stands at the centre of its own 20-hectare park. Offering B&B, it is a wonderfully picturesque place to stay, particularly in spring when the gardens erupt in colour.

Ristorante Mimosa (☎ 0121 742 00; Via San Giuseppe 15; 1st/2nd courses €4.50/5; ⊙ Sun-Fri) This is where locals come for a plate of hearty, no-frills pasta and simple well-cooked meat. Absolutely without pretensions it's a relaxed place where the cooks occasionally pop out to smile at the diners.

Pizzeria Via Trieste (☎ 0121 738 08; Via Trieste 63/65; pizza from €4.20, 1st/2nd courses from €5/8) The cheerful yellow walls and brick ceiling combine to create an atmosphere ideal for munching on a large, bubbling pizza. The wood oven ensures they're correctly charred.

Getting There & Away

Buses run by **Sapav** (☎ 0121 32 20 32; www.sapav .com in Italian) connect with Turin (€2.65; one hour; about 20 daily) and Sestriere (€3.50; one hour 40 minutes; five daily) via Perosa Argentina and Pragelato. The bus stop is outside the **train station** in Piazza Garibaldi.

Pinerolo is on the SS23, which runs from Turin up the Val Chisone to Sestriere.

Around Pinerolo

The small town of **Torre Pellice**, 12km southwest of Pinerolo, is the centre of the Waldensian community (see p95), whose bloody past is well-chronicled at the **Museo Valdese** (☎ 0121 95 02 03; Via Beckwith 3; adult/child €4/2; ☙ 3-6pm Thu, Sat & Sun Feb-Nov).

Flipot (☎ 0121 19 12 36; Corso Antonio Gramsci 17; mains around €25; ☙ Wed-Mon, closed 15-30 Jun & 24 Dec-10 Jan) One of Piedmont's culinary highlights, dishes at this historical restaurant are based on regional ingredients combined to produce stunning combinations and flavours. If a starter of chestnuts, white truffles and crunchy lard doesn't tempt you, then the pigeon *en-croûte* with foie gras might.

To reach Torre Pellice from Pinerolo, take the Stradale Fenestrelle west for about 1.5km and then turn left. Follow the SP164 for about 6km, then turn right onto Via Vittorio Emanuele II and after 2km take the SP 161 for the last 6km.

In the farthest reaches of Val Germanasca, the Alpine village of **Prali** (1415m)

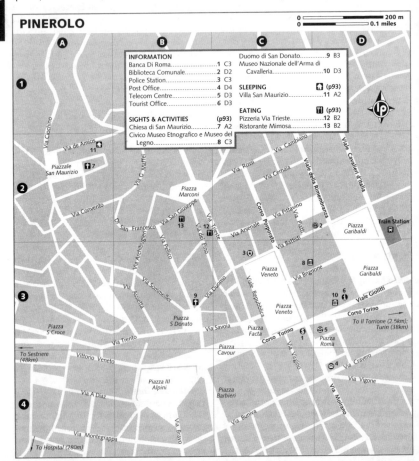

THE WALDENSIAN VALLEYS

Branching off the lower Val Chisone are two valleys that have borne witness to bloodshed and brutal religious persecution, even by historical standards. Known collectively as the Waldensian Valleys, Val Pellice and Val Germanasca are home to the Waldensians, a Protestant sect dating to the 12th century.

The history of the Waldensians begins in 1173, when a wealthy merchant from Lyons, Pietro Valdo (1140–1217), decided to sell all his worldly goods and dedicate himself to a life of full-time preaching. Fed up with the wealth and corruption of the established Catholic Church, he called for a brand of religion based on the gospels and an adherence to poverty. Unsurprisingly, the Archbishop of Lyons was not a fan and in 1184, Valdo and his growing band of disciples (known as the 'Poor of Lyons') were excommunicated from the Church. Forced into hiding and vulnerable to persecution, many decided it was time for new pastures and fled the country.

Just a short hop across the border from France, Val Pellice and Val Germanasca provided ideal sanctuary. Inhospitable and sparsely populated, they were heavily wooded and difficult to get to. The early days were tough but spiritual sustenance came in 1532, when the movement officially joined the Protestant Church.

The Catholic backlash was as brutal as it was predictable. For the next century the French and Savoy authorities led a bloody repression, culminating in a massacre on Easter Saturday 1655, remembered as the 'Piedmontese Easter', which left more than 1,700 Waldensians dead in the hills around Torre Pellice. In 1686 the Waldensians bowed to pressure and fled to Switzerland. But it was a brief interlude as three years later, in 1689, they returned to Piedmont, led in their Glorious Repatriation by Enrico Arnaud.

It wasn't until the 19th century, however, that the right to free worship was finally awarded. On 17 February 1848 – a date still commemorated within the community – King Carlo Alberto issued a royal decree granting the Waldensians full civic and political parity.

The Waldensians continue to practise their religious beliefs in communities dotted around the country but the Waldensian Valleys remain the only place in Italy where the Protestant faith is the dominant creed.

To learn more about the Waldensian faith and its suffered history, Torre Pellice, the movement's spiritual capital, is the place to head for.

---

is an attractive ski resort that has managed, more or less, to withstand the spread of concrete. A small place, it has 11 downhill slopes, of which three are suitable for beginners. Details are available at the **tourist office** (☎ 0121 80 74 18; Fraz. Ghigo 1 bis).

Hotel delle Alpi (☎ 0121 80 75 37; Via Roma 9, Fraz. Ghigo; d €62, half board €52-60; ☷ Nov-Sep; ℗) Ideal for families with kids (there's a 20% reduction for kids under 10) this modest hotel lies within a stone's throw of the ski lifts. The hotel restaurant specialises in local fare.

FORTE DI FENESTRELLE

On the road between Pinerolo and Pragelato, it's worth stopping off at Fenestrelle to investigate the town's extraordinary fort complex near the **Parco Naturale Orsiera Rocciavrè**. Alpine Europe's largest fortification, the 18th-century **Fortezza di Fenestrelle** (☎ 0121 836 00; Via del Forte 1; 1hr/3hrs/all-day guided tours €3.50/6/10; ☷ 10am-noon & 2.30-6pm Mon, Thu-Sun Sep-Jun, daily Aug)

consists of three forts; 1,300,000 sq m; 4000 steps over 2km; and a 635m climb from one end to the other. Guided tours cover three different itineraries.

PRAGELATO
pop 480 / elevation 1524m

Situated at the foot of Mount Albergian, Pragelato has a bloody past. As capital of the French territory in the Val Chisone between 1343 and 1713, it witnessed centuries of conflict. Today it's a somewhat calmer place, enjoying an enviable position on the edge of the **Parco Naturale della Val Troncea**.

The **tourist office** (☎ 0122 74 17 28; Piazza Lantelme; ☷ 9am-noon & 3-6pm) has plenty of information on the park and the town's cross-country pistes and downhill slopes.

Worth a visit, the **Museo del Costume Tradizionale delle Genti Alpine** (☎ 0122 788 44; Fraz. Rivet; admission 8-60/under 8 & over 60 €2.50/free; ☷ 3-6pm Sat, 10am-12.30pm & 3-6pm Sun Sep-Jun,

10am-12.30pm & 3-7pm Sat & Sun Jul, daily Aug) is an interesting trip into the area's sartorial past. Displays feature traditional costumes ranging from 18th-century overalls to 19th-century Sunday suits.

Sleeping & Eating

Relais La Clochette (☎ 0122 74 11 08; Borgata Allevé; s/d €52/104) Open year-round, this three-star hotel offers decent, modern rooms and excellent Piedmontese cuisine. Speciality of the house is the traditional *soupe grasse*, a broth based on bread and onions.

Passet (☎ 0122 789 48; Via Nazionale 5; d €52-62, half board €47-55) Rooms are decidedly rustic at the Passet, a homely hotel with its own garden. The set menu of hearty regional grub is excellent value, starting at €13.

Pragelato is on the main SS23, which heads up the valley from Pinerolo.

SESTRIERE

pop 885 / elevation 2035m

Conceived by Mussolini and built in the 1930s by Giovanni Agnelli, who, it is said, was fed up with his chums popping off to Switzerland or Austria to ski, Sestriere ranks among Europe's sexiest resorts. But while it's certainly chic, it's not exactly attractive.

The townscape is dominated by two concrete cylindrical towers (belonging to the **Valtur** resort), which, while constituting a memorable landmark, add nothing to the resort's charm. Fortunately, its enviable location, in the eastern realms of the vast Via Lattea ski domain, more than makes up for its lack of architectural appeal. Embracing 400km of pistes and five interlinked ski resorts (Sestriere and Sauze d'Oulx, Sansicario, Cesano and Clavière in Italy, and Montegenèvre in France), this prestigious area entices skiers and boarders of all abilities with its enormous range of slopes and exceptionally reliable snow conditions.

Orientation & Information

Sestriere's main square is Piazza Fraiteve, a less than beautiful piazza lined with frighteningly expensive sport shops and places to eat and drink. From here it's an easy walk everywhere.

The efficient **tourist office** (☎ 0122 75 54 44; www.sestriere.it; Via Louset; ☼ 9am-12.30pm & 2.30-7pm) is on the main road to Piazza Fraiteve.

Activities

Sestriere is pure ski. In summer only a handful of hotels remain open, providing for the Ferrari owners who meet here and the cycling enthusiasts eager to catch the Tour de France on the years that it passes through.

A six-day ski pass covering the entire Via Lattea domain costs €138/155 in low/high season and skiing lessons start at €32 per hour for private tuition, €28/135 for a day/week of group lessons. Ski or snowboard/boot/pole hire costs upwards of €10/6/3 a day. A one-day ski-pass for Sestriere costs €28/14 per adult/child. Oodles more Via Lattea information is online at www.vialattea.it.

Sestriere is one of the few resorts that offers floodlit **night skiing** (€10; ☼ 6-9pm) on a regular basis. To this you can add a long list of activities, which includes **heli-skiing**, **bobsledding** and **mushing**, **walking**, **free-climbing** and **mountain biking**. Tourist offices have

---

WHITE GOLD

Formerly known as Valle Scura (Dark Valley), due to it's inaccessability, Val Germanasca is now the Valle Bianca (White Valley), a reference to its two sources of wealth – snow and talc.

The first talc mines were opened in the mid-19th century and quickly became a major source of income despite the considerable logistical problems. At the time there were virtually no roads, and for much of the winter the valley was blocked off by deep snow.

Today you can relive the life of a talc miner at **Scopriminiera** (☎ 0121 80 69 87; www.scopriminiera .it; adult/child Miniera Paola €7.80/6.20, Miniera Gianna €9.80/7.80; ☼ 9.30am-12.30pm & 1.30-5pm Thu-Mon Oct-Feb, 9.30am-12.30pm & 1.30-6pm Wed-Sun Mar-Sep), an operational talc mine until 1995. Underground tours take visitors down two mines, the Paola and the deeper Gianna, providing a grim but fascinating journey into a not-so-distant past. In fact, talc is still mined in the valley and used in the paper, cosmetic, pharmaceutical and ceramic industries.

To get to the Scopriminiera, take the SP169 from Perosa Argentina for Prali, and follow this road for about 15km.

JUST MUSHING AROUND

Learn how to master the noble sport of mushing at the **Scuola Italiana Condut-tori Cani di Slitta** (☎ 0122 83 24 73). The school maintains its own kennel of Alaskan and Siberian huskies, who will happily whisk you away on your command.

Packages on offer include an introductory course (€35), culminating in a 7km run with two or three dogs; a day-long course (€100) that covers theory lessons and up to 20km on the sled; and a sled weekend (€170) comprising lessons and four excursions of 10 km each.

more information on all of these activities. To play a round on Europe's highest **golf course** (☎ 0122 79 94 11; golf.sestrieres@vialattea.it; green fees from €35) is a memorable experience.

For a good sweat, the **Fitness Centre** (☎ 0122 75 50 50; Via Azzurri d'Italia; 1 day €11; ⏰ 11am-10pm) has a sauna, Turkish bath and spa bath.

Sleeping & Eating

Most of Sestriere's hotels are expensive and are very close to Piazza Fraiteve.

Hotel Miramonte (☎ 0122 75 53 33; Via Cesana 3; B&B per person €57-115) Open year-round this is a friendly family-run three-star hotel, 400m from the town centre. It offers few surprises, either good or bad, but rooms are comfortable and it's handy for the golf course.

Grand Hotel Principi di Piemonte (☎ 0122 79 41; www.framon-hotels.com; Via Sauze 3; B&B from €105; 🏊) The place to rub shoulders with VIPs, Sestriere's top hotel is situated in a larch wood and has all you'd expect from a top hotel, including an indoor swimming pool.

The Pinky (☎ 0122 76 441; Piazza Fraiteve 5n; pizza from €4.50) Squeeze yourself between one of the tightly packed wooden tables and tuck into a pizza at this perennially popular spot.

Caffé La Torteria (☎ 0122 77 141; Pizzale Fraiteve 3d; ⏰ 8am-7.30pm; ✗) This bar-cum-café is nothing special beyond the fact that (a) it's packed year-round; (b) has great aperitif nibbles and; (c) serves the thickest hot chocolate this side of Mont Blanc.

Sestriere Café (☎ 0122 77 106; Piazza Agnelli 1; mains €7) The newest addition to life in the square, the Sestriere Café is a popular haunt of the trendy. The metal chairs and sofas draped with fake zebra-skin provide a modern look.

Getting There & Away

Sapav buses (☎ 800 80 19 01, ☎ 0122 75 54 44 Sestriere; www.sapav.com in Italian) connect Sestriere up to five times daily with Cesana (€2.10, 25 minutes), Oulx (€3, 45 minutes) and Turin (€5.10, two to three hours).

CESANA

pop 964 / elevation 1350m

It's the imposing profile of Europe's highest fort on the peak of Mt Chaberton (3130m) that draws the eye as you enter the resort town of Cesana. Lying at the heart of the Via Lattea, Cesana has an impressive network of ski-lifts, which connect with Clavière on one side and San Sicario on the other. Contact the **tourist office** (☎ 0122 892 02; Piazza V Amedeo 3) for details.

San Sicario (1700m) is a purpose-built resort, 5km north of Cesana, which offers little except skiing and sledding, see the boxed text Just Mushing Around (p97).

La Tana degli Orsi (☎ 0122 84 51 49; www.latana degliorsi.it in Italian; Fraz. Ruilles 96; B&B per person €31) You can really get away from the crowds at this converted mountain hut, 6km from Cesana. The thick stone walls and heavy wooden furniture make it a cosy hideaway in winter and a cool retreat in summer. Dinner is included in the price. From the SS23, follow signs for Bousson and continue to the hamlet of Ruilles.

CLAVIÈRE

pop 167 / elevation 1760m

Right on the border with France, Clavière is set amidst abundant larch and fir trees. A Via Lattea ski resort, it offers first class skiing for all abilities and a stunning cross-country circuit. For those who want to up skis for a morning, the **Golf Club of Clavière** (☎ 0122 87 89 17; Via Nazionale 45; green fees €40) boasts a scenic nine-hole course.

For information on the resort and environs check with the **tourist office** (☎ 0122 87 88 56; Via Nazionale 30; ⏰ 9am-noon & 3-6.30pm Mon-Fri, 9am-12.30pm & 3-6.30pm Sat & Sun).

Hotel Pian Del Sole (☎ 0122 87 80 85; fax 0122 87 87 31; Via Nazionale28; d €120) One of the smaller hotels lining Via Nazionale, this chalet-style three-star offers eight simple rooms, which come with TV and telephone. Golfers should manage to carry their clubs the 150m from the hotel to the course.

VALLE DI SUSA

SACRA DI SAN MICHELE

Perched on a hill above the road from Turin is the **Sacra di San Michele** (☎ 011 93 91 30; adult/child €2.50/1.50; ◷ 9.30am-12.30pm & 3-5pm Tue-Fri, 9.30am-noon & 2.40-5pm Sat & Sun mid-Oct–mid-Mar, 9.30am-12.30pm & 3-6pm Tue-Fri, 9.30am-noon & 2.30-6pm Sat & Sun mid-Mar–mid-Oct), a mean and moody, brooding Gothic-Romanesque abbey that has kept sentry atop Monte Pirchiriano (962m) since the 10th century. Inside, don't miss the so-called 'Zodiac Door', a doorway from the 12th-century sculpted with cheeky cherubs pulling each other's hair. Sunday mass is celebrated at noon and 6pm.

The only way to get to the abbey from **Avigliana** (population 11,110), the abbey's closest town 12km east, is by car or on foot. The **tourist office** (☎ 011 932 86 50; avigliana@montagnedoc.it; Piazza del Popolo 2; ◷ 9am-noon & 3-6pm Mon-Fri, 9am-noon Sat) in Avigliana has route maps and information on the area, including the two lakes and marshlands of the **Parco Naturale dei Laghi di Avigliana**.

By foot the shortest walk is actually from Sant'Ambrogio, a village further west, from where an old mule track leads from the foot of the hill to the abbey – a strenuous 90-minute climb. Another route passes by **Il Sentiero dei Franchi** (☎ 011 96 31 747; ilsenti erodeifranchi@tiscali.it; Borgata Cresto 16; 1st/2nd courses €6.70/6.70; ◷ 9am-3pm & 7pm-midnight Wed-Mon), a hiker-friendly bar and restaurant in Borgata Cresto. Reservations are essential.

DETOUR

From Corso Laghi take the road for Giaveno and then Via Monginevro towards Fraz. Bertassi. Just before Fraz. Bertassi, turn right into Via Prole towards the industrial zone and then left down Viale dei Mareschi. At the roundabout at the end of the road take the first right and continue straight to a further roundabout. Take the first right again and then go immediately left. Here you'll find the **Museo del Dinamitifico Nobel** (☎ 011 931 30 00; Via Galiné; adult/child €4/2; ◷ 2-6pm Sun) a fascinating museum dedicated to the building's former life as a dynamite factory.

SUSA
pop 6550 / elevation 205m

On the busiest route between Turin and France, **Susa** started life as a Celtic town (a Druid well remains as testimony) before falling under the Roman Empire's sway. The modest Roman ruins make it a pleasant stop on the way to the ski resorts. In addition to the remains of a Roman **aqueduct**, a still-used **amphitheatre** and the triumphal **Arco d'Augusto**, the town's **cathedral** dates from the early 11th century.

Worth a brief pitstop is the forbidding **Forte di Exilles** (☎ 0122 582 70; adult/child €5/1.50; ◷ 10am-7pm Tue-Sun mid-Apr–Sep, 10am-2pm Tue-Sun Oct–mid-Apr), overlooking the quiet village of Exilles 15km west of Susa. One of the oldest monuments in the Valle di Susa, its origins are uncertain but it was already a formidable fort in the mid-12th-century. Opening hours vary so check with the Susa **tourist office** (☎ / fax 0122 62 24 70; Corso Inghilterra 39; ◷ 9am-12.30pm & 3-5pm Tue-Sat, 10am-noon Sun, 9am-12.30pm Mon).

Hotel Du Parc (☎ 0122 62 22 73; fax 0122 310 27; Via Rocchetta 15; s/d €50/70; **P**) One man and his dogs await you at this homely hotel, just off Susa's main thoroughfare. Despite its position it's a quiet place where the decor is country floral and the welcome gruffly warm.

Sapav buses (☎ 800 80 19 01, in Susa 0122 62 20 15; www.sapav.com in Italian) connect Susa with Oulx (20 minutes), Avigliana (35 minutes), Turin (1¼ hours) and the Via Lattea resorts.

CHIOMONTE
pop 990 / elevation 750m

One of the first tourist centres of the Upper Valle di Susa, Chiomonte is a tiny place known for its stupendous 16th-century fountains. As a ski resort it's well-suited to beginners with four of its nine slopes graded blue.

Grangia Del Courbaval (☎ 328 668 92 29; www .grangiadelcourbaval.it; d €26, half board €36; Strada Vecchia del Frais) Situated 2km out of Chiomonte, this basic *agriturismo* in a former mountain cabin, offers clean white rooms with a minimum of decoration. It's a great place to saddle up and take to the hills on horseback. Dinners are hearty, homemade affairs from €13.

Chiomonte is on the SS24.

OULX & SAUZE D'OULX

Nothing much in itself, **Oulx**, 21km west of Susa, is the main stepping stone to the ski resorts of the Via Lattea. Its **tourist office**

(☎ 0122 83 15 96; oulx@montagnedoc.it; Piazza Garambois 2; ⌚ 9am-noon & 3-6pm) is one of the valley's largest.

A short bus ride away, **Sauze d'Oulx** (1509m) heaves with English tourists in the ski season. One of the Via Lattea resorts, it offers excellent skiing and an aprés-ski that's more British than Italian. In summer, a popular walking trail leads to the hamlet of **Jouvenceaux** where the wooden houses and frescoed chapel remain largely unchanged.

For details contact the **tourist office** (☎ 0122 858 009; Piazza Assietta 18; ⌚ 9am-12.30pm & 3-6.30pm).

B&B Ico's Lodge (☎ 0122 85 95 24; www.bedand breakfast-sauze.it; Via Villaggio Alpino 14; d/t/q €68/83/38; ⌚ closed May, Sep–mid-Nov) Set amongst larch trees this Alpine villa is refreshingly free of concrete. It's a fully-equipped apartment which can be used by up to four people.

Il Capricorno (☎ 0122 85 02 73; Via Case Sparse 21, Localitá Le Clotes; s/d €150/180) For a touch of chalet chic, Il Capricorno does the trick. The polished pine furniture gives the rooms a refined look and the top-notch **restaurant** (mains from €15) serves high-calibre classics such as the delicious homemade fruit flan.

Most aprés-ski is on the Via Assietta, the bar- and pizzeria-lined main drag.

From Oulx train station there are regular departures for Turin (€4.30, one hour 15 minutes, 12 daily), Bardonecchia (€1.55; 10 minutes, 20 daily) and even Paris (€90; four hours 45 minutes, two daily).

BARDONECCHIA
pop 3084 / elevation 1312m
At the head of the Valle di Susa, Bardonecchia is the last stop in Italy before the Fréjus tunnel takes you through to France. Situated in a massive wooded amphitheatre it is divided into two parts, the modern and not terribly attractive Borgonuovo (new town) and the atmospheric Borgovecchio (old town).

A favourite of Turin's weekend skiers, it's also a relaxed summer resort where visitors come to enjoy the lush green hills.

Orientation & Information
Bardonecchia's main strip is Via Medail, which heads uphill from near the train station to the historic centre, the Borgovecchio. For ski-lifts head down Viale delle Vittoria. The **tourist office** (☎ 0122 990 32; www.montagnedoc .it; Viale della Vittoria 4; ⌚ 9am-12.30pm & 2.30-7pm Mon-Sat) has heaps of local information.

Sights & Activities
Although the Borgovecchio is not awash with museums and extravagant churches, it is a picturesque part of town perfect for an early evening stroll.

For more strenuous exercise the **Chalet delle Guide Bardonecchia** (☎ 0122 960 60; Via Medail; ⌚ 5.30-7.30pm Fri & Sat) is an information kiosk run by Alpine guides, who operate excursions ranging from **climbing ice falls** to **trekking with snow rackets**. For a half-day guided trek expect to pay €25.

Cross-country skiing is very popular in the area with well-marked courses at altitude and on the valley floor. A day/week pass costs €10/58. Horse riders can also enjoy the hills with day rides and longer overnight journeys available. For details contact **Silverado** (☎ 333 497 48 51), which charges €16 per horse per hour.

Sleeping & Eating
Bardonecchia is packed with hotels, many of which are characterless mid-range dormitories catering to large groups and ski parties.

Casa Alpina (☎ 0122 99 98 41; Via Giolitti 11; s €25-30 d €45-55) A cosy little pad on the edge of the Borgovecchio, Casa Alpina is, as its name suggests, an Alpine home offering basic rooms for the night. The downstairs **restaurant** (menu €16) specialises in Piedmontese cuisine with a French slant – think fondues and polenta with venison.

Ristorante Biovey (☎ 0122 99 92 15; www.biovey.it; Via Generale Cantore 2; 1st/2nd courses from €7/12; ⌚ Wed-Mon restaurant) An orange mix of the modern and traditional, the decor at this elegant restaurant-cum-hotel is as eye-catching as the food. The warm bread and after-dinner macaroons are a nice touch that add to the ambitious cooking. The well-furnished wine list relies heavily on Piedmontese reds. The eight **rooms** (s/d B&B €45/72) up top fill up fast so book ahead.

Fashionable bars include **Medail** (☎ 0122 99 98 44; Via Stazione 2) and **Miretti** (☎ 0122 90 17 78; Via Medail 79).

Getting There & Away
Bardonecchia is easily reached by both car and train. By car the A32 autostrada leads directly to town, while there are up to 20 trains a day for Oulx (€1.55, 10 minutes) from where you can pick up a train or bus for Turin.

Southern & Eastern Piedmont

CONTENTS

Asti	103
Monferrato	106
Casale Monferrato	106
Alessandria & Around	107
Acqui Terme	108
Alba	110
The Langhe	112
Saluzzo	115
Cuneo	116
Around Cuneo	119

Piedmont's tasty south is capable of bringing out the *bon viveur* in anyone. A mecca for professional gourmets and enthusiastic amateurs, it's an area that understands the good things in life. Noble red wines and sparkling white wines, hazelnuts, precious white truffles and earthy mushrooms are among the gastronomic treasures that are proudly dished up.

Much of the wine is produced in the relatively unexplored hills of the Langhe, around the fascinating town of Alba. An area of green and rolling beauty, it recalls Tuscany's curvaceous countryside. Carpeted with vines, the landscape is peppered with medieval hill-top towns, many of which boast imperious castles. Touring the hills, visiting the castles and tasting the wine are not a bad way of passing your time.

From the gentle peaks of the wine-rich slopes head southwest to the imposing heights of the Alps. Numerous valleys slice through the mountains providing fertile opportunities for fun-seekers. In winter skiers don salopettes and head up to the popular resorts, while in the warmer months the valleys buzz with the hum of hikers, cyclists, climbers and canoeists.

There are caves to explore and striking churches to discover, national parks to tour and thermal baths to enjoy; you can even trek to the source of Italy's longest river, the mighty Po.

HIGHLIGHTS

■ **Race Day**

Cheer at Asti's Palio (p105) and hoot at Alba's donkey derby (p111)

■ **Pedal Power**

Cycle the wine-rich Langhe hill-top villages (p113)

■ **Hot Spring**

Test the hot water's of Acqui Terme's Fontana della Bollente (p109)

■ **Underground**

Tour the caves, the Grotta di Bossea (p120)

■ **Overground**

Walk the cloisters at the vast Certosa di Pesio (p120)

SOUTHERN & EASTERN PIEDMONT

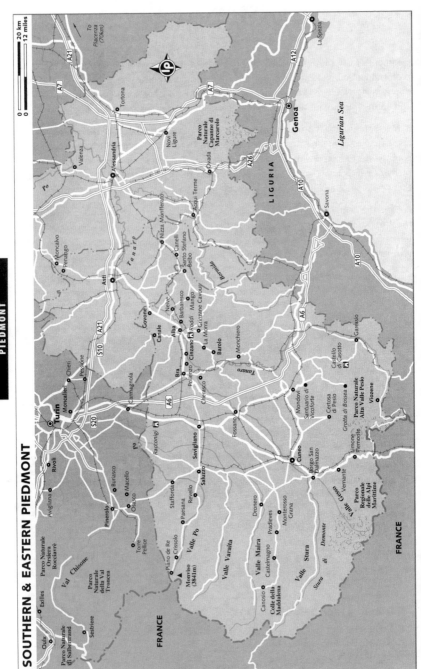

ASTI

pop 73,175 / elevation 123m

The best place in Italy for a bottle of bubbly, Asti is the capital of the sparkling-wine industry. Made rich on the fruits of the surrounding vineyards, it's not a town likely to leave much of a lasting impression, save for the sheer scale of its wine production. But break through the industrial outskirts and you'll find that the bustling centre complete with shops, cafés and a cobbled *centro storico* (historic centre) merits a little exploration.

Come in September, though, and you'll find yourself in the midst of huge crowds gathered to celebrate the town's great festivals. Fuelled by industrial quantities of *spumante* (sparkling wine), the fun peaks with the madcap Palio.

Asti has a rocky history. Its original settlers became part of a Roman colony in 89 BC. After existing as an independent city-state in the 13th and 14th centuries, it was passed around between Spain, Austria, France and finally the Savoys, prior to unification. During the late 13th century the region became one of Italy's wealthiest, with 150-odd towers springing up in Asti alone to show off different families' wealth. Only 12 remain today as reminders of its glorious past.

Orientation

Walking north from the train station through Piazza G Marconi, you can either take Via Cavour to the *centro storico* or skirt around Piazza Campo del Palio to Piazza V. Alfieri to the north. The northernmost point of this triangular piazza meets Corso Vittorio Alfieri, Asti's main drag running east to west. Head left for the historic centre.

Information

EMERGENCY

Police Station (Prefettura; ☎ 0141 41 81 11; Piazza V. Alfieri 30)

INTERNET ACCESS

Internet Point (www.astipoint.it; Via Garibaldi; per hr €5; ☿ 9am-8pm Mon-Fri, 9am-midnight Sat, 5-8pm Sun)

MEDICAL SERVICES

Hospital (☎ 0141 39 21 11; Via Botallo 4)

MONEY

Banca Intesa (☎ 0141 35 38 21; Via Cavour 54; ☿ 8.30am-1.30pm & 3.30-4.30pm Mon-Fri) Bank with ATM.

POST

Post Office (☎ 0141 35 72 51; Corso Dante Alighieri 55; ☿ 8.30am-7pm Mon-Fri, 8.30am-1pm Sat)

SOUTHERN & EASTERN PIEDMONT

FOOD FOR THOUGHT

In an area renowned for its serious dedication to the gastronomic arts, it's only natural that the skills and techniques learned over centuries are passed down to the next generation.

With this in mind, staff at Piedmont's first foodie faculty recently donned their whites to welcome the first wave of wannabe chefs to the **Università di Scienze Gastronomiche** (University of Gastronomic Sciences; ☎ 0172 45 85 11; Piazza Vittorio Emanuele 9). Set in a neo-Gothic palazzo in Pollenzo, 11km west of Alba, the university is set to give credence to the old adage that a 'university is the fountain of knowledge where you go to drink'. In this case, however, the students will be expected to know exactly what they're drinking, where it comes from, what year it was produced and how much they can charge for it.

Lessons in the art of wine-tasting are just one of the joys that await students at the 19th-century campus known as the Agenzia di Pollenzo. A rather striking quadrangular complex, it's an apt choice for a gastronomic centre as it was here in 1842 that King Carlo Alberto founded the region's first Agricultural Association. As well as the university, the red-brick palazzo is set to house a four-star hotel, restaurant and wine bank.

Spread over two sites – the other is in Parma – the university boasts a teaching staff of international experts, including chefs from India, journalists from America and the UK, academics from Israel and wine experts from France and Italy. A formidable body of knowledge covers every angle of the two subjects on offer – Gastronomy and Agro-Ecology. Both degree courses last two years, as does the postgraduate Masters in Food Management and Food and Gastronomy Communication.

An initial intake has been set at 60 students a year. Applicants will be expected to understand Italian and English and have a secondary-school diploma or equivalent. For further information check out the university website www.unisg.it.

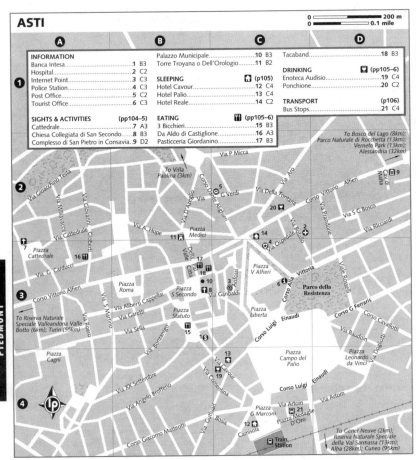

ASTI

0 — 200 m
0 — 0.1 mile

INFORMATION		
Banca Intesa	1	B3
Hospital	2	C2
Internet Point	3	C3
Police Station	4	C3
Post Office	5	C2
Tourist Office	6	C3

SIGHTS & ACTIVITIES		(pp104–5)
Cattedrale	7	A3
Chiesa Collegiata di San Secondo	8	B3
Complesso di San Pietro in Consavia	9	D2

Palazzo Municipale	10	B3
Torre Troyana o Dell'Orologio	11	B2
SLEEPING 🏠		(p105)
Hotel Cavour	12	C4
Hotel Palio	13	C4
Hotel Reale	14	C2
EATING 🍴		(pp105–6)
3 Bicchieri	15	B3
Da Aldo di Castiglione	16	A3
Pasticceria Giordanino	17	B3

Tacaband	18	B3
DRINKING 🍷		(pp105–6)
Enoteca Audisio	19	C4
Ponchione	20	C2
TRANSPORT		(p106)
Bus Stops	21	C4

To Bosco del Lago (8km);
Parco Naturale di Rocchetta (13km);
Verneto Park (13km);
Alessandria (32km)

To Villa
Paolina (3km)

To Gener Neuve (2km);
Riserva Naturale Speciale
della Val Sarmassa (13km);
Alba (28km); Cuneo (95km)

To Riserva Naturale
Speciale Valleandona Valle
Botto (6km); Turin (55km)

TOURIST INFORMATION

Tourist Office (☎ 0141 53 03 57; www.terredasti.it in Italian; Piazza Alfieri 29; ☻ 9am-1pm & 2.30-6.30pm Mon-Sat, 9am-1pm Sun)

Sights

Monument to Asti's 13th-century heyday, the 44m-tall **Torre Troyana o dell'Orologio** (☎ 0141 39 94 60; Piazza Medici; ☻ 10am-1pm & 4-7pm Apr-Sep, 10am-1pm & 3-6pm Sat & Sun Oct) towers over Piazza Medici. Restored between 1997 and 1999, it's now possible to scale the 199 steps to a 37m-high viewing platform.

Gracing Piazza San Secondo, the Roman-esque-Gothic **Chiesa Collegiata di San Secondo** (☎ 0141 53 00 66; Piazza San Secondo; ☻ 10.45am-noon & 3.30-5.30pm Mon-Sat, 3.30-5.30pm Sun) houses the

bones of the city's patron saint; legend has it that Secondo was martyred and buried here in AD 119. Adjoining the church is the **Palazzo Municipale**, a splendid 18th-century office building that is not open to the public.

Further afield lies Asti's red-brick **cattedrale** (☎ 0141 59 29 24; Piazza Cattedrale; ☻ 8.30am-noon, 3.30-5.30pm). From the 8th century, it sports three beautiful stained-glass windows.

Museum buffs might want to head down to the **Complesso di San Pietro in Consavia** (☎ 0141 39 94 60; Corso Vittorio Alfieri 2; adult/child €2.50/0.50; ☻ 10am-1pm & 3-6pm Tue-Sun), a 14th-century religious complex with three museums: one dedicated to local archaeological finds; one to fossils and palaeontological goodies; and the third to various Egyptian pieces.

Hotel accommodation, Stresa (p124)

MARTIN MOOS

JUDI WILLOUGHBY

Isola San Giulio, Lago D'Orta (p130)

An angel atop a building, Stresa (p124)

MARTIN MOOS

NICK TAPP

Mountain refuge, Parco Naturale delle Alpi Marittime (p119)

NICK TAPP

Cascading waters, Parco Naturale delle Alpi Marittime (p119)

Medieval brick towers, Alba (p111)

MARTIN MOOS

A sight in itself, Asti's chaotic Wednesday- and Saturday-morning market on Piazza Alfieri and Piazza Campo del Palio sells everything from food and clothes to tractors, vines and lawnmowers.

Festivals & Events

Asti is big on *feste* (festivals). September's flurry of festivals offers ample wine-tasting opportunities: the 10-day **Douja d'Or** (a *douja* being a terracotta wine jug unique to Asti) is followed by the one-day **Delle Sagre** food festival on the second Sunday of the month (a mind-blowing 500,000 people sat down to eat on Piazza Campo del Palio in 2002).

The **Palio**, held in the third weekend in September, sees horses race around Piazza Alfieri. The first mention of horse racing in Asti dates to 1275. Historians tell of townsmen racing beneath the town walls of Alba, their historic enemy. Today the race is strictly within Asti's town limits. On the third Sunday of September, 21 costumed jockeys, from each of the town's historic quarters, gallop bareback around the course set up in Piazza Alfieri. The winner is presented with the Palio, a crimson standard bearing the town's insignia. The race comes at the end of weeks of build-up, with entire town quarters banqueting at huge tables set up in the streets. On the big day, the race is preceded by a spectacular procession of more than 1,200 people, all dressed in medieval garb, through the historic centre.

Sleeping

Booking ahead is always a good idea in Asti; around Palio time (September) it's essential.

Hotel Cavour (☎ /fax 0141 53 02 22; Piazza G Marconi; s €39-44, d €58-64) Opposite the train station, this is a family-run affair that is welcoming and comfortable. The two-star rooms are modern and all come with TV and telephone.

Hotel Reale (☎ 0141 53 0240; fax 0141 343 57; www .hotel-reale.com; Piazza Alfieri 6; s €75-85, d €110-140; ⚓) The rather grand Royal Hotel languishes in a majestic 18th-century mansion on Asti's central square. The hallmark is old-world style with 21st-century comfort.

Hotel Palio (☎ 0141 343 71; www.hotelpalio.com; Via Cavour 106; s/d €70/140; Ⓟ ⚓) Don't be put off by the less than promising exterior. This friendly hotel has good-sized rooms furnished with antique furniture; one room even boasts a handsome wrought-iron bedstead. There is also wheelchair access.

Eating & Drinking

Since the 1850s the grapes grown on the largely flat plains around Asti have produced Italy's top sparkling wine – Asti (better known, incorrectly, since 1993, as Asti Spumante). The sweet white wine is best drunk young and at a chilled 6°C to 8°C, like its less-fizzy cousin Moscato d'Asti. There are numerous places to sample it, either in or out of town in Asti's 9120 hectares of vineyards, tended by 6800 wine growers. The tourist office has a complete list.

Enoteca Audisio (☎ 0141 43 63 26; Via Cavour 83; ⏱ 8am-9pm Tue-Sun) A simple brick and wooden wine-bar-cum-café, this laid-back place maintains a choice collection of locally produced wines. Tasters are welcome, as are purchasers who are after a case or two of something special.

FUN IN THE FLORA

In Asti's green environs, nature lovers can take to the woods in the **Parchi e Riserve Astigiani**, a 650-hectare protected area that comprises three different parks: the **Parco Naturale di Rocchetta**, 13km east of Asti in Rocchetta Tanaro; the **Riserva Naturale Speciale Valleandona Valle Botto**, 6km west of Asti in Valleandona; and the **Riserva Naturale Speciale della Val Sarmassa** in Incisa Scapaccino, 14km southeast of Alba. All three are characterised by the hilly landscape typical of the area and provide homes to a host of woodland creatures and up to 40 species of nesting birds.

There are also three oases run by the WWF. In Poggio di Castello d'Annone, 8km east of Asti, the 10 hectares of woodland at **Bosco del Lago** (☎ 0141 11 13) contain some magnificently gnarled 200-year-old oak trees while it is the Art Nouveau **Villa Paolina** that stands out at the 10-hectare **park** (☎ 0141 59 32 81) in Valmanera, in the northern suburbs of Asti. The last in the trio is the **Verneto park** (☎ 0141 59 32 81), a soggy paradise for a thriving insect population, in Rocchetta Tanaro, 13km east of Asti.

Da Aldo di Castiglione (☎ 0141 35 49 05; Via Giovanni Gioberti 8; mains around €13; ⏰ Fri-Wed) Pass through the forbidding door and you enter a spacious dining hall with tables set simply in white. The local meat dishes are succulent and tasty – the *stinco di maialetto* (pig's shinbone) is a winner but the star of the show is the *mousse all'Amaretto* (Amaretto mousse); it is quite simply fantastic. Wine advice comes with the service when you order Barbera d'Asti Superiore (from €13 per bottle).

Tacaband (☎ 0141 53 09 99; Via al Teatro Alfieri 5; 1st/2nd courses €8/10; ⏰ noon-2pm & 8-9.30pm Thu-Tue) Pick and choose from 500 different wines at this select wine bar, next to the theatre off Corso Alfieri. To aid the tasting process it offers a good-value range of fixed lunchtime menus Monday to Friday (€12 to €18), a *menu degustazione* (tasting menu; €30) and a superb antipasti (€20).

3 Bicchieri (☎ 0141 32 41 37; Piazza Statuto 37; mixed platters €6, salads from €3.60; ⏰ 7.30am-last customer Tue-Sun) Though nestled inside a 16th-century red-brick tower, its contemporary, clean-cut minimalist furnishings perfectly set off its platters of melt-in-the-mouth *bresaola* (dried seasoned meat), mixed salami and cheese. Wine by the glass costs from €2.60.

Gener Neuve (☎ 0141 55 72 70; Lungo Tarno 4; set menu €60; ⏰ Tue-Sat) Folk drive hundreds of kilometres to dine at this Michelin-starred restaurant. The menu fluctuates with the season, so diners wanting to taste the legendary white truffle should book for sometime between September and December. The wine list veers towards the great Piedmontese reds and the decor towards the rustic. It is located about 2km south of Piazza Campo del Palio.

Worth popping into for a quick choc is **Pasticceria Giordanino** (☎ 0141 59 38 02; Corso Vittorio Alfieri 254), while coffee addicts should head to **Ponchione** (☎ 0141 59 24 69; Corso Vittorio Alfieri 149).

Getting There & Around
SATTI (www.satti.it in Italian) buses connect Asti with towns in the province. They depart from the bus stops in Piazza Medaglie d'Oro, just to the east of the train station. Urban bus services are run by **ASP** (☎ 0141 348 27).

By car Asti is easily reached via the A10 or the parallel SS10, which connects Turin with Alessandria. For Alba, Cuneo and the south, take the SS231.

Asti is served by regular trains to and from Turin (€3.50, 30 to 55 minutes,

hourly) and Alessandria (€2.45, one hour 20 minutes, hourly).

MONFERRATO
Little visited yet beautiful, this pocket of vineyards and hill-top villages is one of Italy's most important wine-producing areas.

Spread-eagled between Asti and Casale Monferrato, it is divided into two parts: the Lower Monferrato, north of Asti, and home of the great Barbera del Monferrato wines, is characterised by a gentle undulating landscape, while further south the Upper Monferrato becomes increasingly rugged.

CASALE MONFERRATO
pop 38,545 / elevation 116m
An important agricultural centre, Casale Monferrato sits on the right bank of the River Po, 30km northeast of Asti. Unexceptional, and for the most part workmanlike, it's worth passing through to have a look at its spectacular **synagogue** and, on the second Sunday of every month, its antique market.

Information
The **tourist office** (☎ 0142 44 43 30; Piazza Castello; ⏰ 8am-6pm Mon-Sat, 10am-12.30pm & 3-6.30pm Sun) offers a hotel booking service and sells a guide to walking in the area, *Camminare in Monferrato* (€10), which lists 50 itineraries.

Sights
Casale's major attraction is its 16th-century **synagogue** (☎ 0142 718 07; Vicolo Salomone Olper 44; admission free; ⏰ 10am-noon & 3-5pm Sun) in the heart of the old Jewish ghetto. Dating to 1595 the bare facade (in the 16th-century Jews were forbidden to decorate the exterior of their synagogues) gives no indication of the sumptuous interior. Revamped between 1857 and 1866 it's a stunning example of rococo excess with an abundance of gold-leaf and elaborate carving. The synagogue also houses the **Museo d'Arte e Storia Ebraico** (Museum of Jewish Art and History; ☎ 0142 718 07; Vicolo Salomone Olper 44; admission €4; ⏰ 10am-noon & 3-5pm Sun), where you'll find a collection of Jewish artefacts from the 17th and 18th centuries.

Sleeping & Eating
Hotel Leon d'Oro (☎ 0142 763 61; fax 0142 763 63; Via Roma 62; s/d €36.50/72) In the heart of the historic centre this friendly hotel has rooms spread over four floors. The reception is on

the 3rd floor and sports a rather alarming 1970s-style décor, which, fortunately, the simple, old-style rooms have been spared.

Taverna Paradiso (☎ 0142 755 44; Piazza Santa Stefano; 1st/2nd courses from €6/8) Nestled into the corner of a tiny little piazza, this is a bright and cheery place to sit down to a meaty Piedmontese menu. There are few surprises on offer, just hearty local fare.

Getting There & Away
Casale sits on the SS31, which links Alessandra with Chivasso. The A26 is also close by. There are direct trains to Alessandria (€2.45, 30 minutes, 16 daily) and Vercelli (€2, 20 minutes, 11 daily). For Turin it's easier to take a bus. **STAT** (☎ 0412 45 28 54) runs to Turin (€4.30, one hour 50 minutes, six daily).

Around Casale Monferrato
For the best of the area's wine head for the **Enoteca Regionale del Monferrato** (☎ 0142 93 32 43; Palazzo Callori; ☺ 9am-1pm & 1.30-4.30pm Mon & Wed-Fri, 10am-noon & 3-7pm Sat & Sun Feb-Dec) in Vignale Monferrato, 15km south of Casale. The austere 17th-century palazzo not only houses the extensive cellar but also plays host each June and July to the Vignale Danza festival. The international dance festival stages a series of performances spanning classical ballet to modern-jazz inspired choreography.

Just down the road in Altavilla Monferrato, the **Museo della Grappa Mazzetti** (☎ 0142 92 61 85; www.altavilla.com in Italian; Località Cittadella 1; admission free; ☺ 9am-noon & 2-6pm) is housed in the working Mazzetti grappa distillery. The century-old distillation equipment on display vividly shows how this firey liquid is produced. Aficionados might also enjoy the collection of prestigious grappa labels.

Back on the wine trail, the **Cooperativa Sette Colli** (☎ 0141 91 72 06; www.vinisettecollimoncalvo.it in Italian; ☺ 9am-noon & 3-6pm Mon-Sat, 9am-noon Sun) in Moncalvo, 15km north of Asti, is one of hundreds of places where you can taste (free) and buy. Otherwise many of the dozens of *agriturismi* (farmstay accommodation) in this rural region run informal cellar tours; the **Consorzio Operatori Turistici Asti e Monferrato** (☎ 0141 53 03 57; www.terredasti .it in Italian; Piazza Alfieri 29) in Asti has a list.

SLEEPING
La Brenta di Cavalla Angela (☎ 0142 93 32 01; Ca' Arfinotto; s/d €45/70; ☺ Mar–mid-Nov; **P**) To rest

your heavy head after a hard day's tasting, this homely B&B in Vignale is just the ticket. The welcoming 17th-century farmhouse is a picture of rural perfection, as the ivy threatens to drown the grey-stone walls.

Tenuta del Barone (☎ 0141 91 01 61; Via Barone 18, Penango; www.tenutadelbarone.com; s/d with breakfast low season €44/62, high season €55/77.50, dinner with wine €25; **P**) Very much a family affair, this old and rambling farm dating to 1550 has been converted over the past decade into a cheery and down-to-earth B&B. Sleep in the old stables and feast on enormous amounts of homemade food cooked up by Mother.

Penango, 2km from Moncalvo, is signposted from Moncalvo's southern end.

Locanda del Sant'Uffizio (☎ 0141 91 62 92; www.thi.it; Strada Sant'Uffizio 1, Cioccaro di Penango; s/d €158/215; **P** ⚡ 🖳 ⚮) This upmarket haven of peace comes in the form of a restored 17th-century convent with 4 hectares of working vineyards. Stylish rooms – some with original frescoes – reflect the colour of the flowers after which they are named.

ALESSANDRIA & AROUND
Provincial capital and Piedmont's third largest city, Alessandria doesn't have a whole lot to offer. An important manufacturing (wine, machinery, paper, furniture and hats) and agricultural centre, it's not likely to feature on your must-see list. However, if you do find yourself here, don't despair. Simply wandering the vivacious streets can be fun in itself.

Orientation & Information
Orientate yourself around Alessandria's large and plain central square Piazza Libertá. From here it's a short walk west to Via Milano, the central shopping strip, and to Corso Roma which leads south to Piazza Garibaldi.

The **city tourist office** (☎ / fax 0131 23 47 94; Via Gagliaudo 2; ☺ 10am-1pm & 2-6pm Mon-Sat) gives out information on the town, while the **provincial tourist office** (☎ 0131 28 80 95; www.alexala.it; Piazza S.Maria di Castello 14; ☺ 9am-1pm & 2-6pm Mon-Fri) is also involved in actively promoting the Province of Alessandria.

Sights
Alessandria's major claim to fame is the **Museo del Cappello** (☎ 0131 400 35; Corso Borsalino 54). Here you can admire up to 5000 hats produced by Giuseppe Borsalino (1842–1900). A legend in the world of millinery,

Borsalino's name lives on in his famous hat, still a favourite of Piedmontese business-man. At the time of writing, the museum was closed indefinitely for restoration.

For artefacts of a more traditional nature, head out to the **Antiquarium di Villa del Foro** (☎ 0131 23 47 94; Via Oviglio 10; admission free; ☽ 4-7pm Wed & Fri, 9am-noon & 4-7pm Sat, 10am-1pm & 4-7pm Sun), 10km west of town. This small museum dis-plays the Roman bits and bobs dug up at the Via Fulva excavation. These include some dinky coloured vases and various bits of chipped pottery. If you're without a car, take bus No 15 from outside the train station.

The small town of Marengo, 4km east of Alessandria, owes its fame to Napoleon's battle against the Austrians. The Battle of Marengo was fought on 14 June 1800 and is remembered at the **Museo della Battaglia di Marengo** (☎ 0131 61 95 89; Via Genova 8; admission free; ☽ 3-6pm Mon-Sat, 10am-noon & 3-6pm Sun). Here you'll find various documents and relics.

Sleeping & Eating

Ostello Santa Maria di Castello (☎ 0131 28 81 87; www.hostels-aig.org; Piazza Santa Maria di Castello; dm €10.50) Prettily ensconced in the cloistered square next to the church of the same name, this youth hostel offers 70 dorm beds. The reception is on the ground floor next to the provincial tourist office.

Osteria della Luna nel Brodo (☎ 0131 23 18 98; Via Legnano 12; 1st/2nd courses from €6/8; ☽ Tue-Sun) Apart from its delightfully poetic name, Osteria of the Moon in the Soup, this place is a sure-fire winner. Much frequented by young locals, it serves innovative dishes on traditional themes. As a first course, the *risotto montecato alle rape rosse e timo* (risotto with red turnips and thyme) takes some beating. Booking is a must.

Pasticceria Giraudi (☎ 0131 27 55 63; Via San Lorenzo 102; ☽ 8.30am-12.45pm & 3.45-7.45pm Tue-Sat,

8.30am-12.45pm Sun) This is the place to pick up a delicious box of chocolate goodies. If ac-companied by someone with a sweet tooth, be wary of your wallet.

Getting There & Around

The easiest way to get to Alessandria by car is via the A26 from east or west of Alessan-dria, or A21 from the north or south.

Alessandria is an important train junc-tion, with regular services to Turin (€10.38, one hour 20 minutes), Asti (€3.91, 30 min-utes), Novara (€3.90, one hour 15 minutes) and Acqui Terme (€2.45, 45 minutes).

ACQUI TERME
pop 20,215/ elevation 156m

The famed waters of Acqui Terme have been drawing visitors to this spa town since Roman times. Situated in the hills of the Upper Monferrato, 30km southwest of Ales-sandria, it's a genteel place that, while pretty enough, won't keep you busy for very long.

The beneficial effects of the thermal baths were first discovered by the Romans, who built Acqui into a thriving city. Today little remains of their presence but the spring wa-ters continue to flow. The baths are centred on the area to the south of the River Bor-mida. Here you can enjoy the curative effects of the highly sulphurous waters or simply bath yourself in the gloriously gloopy mud.

Orientation & Information

The historic centre consists of a medley of streets branching off the Corso Italia, which connects Piazza Italia with Piazza San Franc-esco and Corso Roma. To get to the *zona bagni* (bath zone), take Corso Bagni across the river and turn left into Viale Einaudi.

The helpful **tourist office** (☎ 0144 32 21 42; www.acquiterme.it in Italian; Via Maggiorino Ferraris 5; ☽ 9.30am-12.30pm & 3.30-6.30pm Mon-Sat all year, 10am-

---

MUSEO DEI CAMPIONISSIMI

Cycling in Piedmont has a long and distinguished tradition, with champions fêted as heroes and races followed fervently. It was with this in mind that the high-tech temple of cycling, the **Museo dei Campionissimi** (☎ 0143 725 85; www.museodeicampionissimi.it in Italian; Viale dei Campionissimi; adult/child €7/4; ☽ 3-8pm Fri, 10am-8pm Sat & Sun, other days on request) was inaugurated in 2003, in a disused factory complex in Novi Ligure, 22km southeast of Alessandria. Here you can compete in a virtual race, marvel at the exploits of local greats Costante Girardengo and Fausto Coppi, and contemplate the role of the bicycle in the history of art. The museum also proposes a number of cycling itineraries, one of which passes through Castellania, birthplace of Coppi.

1pm Sun Mar-Dec) can help with accommodation and provide details for the thermal centres.

Sights & Activities

Smell the sulphur in the air at Acqui's symbolic **Fontana della Bollente** (Piazza Della Bollente). The 19th-century fountain spouts out 500L a minute of hot thermal water. Measured at 74.5°C, the bubbling water gives off a distinct whiff of rotting eggs.

For more fun in the wet stuff, contact one of the town's two major thermal centres, **Stabilimento Termale Nuove Terme** (☎ 0144 32 43 90; Via XX Settembre 5) in the centre of town or the **Stabilimento Termale Regina** (☎ 0144 32 43 90; Viale Donati) in the *zona bagni*. Expect to pay around €25 for a sulphur bath, €35 for a mud bath or €49 for an anti-cellulite massage.

For those who prefer their liquid pleasures poured out of a bottle, the **Enoteca Regionale di Acqui Terme** (☎ 0144 77 02 73; Piazza Levi 7; ⏱ 10am-noon & 3-6.30pm Tue & Fri-Sat, 3-6.30pm Thu) should be able to help. Hidden in the belly of an 11th-century palazzo, the cellar's speciality is the local Brachetto d'Acqui, a wine the Romans quaffed for its properties as an aphrodisiac.

Sleeping & Eating

Relais dell'Osso (☎ 0144 568 77; www.osso.it in Italian; Via dei Dottore 5; s/d €42/73) This charming place is right in the heart of the tranquil old town. Rooms are sunny and bright despite the wood-beam ceilings and wooden furniture. Breakfast is an additional €5.

Grand Hotel Nuove Terme (☎ 0144 585 55; www.grandhotelnuoveterme.it; Piazza Italia 1; s/d €100/130) Dominating Piazza Italia, this glamorous Art Nouveau hotel has been in business for more than a century. Counting Winston Churchill among its legion of former guests, it offers stylish and comfortable rooms as well as a well-equipped beauty centre.

Antica Hosteria da Bigât (☎ 0144 32 42 83; Via Mazzini 30/32; 1st/2nd courses from €6/5.50; ⏱ Thu-Tue) Warm wooden beams and brick walls welcome you to this tasty trattoria in the historic centre. Known for its *farinata* (a type of thin focaccia), it also serves a mean fish curry disguised on the menu as *stoccafisso*.

Getting There & Away

By car, Acqui can be reached on the SP30. Alternatively, exit the A26 at Ovada and follow the signs.

There are frequent trains from the **train station** (☎ 0144 525 83; Piazza Vittorio Veneto) to Asti (€3.10, one hour) and Alessandria (€2.45, 45 minutes), from where you can pick up a connection to Turin (€6.25).

Around Acqui Terme

Those following the wine trail shouldn't miss what is considered to be the region's premier wine museum in **Nizza Monferrato**, 14km northwest of Acqui. The **Museo Borsano** (☎ 0141 72 12 73; Piazza Dante; admission free; ⏱ 9-11am) chronicles the history of wine production in the region. The old wooden presses on display are intriguing and the collection of labels and prints is well worth a look. Visits are by appointment only.

While in this neck of the hills try to get hold of the local speciality *cardo* (in the local dialect, *gobbo*; in English, thistle). The prickly veg is available from greengrocer **Da Elisa** (Via Carlo Alberto 75; ⏱ 8am-12.45pm & 3.30-7.30pm Mon-Sat, closed Thu afternoon) between November and December.

SLEEPING

Near the small town of Ponzone, 12km to the south of Acqui Terme, there are two good options, while further afield in Bergolo, 38km southeast of Acqui Terme, there's a second youth hostel.

Ostello Ciglione (☎ 0144 37 87 25; Via Ciglione 12, Ciglione; dm €9; [P]) This recently inaugurated youth hostel offers basic dorm accommodation, use of a kitchen and a **dining room** (dinner €7). To get here from Acqui take the bus for Ponzone (20 minutes) from outside the train station.

Cascina Piagge (☎ 0144 37 88 86; Via Cascinalli 257; www.agriturismolepiagge.it in Italian; B&B per person €25, children under 3 free, aged 4-12 50% discount, dinner €20) Guests at this child-friendly *agriturismo* in the hills are encouraged to lend a hand with the everyday work of the farm. Farmhouse rooms are simple but not without charm, and the panoramic terrace is a definite plus. You'll need your own wheels to get here.

Ostello Le Langhe Bergolo (☎ 0173 872 22; Via Roma 22, Bergolo; dm bed €12, in family room €14) In the village of Bergolo, this HI youth hostel is an ideal base for exploring the surrounding hills. A difficult place to reach by public transport, your best bet is to take one of the three daily buses from Acqui Terme (two hours).

ALBA

pop 30,000 / elevation 172m

In a region noted for its food and wine, Alba manages to stand out. A gastronomic mecca in the heart of red-wine country, it's famed throughout Italy for its highly sought-after white truffles. For sweeter pleasures, there's the world's most famous chocolate factory, Ferrero.

Food and drink apart, Alba still merits a visit. The characteristic red-brick towers that rise above the cobbled squares make a fine backdrop to the pretty porticoed streets.

Alba reached a zenith of prosperity in the 15th and 16th centuries, when it was the scene of bloody fighting between the Spanish and French. The Savoys duly entered the fray and in 1628 took control of the town. During WWII citizens proclaimed an independent republic for 23 days, after partisans liberated it from the Germans.

Alba is surrounded by some of Piedmont's most suggestive and productive countryside. Extending south and east of town, the green hills of the Langhe are famous for their majestic red wines.

Orientation

Alba's town centre is compact and easily explored on foot. The main strip, Via Vittorio Emanuele II, connects the two central squares, Piazza Savona and Piazza Risorgimento. From Piazza Risorgimento head northwest along Via Cavour for Piazza Medford. To get to the town centre from the train station, cross Corso F Bandieri, turn right and then immediately left down Via Roma.

Information

EMERGENCY

Carabinieri Police Station (☎ 0173 44 13 33; Via Tanaro 1)

MEDICAL SERVICES

Hospital (☎ 0173 31 61 11; Via Pierino Belli 26)

MONEY

Banca Popolare di Novara (☎ 0173 44 43 11; Via Roma 14) Bank with ATM.

POST

Post Office (☎ 0173 44 47 31; Via XX Settembre 5; ⊗ 8.30am-7pm Mon-Fri, 8.30am-1pm Sat)

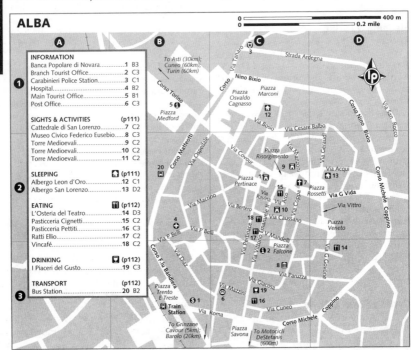

ALBA

INFORMATION
Banca Popolare di Novara.............1 B3
Branch Tourist Office....................2 C3
Carabinieri Police Station............3 C1
Hospital...4 B2
Main Tourist Office.......................5 B1
Post Office....................................6 C3

SIGHTS & ACTIVITIES   (p111)
Cattedrale di San Lorenzo............7 C2
Museo Civico Federico Eusebio.....8 C3
Torre Medioevali...........................9 C2
Torre Medioevali.........................10 C2
Torre Medioevali.........................11 C2

SLEEPING   (p111)
Albergo Leon d'Oro.....................12 C1
Albergo San Lorenzo...................13 D2

EATING   (p112)
L'Osteria del Teatro.....................14 D3
Pasticceria Cignetti.....................15 C2
Pasticceria Pettiti.......................16 C3
Ratti Ellio..................................17 C2
Vincafé......................................18 C2

DRINKING   (p112)
I Piaceri del Gusto......................19 C3

TRANSPORT   (p112)
Bus Station................................20 B2

SOME FACTS TO CHEW ON

The chocolate business has come a long way since Pietro Ferrero established the company bearing his name in 1946. Now a multinational confectionary giant, its products include Ferrero Rocher, Nutella (made from locally harvested hazelnuts) and, oddly enough, Tic Tacs. The Alba site is the headquarters of Ferrero as well as a massive chocolate factory.

Chocoholics might be interested to know that in one year Ferrero uses 70,000 tonnes of cocoa; 56,000 tonnes of hazelnuts (making it the world's largest consumer); 102,000 tonnes of milk; and an enormous number of jars for the 179,000 tonnes of Nutella it produces.

TOURIST INFORMATION

Main Tourist Office (☎ 0173 3 58 33, B&B booking ☎ 0173 36 15 38; www.langheroero.it; Piazza Medford 3; ☺ 9am-12.30pm & 2.30-6.30pm Mon-Fri, 9am-12.30pm Sat) Plentiful information and a B&B booking service.

Branch Tourist Office (☎ 0173 36 25 62; www.turismodoc.it; Via Vittorio Emanuele II 19; ☺ 9am-1pm & 2-6pm Mon-Sat)

Sights

Alba's most photographed landmarks are its red-brick **Torre Medioevale** (medieval towers), which loom over Piazza Risorgimento. Originally built as monuments to the wealth and taste of the town's 14th- and 15th-century nobility, only about 20 remain today. The best-preserved are still impressive, particularly when lit up at night. Unfortunately it is not possible to climb any of the towers.

Nearby, and currently under wraps, the **Cattedrale di San Lorenzo** (Piazza Risorgimento) dates to the early 12th century. Much altered from its original Gothic style, it's currently undergoing its umpteenth restoration, due for completion in September 2005.

Dedicated museum-goers can investigate Alba's Roman and prehistoric past at the **Museo Civico Federico Eusebio** (☎ 0173 29 24 73; Via Paruzza 1; adult/child €4/2.50; ☺ 4-7pm Mon-Fri, 9.30am-12.30pm & 4-7pm Sat & Sun), which houses a modest collection of prehistoric and Roman artefacts as well as a selection of minerals and fossilised bugs.

Alas, it's not possible to visit the **Ferrero factory** (see above) but for those eager for a look, follow your nose and you'll find it west of the town centre in Via Vivaro.

Activities

With picturesque vineyards to see and wine cellars to visit, **cycling** and **walking** in the surrounding Langhe hills is a true pleasure. The tourist office sells walking maps and a brochure with six cycling itineraries (€1.50)

themed on Barolo, cheese, hazelnuts, stone, Moscato (a sweet golden wine) and religion. Bikes are available for hire at **Motocicli DeStefanis** (☎ 0173 44 04 62; Via S Margherita 2; per day €13).

Festivals & Events

Alba's big event of the year is its **truffle fair** (see p112) in October and the **Palio degli Asini** (Donkey Derby) in the same month. The latter was inaugurated in 1932, as a snub to arch-rival Asti (see p105) and provides the hilarious spectacle of jockeys clad in medieval garb vigorously urging on their stubbornly stationary asses.

In late May and early June the town is flooded with puppets as marionette maestros take to the streets and stages of Alba, Bra and the Langhe hills as part of the annual **Burattinarte festival** (☎ 0173 50 93 45).

Sleeping

You shouldn't have any problems finding a room unless you're coming in October, when an advance booking is essential. A popular alternative to staying in town is to lodge in one of the many *agriturismi* in the surrounding countryside. The tourist office stocks extensive lists of local *agriturismi*.

Albergo San Lorenzo (☎ 0173 36 24 06; fax 0173 36 69 95; Piazza Rossetti 6; s €60-70, d €80-90) A gem of a hotel, this may be the swishest two-star in Piedmont. At first glance it seems more modern-art gallery than hotel but head to the rooms and you'll find them tastefully simple, with the parquet floor and stylish furniture adding warmth to the white decor.

Albergo Leon d'Oro (☎ /fax 0173 44 19 01; Piazza Marconi 2; s €28-42, d €45-60) The Golden Lion, overlooking the fresh-food market, surprises: white wooden shutters hide a flower-filled terrace and spotlessly clean, if old-fashioned, rooms. The cheap self-service restaurant on the ground floor has nothing to do with the hotel.

Eating & Drinking

There are numerous restaurants and trattorie in the area around Via Vittorio Emanuele II.

L'Osteria del Teatro (☎ 0173 36 46 03; Via Generale Govone 7; mains about €12; ✷ Thu-Tue) Tucked away in the heart of the *centro storico*, this is a classical Piedmontese restaurant. The decor is rustic smart (wood tables, cream walls and soft lighting), the menu is traditional and the wine list enough to satisfy most amateurs. Unoriginal but tasty, the *agnolotti del plin* (small pockets of pasta filled with meat, eggs, Parmesan cheese and herbs) slips down a treat with a bottle of Dolcetto d'Alba (€11).

Vincafé (☎ 0173 36 46 03; Via Vittorio Emanuele II 12; cheese & meat platters €8-16) A clever mix of old and new, this contemporary wine bar cooks up a splendid feast of mixed cheese and meat platters in a vaulted stone cellar. Thirsty diners can choose from the 350-label wine list.

For a delicious bag of something sticky and sweet, head for **Pasticceria Cignetti** (☎ 0173 44 02 18; Via Vittorio Emanuele II 5) or **Pasticceria Pettiti** (☎ 0173 44 16 12; Via Vittorio Emanuele II 25), both Alba institutions. For cheese, cured meat and, at €52 for a 17g knob, white truffle, try **Ratti Elio** (☎ 0173 44 05 40; Via Vittorio Emanuele II 18); for a bottle of local red, dip into the friendly *enoteca*-cum-bookshop **I Piaceri del Gusto** (☎ 0173 44 01 66; Via Vittorio Emanuele II 23).

Getting There & Around

BUS

From the **bus station** (☎ 800 99 00 97; Corso Matteotti 10) Satti runs buses to/from Turin (€3.70, one hour 45 minutes, up to 10 daily) and to/from Barolo (€1.60, 25 minutes, up to 10 daily), through Grinzane Cavour and La Morra.

CAR & MOTORCYCLE

Alba is on the SS 231, which connects Asti with Cuneo.

TRAIN

From Alba **train station** (Piazza Trento e Trieste) there are hourly trains to and from Turin (via Bra/Asti €3.90/5.10, 50 minutes) and about 10 trains a day to Alessandria (€3.90, 20 minutes).

THE LANGHE

The gently rolling Langhe hills around Alba are a gourmet's paradise. Some of Italy's best reds come from this fertile area; Barbaresco, Barolo and La Morra are all big names to look for. Many of the medieval hill-top towns that pepper the landscape boast castles that have stood for centuries, guarding the region from uninvited guests.

The area is best explored by car or, as is very popular, by bike. The slopes are not too ferocious and you are assured a tasty welcome almost everywhere you go.

TRUFFLE HUNTING WITH A PIEDMONT CHAMP

When autumn comes to Piedmont, it's time to *andare a funghi* (mushroom-pick). Mushrooms, especially the popular porcini (boletus) and the harder to find *tartufo* (truffle), are considered something of a delicacy. Black truffles are precious, but it is the white truffle of Alba that is the most prized of all.

The white truffle is celebrated each year with the **Fiera del Tartufo Bianco d'Alba** (Alba White Truffle Fair), held every Saturday and Sunday for four weeks from early October to early November. The open-air truffle feast fills Piazza Medford, while truffle and mushroom traders haggle over whopping 2kg slabs of porcini and fist-sized truffles at the market in Coro della Maddalena (Maddelena Courtyard). The fair closes with a world white truffle auction at Castello di Grinzane Cavour (see p114). In 2003 white truffles sold for around €200 per 100g (compared to around €40 for 100g of black).

Trifolao (truffle-hunters) only hunt for truffles, with the help of a specially trained truffle-sniffing dog, at night. Piedmont's champion dog, Bricciola, is one of three dogs that sniff out black and white truffles with Signor Ezio on the land around **Tra Arte e Querce** (☎ 0173 79 21 56; www.traarteequerce .com in Italian; Via Monchiero Alto 11, Monchiero; d with truffle breakfast low/high season €80/130, mains €15; ✷ on reservation Mar-Dec), a 17th-century stone house 17km southwest of Alba, with a truffle restaurant and several stylish rooms above. Guests can feast on Signora Clelia's truffle-inspired homemade cooking, and join Signor Ezio on a truffle-hunting expedition. He hunts white truffles between September and December, and black truffles in spring, winter and autumn.

Barbaresco

After about 5km heading north from Alba along the SS231, you'll find signs for Barbaresco, a hill-top village whose name sends shivers down the spines of wine aficionados everywhere. Within the village's tiny enclaves there are numerous fine-dining options and the **Enoteca Regionale del Barbaresco** (☎ 0173 63 52 51; Via Torino 8/a; ☺ 9.30am-1pm & 2.30-6pm Thu-Tue Feb-Dec). The cellar is housed appropriately enough, in a church built by the villagers in the mid-19th century to give thanks for the area's exceptional wine harvest.

The **tourist office** (☎ 0173 63 50 13; Via Torino 5; ☺ 10am-6pm Mon-Wed & Fri-Sat, 11am-1pm & 3-6pm) has plenty of helpful information on where to eat, drink and sleep.

Albergo Ristorante Vecchio Tre Stelle (☎ 0173 63 81 92; www.vecchiotrestelle.it; s/d from €57/75) On the outer edges of the village this smart little hotel doubles as a Michelin-starred restaurant. The yellow **dining room** (set menu from €38) seats 40 lucky devils, who tuck into such creations as *millefoglie di baccalá con patate e olive* (a pastry lasagne with a white fish, potato and olive filling). Bookings are essential.

From Barbaresco continue 5km east and you come to **Neive**, a town divided into two. At the top of the hill is the medieval old town, and down the hill, the modern new part. The town's major claim to fame is the **Distilleria di Romano Levi** (p113).

Should you want to stay the night, up in the historic centre **L'Aromatario** (☎ 0173 67 72 06; Piazza Negro 4; d €53-68) is a pretty place in which to bed down for the night. A lovely 17th-century palazzo drowning in ivy, it will sell you wine on the ground floor and do you a comfortable room upstairs.

Govone

From the **Castello Reale di Carlo Felice di Casa Savoia** (☎ 0173 581 03; adult/child €3/2; ☺ 10am-noon & 3-6pm Sun May-Oct, 10am-noon & 4-7pm Sun Jul & Aug) in Govone you can enjoy exceptional views over the hills. Originally a medieval fortress it was given a baroque makeover by architects Guarini and Alfieri and was later used by Carlo Felice as his country residence.

Il Molino (☎ 0173 62 16 38; www.ilmolinoalba.it in Italian; Via XX Settembre 15; s €55-65, d €75-95) Admire the views over the castle park from this charming B&B. Rooms in the restored

mill have kept their original brick-vaulted ceilings, which beautifully complement the classical furnishings.

Govone is just off the SS231, 9km north of Barbaresco.

Canale

Serious gourmets should not bypass Canale, 10km north of Alba. In particular, they should make for Via Roma 57, where the **Enoteca Regionale del Roero** (☎ 0173 97 82 28; Via Roma 57; ☺ 9.30am-12.30pm & 3.30-7.30pm Thu-Tue) houses a gastronomic pleasure palace. On the ground floor you can select your tipple from the extensive collection of Roero wines, while upstairs chef Davide Pallude rules the roost at his Michelin-starred restaurant.

All'Enoteca (☎ 0173 958 57; Via Roma 57; mains from €20; closed Wed & Thu lunch, Jan & Aug) Known well-beyond regional borders, this refined restaurant continues to serve its own brand of high cuisine. Typical of chef Pallude's traditional but innovative outlook is the unbelievably smooth *mille foglie* (a type of lasagne with pastry instead of pasta) of duck's liver and figs. To follow, the chocolate puddings are as light as they are delicious.

Santo Stefano Belbo

The name of author Cesare Pavese will forever be linked with this small town 15km east of Alba. Today an important centre for the production of Moscato, it was here that the tragic writer was born in 1908.

Fans should take an hour or two to visit the **Centro Studi Cesare Pavese** (☎ 0141 84 08 94; Piazza Confraternia 1; admission free; ✆ 9am-1pm & 2-5pm Mon, 10am-12.30pm & 3-6.30pm Tue, Wed, Fri & Sat, 10am-1pm Thu), where you can see original manuscripts and the copy of *I dialoghi con Leucó*, in which he wrote his last words before committing suicide in Turin in 1950. It's also possible to visit the house where he was born. Call ☎ 0141 84 49 42 to book.

Relais San Maurizio (☎ 0141 84 19 00; www.relais sanmaurizio.it; localitá San Maurizio; s €140-185 d €160-240; **P** ✆) Treat yourself to a grape facial at this five-star retreat, just outside town. Set in a centuries-old park, this former monastery is an oasis of luxury, where guests can enjoy treatments based on wine extracts in the so-called 'eno-thermarium'.

To research the local Moscato continue the wine trail to **Mango**, 6km to the west. The **Enoteca Colline del Moscato** (☎ 0141 892 91; Piazza Castello; tastings €1.50 a glass; ✆ 10.30am-7pm Wed-Sun mid-Feb-Dec) features both Moscato d'Asti and the sparkling wines of Piedmont. It is housed in the baroque **Castello** (☎ 0141 892 91; admission free; ✆ 10am-12.30pm & 3.30-7pm Wed-Sun) which you can visit by appointment only.

Alternatively, head north to **Canelli** and the **Enoteca Regionale di Canelli** (☎ 0141 83 21 82; Corso Libertá; ✆ 9.30am-12.30pm & 4-7pm Tue-Sun) a second cellar specialising in Moscato wines.

Grinzane Cavour

Located 5km southwest of Alba, some of Piedmont's most sought-after wines are stashed in the prestigious **Enoteca Regionale Cavour** inside the **Castello Grinzane Cavour** (☎ 0173 26 21 59; Piazza Castello 5; admission €3.50; ✆ 7 guided castle tours daily 10am-5.30pm Wed-Mon). Italian statesman and village mayor Camillo Cavour lived here in the 1850s.

If you happen to pass by Grinzane between July and September, you'll find the place a hive of cultural activity. The **Grinzane Festival** (www.grinzane.it) encompasses theatrical performances and book readings in an annual celebration of the area's literary heritage.

From Grinzane it's a 3km hop north to the **Castello di Roddi** (☎ 0173 61 53 63; adult/child under 12 €2.60/free; ✆ 11am-1pm & 2-5.30pm Sun 25 May–26 Oct). Dating to the 11th century it was completely revamped in the 15th century, and between

---

MARTINI & ROSSI

Martini (an alcohol salesman) and Rossi (a distillery supplier) were two men from Turin who teamed up in the 1850s to create a wine and liqueur distillery of their own in 1879. What happened after that can be discovered at the **Museo Martini di Storia dell'Enologia** (☎ 011 941 92 17; Piazzale Luigi Rossi 1; admission free; ✆ 2-5pm Tue-Fri, 9am-noon & 2-5pm Sat & Sun Sep-Jul), about 20km southeast of Turin in Pessione. The museum is housed in the cellars of an 18th-century villa. One of Martini's largest production plants is also here but guided tours and tasting sessions have to be arranged in advance.

1880 and 1960 was home to the very serious University of Truffle Hounds.

Cinzano

Cinzano is made and bottled 10km west of Alba in Cinzano, below the Santa Vittoria d'Alba area on the SS231. The monstrous distilling plant of United Distillers & Vintners (UDV) cannot be visited but individuals can try to join a group to tour the **Villa Cinzano** (☎ 0172 47 71 11). Artefacts documenting the history of a company that started as a small distilling operation in Turin's hills in 1757 are displayed in the villa, a former hunting lodge of Savoy king, Carlo Alberto.

Bra

A pretty enough market place, Bra is a foodie town. Home to Slow Food (p51), the organisation that promotes the joys of sitting down to a properly prepared meal, it stages two festivals celebrating the joys of food. In April the **Corto in Bra** short-film festival looks at food in celluloid, while the biennial **Cheese** needs no explanation. The next *formaggio* festival is set for September 2007.

Bra's **tourist office** (☎ 0172 43 01 84; Via Moffa di Lisio 14; ✆ 9am-1pm & 3-6pm Mon-Fri, 9am-noon Sat, plus 9am-noon Sun Mar-Nov) has details on these and plenty of information on the district.

Osteria Boccondivino (☎ 0172 42 56 74; Via Mendicità Istruita 14; mains about €13; ✆ Tue-Sat) It was in the beautiful 17th-century courtyard of Boccondivino that the Slow Food movement was born in July 1986. Specialising in Piedmontese dishes, this atmospheric restaurant is the ideal place to try a bit of the local Bra sausage or a platter of smelly cheeses. Booking ahead is advised.

Cherasco

Lumache (snails) are an integral part of Langhe cuisine. And nowhere more so than in Cherasco, Italy's self-proclaimed snail capital 23km west of Alba, where the molluscs are not actually grown (it's too cold) but simply marketed and sold.

Snails in this neck of the woods are dished up without their shells or as the locals put it *nudo* (nude). They can be pan-fried, roasted on a spit, dressed in an artichoke sauce or minced inside ravioli.

Two tasty trattorie to try these dishes at are **La Lumaca** (☎ 0172 48 94 21; cnr Via San Pietro & Via Cavour; 1st/2nd courses €5/8-10; ☺ noon/12.30-2pm & 8-9.30pm Wed-Sun) and **Osteria della Rosa Rossa** (☎ 0172 48 81 33; Via San Pietro 31; 1st/2nd courses €5/8; ☺ 12.30-2pm & 8-9pm Fri-Tue). Reservations are essential at both.

Cherasco's **Istituto Internazionale di Elicicoltura** (☎ 0172 48 92 18; Via Vittorio Emanuele 55) has more heliciculture (snail farming) facts.

Barolo

Robust, velvety, truffle-scented with orange reflections, and the 'wine of kings and king of wines' are among the compliments piled onto this extraordinary red wine, produced around Barolo, 20km southwest of Alba. To sample a glass or two, time your visit for early September when the village celebrates the Festa del Vino Barolo. Tastings are held at the **Enoteca Regionale del Barolo** (☎ 0173 562 77; www.baroloworld.it; ☺ 10am-12.30pm & 3-6.30pm Fri-Wed), inside **Castello di Barolo**.

No, you aren't that drunk. **Capella Sol Le-Witt-David Tremlett** (☎ 0173 28 25 82), a chapel on top of a vine-covered hill between Barolo and **La Morra**, really is painted all the colours of the rainbow. Built by a farmer in 1914, the ruined church (never consecrated) was restored and painted with symmetrical patterns in red, blue, green, yellow and orange by English and American artists in 1999. The chapel is 1.6km southeast of La Morra along a dirt track, signposted off Via Roma at the southern end of the village.

Southwest of Barolo, the ruins of what was once one of the major Roman cities in the area, Augusta Bagiennorum, are free to visit. Set in the beautiful countryside that surrounds the village of Roncaglia, they, and the area, merit a fleeting visit. Particularly impressive are the remains of the huge Roman amphitheatre, which form part of the **Riserva Naturale Speciale dell'Area Augusta Bagiennorum** (☎ 0171 73 40 21; Via S. Anna 34, Chiusa Pesio).

SALUZZO

pop 15,740 / elevation 395m

Once a feisty medieval stronghold, the charming town of Saluzzo sits in the long shade of the Monviso range. Characterised by its red-brick old town, it has a history of defiance, managing to retain its independence – no mean feat in the medieval mayhem that raged in these parts – until the Savoys won it in a 1601 treaty with France.

Information

MONEY

Banks and ATMs abound on Corso Italia.

TOURIST INFORMATION

Tourist Office (☎ 0175 467 10; Piazza dei Mondagli 5; ☺ 9am-12.30pm & 3-6.30pm Mon-Sat, 9am-noon & 3-7pm Sun Apr-Sep, 9am-12.30pm & 2-5.30pm Mon-Sat, 9am-noon & 2-6pm Sun Oct-Mar)

Sights & Activities

The burnt-red tiled rooftops of Saluzzo's charming old town make a pretty picture from the top of the 48m-high **Torre Civica** (☎ 0175 414 55; Via San Giovanni; admission €2.50, combined Torre & Museo €5; ☺ 9.30am-12.30pm & 2.30-6.30pm Thu-Sun Mar-Sep, 9.30am-12.30pm & 2.30-6.30pm Sat-Sun Oct-Feb), a 15th-century tower, where the town administration once sat.

Further along the same street, the **Museo Civico di Casa Cavassa** (☎ 0175 414 55; Via San Giovanni 5; adult/child €4/2, combined Torre & Museo €5; ☺ 10am-1pm & 2-6pm Thu-Sun Apr-Sep, 10am-1pm & 2-5pm Tue-Wed Oct-Mar) is a fine example of a 16th-century noble's residence. While you're on this street just duck in to the **Chiesa di San Giovanni** to have a look at the enormous *presepe* (nativity scene). Drop a coin into the slot and watch the elaborate sight light up.

It's not difficult to imagine the Marchesi, Saluzzo's medieval rulers, meting out justice from **La Castiglia** (Piazza Castello) a 13th-century red-brick castle that inspires a foreboding sense of fear. It is currently closed to the public.

Sleeping & Eating

Hotel Persico (☎ 0175 412 13; persico@libero.it; Vicolo Mercati 10; s/d from €38/56; **P**) You're assured a rousing welcome when you turn up at this no-frills two-star pad on Piazza Cavour. The ground floor restaurant is popular at weekends (go for the 11-dish €7 antipasto if you're hungry) while the upstairs rooms are functional and clean.

Hotel Astor (☎ 0175 455 06; fax 0175 474 50; Piazza Garibaldi 39; s/d €65/93; **P** **✗**) Ring the bell to enter this three-star hotel, overlooking one of main squares in the new part of town but just a few minutes' walk from Saluzzo's medieval treasures.

Trattoria Përpôin (☎ 0175 423 83; Via Spielberg 19-27; s/d €45/80; **P**) Enjoy hearty home-cooking at shared tables in this cheerful eating and sleeping option. There is no hotel reception; call ahead if you intend arriving outside **restaurant** (menus €12-25) opening hours.

Taverna dell'Artista (☎ 0175 420 31; Via Gualtieri 8; 1st/2nd courses €5/10, pizza €4-6) Packed with youngsters out for their Saturday-night dinner, this is a lively and well-known spot for a plate of simple pasta or a bubbling pizza. A good bet is the *gnocchi al castelmango* (gnocchi baked in a nutty blue cheese unique to Piedmont).

A divine selection of cheese, sausages, dried meat, wine and oils are displayed at **I Formaggi** (☎ 0175 24 82 62; Piazza XX Settembre 6; ⏲ 8am-12.30pm & 4-7.30pm Tue-Sat).

Getting There & Away

Saluzzo is 32km north of Cuneo and 60km south of Turin. There are hourly **buses** (☎ 0175 437 44) to and from Turin (€3.50, 1½ hours, hourly). Otherwise, take a train from the **train station** (Piazza Vittorio Veneto) to Cuneo (€2.45, 30 minutes, up to six daily), from where there are connections for Turin.

By car you should take the SS20 for Savigliano and then turn off west for 12km.

Around Saluzzo

A 12km drive north of Saluzzo brings you to the **Abbazia di Santa Maria di Staffarda** (☎ 0175 27 32 15; adult/child €5.15/4.10; ⏲ 9am-12.30pm & 2.30-6.30pm Tue-Sun Apr-Oct, 9am-12.30pm & 2-5pm Tue-Sun Nov-Mar), an atmospheric 12th-century abbey. Almost destroyed by French troops in 1690, it was subsequently rebuilt by King Vittorio Amedeo. For a quiet moment, slip off to the lovely cloistered square.

Set in its own magnificent park, the **Castello Reale di Racconigi** (☎ 0172 71 71 85; Piazza Carlo Alberto; adult/child €5/3, park €2/1; ⏲ by appointment only 8.30am-6.30pm Tue-Sun, park ⏲ 10am-7pm Tue-Sun Mar-Nov) is a lavish Savoy residence that dominates the approach to Racconigi, 18km northeast of Saluzzo.

Nearby the **Centro Cicogne e Anatidi** (Stork Sanctuary; ☎ 0172 834 57; www.cicogneracconigi.it; Via Stramiano 30; admission €4; ⏲ 10am-sunset) is one of two nature attractions in the area. The other is in Carmagnola, 10km further north, where the **Museo Civico di Storia Naturale** (☎ 011 972 43 90; www.storianaturale.org in Italian; Via San Francesco di Sales 188; adult/child €2/0.50; ⏲ 9am-12.30pm Mon-Thu, 3-6pm Thu, Sat & Sun Aug & Jul, by appointment only) houses an eclectic collection of flora and fauna, including a human skeleton, a rhino's skull and numerous snakes in jars. The museum can also provide itineraries for cycling in the **Parco Fluviale del Po Torinese**, the protected area that runs alongside the River Po.

Returning south, the **Castello di Manta** (☎ 0175 878 22; adult/child €5/2.50; ⏲ 10am-1pm & 2-6pm Tue-Sun Dec-Sep, 10am-1pm & 2-5pm Tue-Sun Oct-Jan, free guided tours 3pm Sun) is 5km south of Saluzzo in Mantua. Built in the 13th century, the castle was given a thorough makeover 200 years later. Not to be missed are the magnificent frescoes in the Sala Baronale.

West of town, the River Po winds along the Valle Po from its source on the Pian del Re, below the **Monviso** (3841m) peak. For information about trekking and a multitude of other sports, make for **Paesana,** where the **tourist office** (☎ 0175 94 58 57; www.vallipo.cn.it in Italian; Piazza Vittorio Veneto) can fill you in. **Crissolo** is the other main resort in this enticing valley.

L'Ciabot (☎ 0175 94 58 13; www.lciabot.it; località Colletta 40; B&B per person €25) In Paesana, this mountainside *agriturismo* offers three self-contained apartments, each with its own balcony. Ideal for families, there is fruit for sale and swings for the kids. Campers can pitch their tent in one of three spaces available.

There are also couple of Alpine ski resorts in the more southern **Valle Varaita**. For more information, contact the Provincial Tourist Office in Cuneo (p117).

CUNEO

pop 55,415 / elevation 543m

Cuneo doesn't feature on many travellers' itineraries. The capital of Piedmont's southernmost province is not an unpleas-

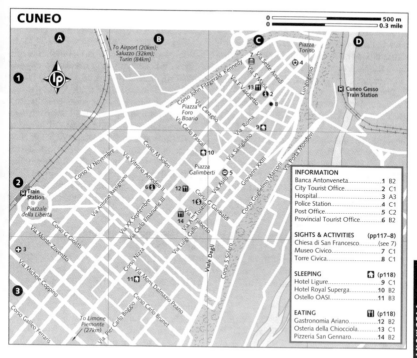

CUNEO

INFORMATION
Banca Antonveneta..................1 B2
City Tourist Office...................2 C1
Hospital................................3 A3
Police Station........................4 C1
Post Office............................5 C2
Provincial Tourist Office.........6 B2

SIGHTS & ACTIVITIES   (pp117–8)
Chiesa di San Francesco.......(see 7)
Museo Civico.........................7 C1
Torre Civica..........................8 C1

SLEEPING   (p118)
Hotel Ligure.........................9 C1
Hotel Royal Superga.............10 B2
Ostello OASI........................11 B3

EATING   (p118)
Gastronomia Ariano..............12 B2
Osteria della Chiocciola........13 C1
Pizzeria San Gennaro...........14 B2

ant place, it simply doesn't offer much that isn't better elsewhere. The small medieval quarter in the northern wedge of the city is the usual mix of cobbles, porticoes and tiny alleyways, while the city's most impressive landmark is its vast central square.

An important transport hub, Cuneo is ideally suited as a base for exploring the stunning southern valleys, which radiate out into the surrounding mountains.

Orientation

Shaped like a wedge (*cuneo* means wedge in Italian) Cuneo is easy to navigate. Starting at the central square, Piazza Galimberti, the *centro storico* forms the tip of the wedge to the northeast and the geometric modern town flares out to your south. Via Roma runs from the tip of town into Piazza Galimberti, while on the other side of the square, the city's major artery, Corso Nizza, shoots dead straight out of town.

To get from the train station to Piazza Galimberti, cross Piazzale della Libertá, go straight down Corso G. Giolitti, then turn left down Corso Nizza.

Information

EMERGENCY
Police Station (☎ 0171 44 44 42; Via Roma 6)

MEDICAL SERVICES
Hospital (☎ 0171 44 11; Via M Coppino 26)

MONEY
Banca Antonveneta (☎ 0171 69 02 38; Piazza Galimberti 7) Bank with ATM.

POST
Post Office (☎ 0171 46 03 60; Via Bonelli 6; 8.30am-7pm Mon-Fri, 8.30am-1pm Sat)

TOURIST INFORMATION
City Tourist Office (☎ / fax 0171 69 32 58; Via Roma 28; 9.30am-12.30pm & 3-6.30pm Mon-Sat)
Provincial Tourist Office (ATL; ☎ 0171 69 02 17; www .cuneoholiday.com; Via Vittorio Amedeo II 13; 8.30am-1pm & 2.30-6pm Mon-Fri) For province information, such as accommodation lists and details of outdoor activities.

Sights

The city's best-known 'sight' is the **Museo Civico** (☎ 0171 63 41 75; Via Santa Maria 10; adult/child €2.60/1.55;

8.30am-1pm & 2.30-5.30pm Tue & Sat, 8.30am-1pm & 2.30-5pm Wed-Fri, 10am-12.30pm & 3-6.30pm Sun Jun-Sep, 10am-12.30pm & 2.30-6pm Sun Oct-May) in the Gothic **Chiesa di San Francesco**. The eclectic collection of artefacts, recount the history and traditions of life in the province.

If you're in town on a Sunday, the 14th-century **Torre Civica** (Via Roma 19; adult/child €2.10/1.55; 3-6pm Sun) affords some fine views over the rooftops to the mountains beyond. It's said that on a clear day you can see the summit of Monte Rosa.

Sleeping

Finding a room in Cuneo is not a problem, although the range of options is limited as hotels are primarily geared to the business market.

Ostello OASI (0171 673 90, after hours 338 209 78 93; Via Mons. Peano 8; s with shared bathroom €20; 9am-noon Mon-Sat) The nearest thing Cuneo has to a youth hostel is this religious institute. Situated within a stone's throw of the *centro storico*, it has 11 simple, clean rooms.

Hotel Royal Superga (0171 69 32 23; Via Pascal 3; s €52-57 d €68-82; **P**) Just off Piazza Galimberti, this 19th-century hotel is a welcoming place with charming and spacious three-star rooms. Decorated simply and without fuss, the rooms are of the old school with solid doors and wooden window shutters, which are useful for keeping out the noise of the Tuesday and Friday market.

Hotel Ligure (0171 68 19 42; www.ligurehotel.it in Italian & German; Via Savigliano 11; s/d €42/58, half-board €45; **P**) Tucked away in the back streets of the *centro storico*, this friendly little hotel offers good value for money. The rooms are unspectacular but, surprisingly for a two-star, come with most of the trimmings, including satellite TV. The in-house restaurant is also a definite plus.

Eating

Head to the *centro storico* and its narrow alleyways for your typical trattoria.

Osteria della Chiocciola (0171 662 77; Via Fossano; mains €12; Mon-Sat) Half-*enoteca*, half-restaurant, this is a wine lovers kinda place. Browse the comprehensive wine collection downstairs before heading upstairs to tuck into the regional cuisine. Particularly good is the *carne cruda* (raw meat) and the *vitello con sale marino e rosmarino* (veal with sea

salt and rosemary), which is tender and tasty.

Pizzeria San Gennaro (0171 60 20 88; Via Emanuele Filiberto 2; pizza from €4.50) For a good old pizza and beer, you can't beat this noisy and bustling pizzeria. Come on a Saturday night and you'll be waiting for a table but the pizzas are excellent and the service is attentive and cheerful. You can also choose from a selection of *antipasti* and pasta dishes.

Gastronomia Ariano (0171 69 35 22; Piazza Galimberti 2) Hemingway stopped off at this historic delicatessen on the advice of his chum, Italian publisher Mondadori. The tempting array of gourmet delights include smoked fish, cured hams, pâtès and Alpine cheese.

Getting There & Around

AIR

The city's **airport** (Aeroporto di Cuneo; CUF; 0171 37 43 74) is at Levaldigi, 20km to the north. Air Excel has daily flights to Rome and weekday services to Strasbourg. To reach the airport take the SS20 in the direction of Levaldigi, or take one of the hourly trains to Savigliano (€2.65, 35 minutes), from where shuttle buses run to the airport.

BUS

Buses depart from in front of the train station in Piazzale Libertá. **ATI** (0171 674 00; www.atibus .it in Italian) operates buses for Saluzzo (€2.25, one hour, about 20 daily) while **Autolinee Valle Pesio** (0171 73 44 96) plies the Valle Pesio.

CAR & MOTORCYCLE

The main road into town, the SS20, connects Cuneo with the skiing resort of Limone Piemonte to the south, and Savigliano and Racconigi to the north. Coming in from Asti and Alba, the SS231 merges with the SS20 a few kilometres north of town.

TRAIN

Regular trains from the central **train station** (Piazzale Libertà) run to Limone (€2.25, 35 minutes, seven daily), Saluzzo (€2.45, 35 minutes, up to six daily), Turin (€4.70, 1¼ hours, up to eight daily). There is a second train station for the Cuneo–Gesso line, serving small towns in that valley to the southwest. The Cuneo Gesso station (known as the Stazione Vecchia) is on Piazzale Stazione Gesso to the east of the historic centre.

AROUND CUNEO
Val Stura & Val Maira

From Cuneo, a clutch of valleys radiates south and west. The longest, **Val Stura**, leads 70km to the Colle della Maddalena (1996m), a mountain pass, open from May to September, linking Italy with France.

Ostello Al Tenibres Pietraporzio (☎ 0171 966 02; Via Nazionale 8, Pietraporzio; dm bed €14) Deep in the Val Strura, this HI youth hostel at altitude provides a decent bed and a hot meal (€8.50). To get here without your own wheels, take the ATI bus from Cuneo to Pietraporzio (€3.50, 2½ hours, five daily).

Northwest of Cuneo, the dead-end **Val Maira** climbs past **Dronero** (population 7035, elevation 622m), a pretty medieval village with houses topped by precarious-looking grey slate roofs. A popular area for cross-country skiers in winter and hikers in summer, its further reaches remain pleasantly unspoiled.

La Meja (☎ 0171 99 81 16; Via Pianesio 1, Canosio; half-board per person €46; ☑ 30 Jun-30 Sep) The accommodation couldn't get any more basic than at this cheerfully modest mountain-top *agriturismo* in the middle of nowhere. The friendly owner makes you feel like one of the family as she piles your plate with yet more steaming food. You'll need your own wheels to get to **Canosio** (elevation 1275m), which lies in the western reaches of Val Maira.

Cheese addicts should make the pilgrimage to three little villages in **Val Grana**, north of Val Stura and south of the Val Maira, where the famous Castelmagno cheese is produced. The strict quality controls that regulate the manufacture of this cheese dictate that it can only be made with milk from cows grazed on the pastures around **Castelmagno**, **Pradleves** and **Monterosso Grana**. To buy a sample, try **Azienda Agricola Marco Arneodo** (☎ 0171 98 62 34;

DETOUR

Not really a detour so much as a pit stop, Vernante (785m) merits a quick look for its original street art. Many of the houses in this mountain town have been adorned with colourful depictions of the world's favourite marionette, Pinocchio. Getting to Vernante couldn't be simpler – about 6km out of Limone you'll see the town signposted from the SS20; very simply, follow the signs.

JEANS & THINGS

Around Cuneo there are two factory outlets worth stopping by. In Borgo San Dalmazzo, the vast **Nike factory store** (☎ 0171 26 80 22; Via Cuneo 72; ☑ 2-7.30pm) stands on the SS20 as it skirts the town centre. Here you'll find a vast array of sporting goods at considerably discounted prices. Further north, the jeans giant **Levi's** (☎ 0172 63 71 84; Via Oreglia 21; ☑ 3.30-7.30pm Mon 9.30am-1pm & 3-7.30pm Tue-Fri 9.30am-7.30pm Sat) has a megastore in the town of Fossano, 21km north of Cuneo.

Via Vittorio Veneto 1, Fraz. Chiotti), a well-known local producer in Castelmagno.

Valle Vermenagna

Borgo San Dalmazzo, 3km from Cuneo, is somewhere you probably won't stop unless you're into shoes or snails. Shoe fans should make for the **Nike factory outlet** (p119), while snail enthusiasts should time their visit for late November or early December, when the town plays host to the annual **Fiera Fredda Regionale della Lumaca**, a 10-day snail fair.

The province's top ski resort **Limone Piemonte** (population 1587, elevation 1009) sits in the Alpi Marittime, 23km beyond Borgo San Dalmazio (p120).

Relais de Charme Arrucador (☎ 348 290 22 63; www.arrucador.it; Borgata San Lorenzo, Limonetto; d B&B €180) A luxury retreat in the snow, this converted mountain cabin sits at 1500m in the midst of the ski slopes. Offering four beautifully decorated rooms and a Turkish bath it's the perfect place to woo your loved one. Open year-round the owner collects you from Limonetto on his snowmobile.

Valle Gesso

Snaking southwest from Cuneo, this valley of bare rock cliffs and sheer drops leads you into the spectacular landscape of the **Parco Naturale delle Alpi Marittime**. Information on the park is available in Entracque at the **information point** (☎ 0171 97 86 16; Piazza Giustizia e Libertà 7)

A convenient stepping stone is the tiny town of **Entracque** (population 878, elevation 894m), 18km from Cuneo. A point of departure for numerous walking and skiing trails, it's also home to the **Centro Informazione della Centrale Luigi Einaudi** (☎ 0171 97 88 11; Strada San Giacomo), a visitor centre that organises guided

SKIING IN THE SOUTH

Piedmont's southern Alps provide plenty of skiing. The main resort is **Limone Piemonte** (1400m), 26km south of Cuneo in the **Valle Vermenagna**. Offering up to 80km of pistes, it's the only resort in the Alpi Marittime that's accessible by train and car and as a result heaves in season and at weekends. A day/week ski pass costs €26/134 while private lessons start at €31. For further details on skiing, summer activities and accommodation contact the **tourist office** (☎ 0171 92 95 15; www .infolimone.it; Piazza Municipio; ☼ 9.30am-noon & 3-6.30pm Thu-Tue) in the town's central piazza.

To the southeast of Cuneo, **Frabosa Sottana** (641m) and **Frabosa Soprana** (891m) lie in the **Valle Maudagna** on the slopes of Monte Moro (1739m). Together they constitute a modern ski centre that provides up to 30km of slopes. From here you can connect with the larger and higher Mondolè domain, which centres on the resorts of **Artesina** (1,300m) and **Prato Nevoso** (1,500m).

tours of the gigantic hydro-electric power plant nearby. Visitors are accompanied on a small train into the depths of Europe's largest turbine-pump complex. Contact the centre directly to book a tour.

Valle Pesio

An unfeasible sight on the edge of the Parco Naturale Alta Valle Pesio, the **Certosa di Pesio** (☎ 0171 73 81 23; ☼ 9am-1pm & 2.30-6.30pm) is a massive 12th-century religious complex which, in its heyday, was an important point of pilgrimage. The French put a stop to that in 1802 closing it down before it re-emerged in 1840 as a weather station. Today, thanks to a complete restoration, it's an imposing sight with tranquil cloisters and frescoed chapels. The complex accommodates religious tourists.

Il Monregalese

Most exploration of this area, to the south and east of Cuneo, starts with the unexciting town of **Mondovì**. Split into two parts (the medieval upper half, known as Piazza, and the industrial lower half, Breo), it's not a place to detain you long. The baroque palaces of the historic centre have seen better days and the modern quarter offers no great thrills.

The **tourist office** (☎ 017440389; turistico@comune. mondovi.cn.it; Corso Statuto 19; ☼ 10am-12.30pm & 3-6.30pm Tue-Sun) can help with accommodation

lists and information on the surrounding area.

It's the sheer scale of the **Santuario di Vicoforte** (☼ 10am-noon & 2.30-5.30pm Mon-Sat, 2.30-4pm Sun), 6km up the road from Mondoví, that sets the heart racing. One of Piedmont's most important monuments, it's a massive baroque church topped by the world's largest elliptical dome. Built over 294 years (between 1596 and 1890), it's relatively subdued by baroque standards and well worth the not-great effort required to get here. Souvenir-hunters can peruse the twee piazza that fronts the sanctuary.

In the bowels of **Valle Corsaglia**, the underground cave complex, **Grotta di Bossea** (☎ 0174 34 92 40; €7.80; ☼ guided visits 10am, 11.30am, 2.30pm, 4pm, 5.30pm in Italian) is not to be missed. The highlight of the 2km itinerary is the huge hall (150m long, 50m high and 60m wide) in which you can admire the Missile, a 10m stalagmite set to fire off at a 45-degree angle, or the 25m knoll known as the Buddha.

Further east, **Valle Tanaro** snakes through the mountains to the pleasant town of **Garessio**, a popular resort that has managed to retain its Alpine character despite the encroaching factories. On your way down the valley, stop off for an hour or two at the **Castello Reale di Casotto** (☎ 0174 35 11 31; Casotto; adult/child €3/2; ☼ 9am-noon & 2-7pm), a 12th-century monastery that Vittorio Emanuele II later transformed into one of his many royal hunting lodges.

Northern Piedmont & the Lakes

CONTENTS

Lago Maggiore	124
Lago D'Orta	130
Valsesia	131
Val D'Ossola	133
Novara	134
Vercelli	136
Ivrea	138
Biella	140
Sordevolo	141
Gattinara	141

Piedmont's northern reaches provide a spectacular outdoor playground. A mountainous terrain of valleys and lakes, it combines the rugged natural beauty of the Alps with the manicured elegance of historic gardens and *belle époque* palaces.

Piercing Switzerland in the north, and bordered by Lombardy to the east and Valle d'Aosta to the west, it is an area of marked geographical divisions. As the Alpine slopes of the north give way to the endlessly flat plains of the Lombard plain, so the scenery becomes increasingly barren.

The jewel in the crown is the picturesque Lago Maggiore, a long-time haunt of the Milanese rich and tourists from all over northern Europe. Stretching up into Switzerland, it's a popular day-trip in winter and a heaving resort area in summer. Cross over Monte Mottarone and you'll find the lesser-known Lago d'Orta. Not as spectacular as its more celebrated neighbour and considerably smaller, it's nevertheless an inviting spot.

Many visitors stick to the lakes, which beautiful as they are, means missing out on some magnificent Alpine adventures. Some of the most thrilling scenery is to be found in the Valsesia, which winds its way west from Varallo towards the Parco Naturale Alta Valsesia. An area of outstanding beauty, it is very popular with skiers and the summer-sports brigade.

The southern plains, by contrast, are anything but spectacular. Soggy and flat, they are perfect for cultivating rice, one of the area's major agricultural concerns.

HIGHLIGHTS

- **Island Hopping**
  Explore Lago Maggiore's elegant islands (p127)
- **Flower Power**
  Immerse yourself in Villa Taranto's famed gardens (p129)
- **Festival Fury**
  Dodge the oranges at Ivrea's annual battle (p138)
- **White Water**
  Canoe the rapids in the Valsesia (p131)
- **Rice Recipe**
  Tuck into a risotto in Vercelli, Europe's rice capital (p137)
- **Best Beer**
  Gulp down the world's best lager in Biella (p140)

★ Valsesia

★ Biella

Vercelli
★

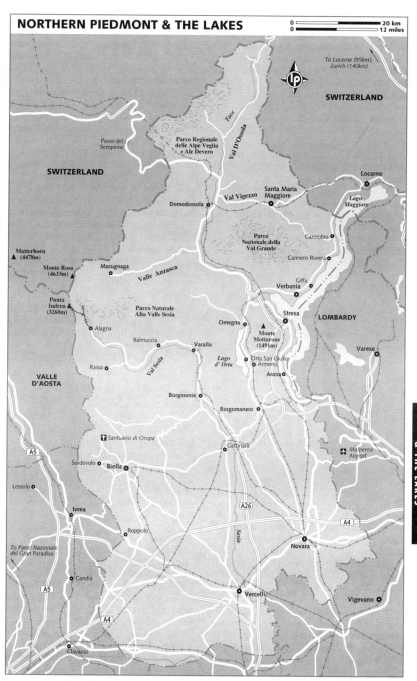

NORTHERN PIEDMONT & THE LAKES

0 ———————— 20 km
0 ———————— 12 miles

To Lucerne (95km);
Zurich (140km)

SWITZERLAND

Passo del
Sempione

Parco Regionale
delle Alpe Veglia
e Ale Devero

Toce

Val D'Ossola

SWITZERLAND

Locarno

Santa Maria
Maggiore

Val Vigezzo

Lago
Maggiore

Domodossola

Parco
Nazionale della
Val Grande

Cannobio

Matterhorn
▲ (4478m)

Cannero Riviera

Monte Rosa
(4633m) ▲

Macugnaga

Valle Anzasca

Giffa
Verbania

Punta
Indren ▲
(3260m)

Parco Naturale
Alta Valle Sesia

Stresa

LOMBARDY

Alagna

Omegna

▲
Monte
Mottarone
(1491m)

Varese

Balmuccia

Varallo

Lago
d' Orta

Orta San Giulio
Armeno

Rassa

Val Sesia

**VALLE
D'AOSTA**

Arona

Borgosesia

Borgomanero

Santuario di Oropa

Gattinara

Malpensa
Airport

A5

Sordevolo

Biella

Lessolo

Ivrea

A26

A4

Roppolo

Sesia

Novara

To Parco Nazionale
del Gran Paradiso

Candia

A5

Vercelli

Vigevano

A4

Chivasso

LAGO MAGGIORE

A captivating lake, Maggiore (also known as Lago Verbano) is stunning in parts, although its shores are flatter and less spectacular than its pre-Alpine counterparts. Fed principally by the Rivers Ticino and Tresa, this lovely lake is about 65km long and lures stifling crowds in July and August.

Adding to the summer-time fun are the area's two principal festivals. The **Lago Maggiore Jazz Festival** attracts big-name artists and equally big crowds, while the **Festival dei Laghi** is a bonanza of flowers and dance. Both take place during July and August.

Stresa is the main lakeside resort, while to the south Arona sits on the southern edges of the lake; further to the north Verbania is the largest town and provincial capital.

We only cover the western shore here as the eastern shore falls into Lombardy and the northern tip lies in Switzerland. For further information on Lago Maggiore and the entire Italian lake district, consult the comprehensive website www.distrettolaghi.it.

Stresa

pop 4885 / elevation 205m

Beloved of Brits, Germans and the fur-coat brigade, Stresa, 80km northwest of Milan on the lake's western shore, is like one great English tearoom – prim and not unattractive but staid and insipid. Out of season it can be melancholic as many hotels shut but on a cold clear winter's day it can be magnificent as you stare out over the mountains sparkling white against the azure background.

Commonly touted as a base for visiting the Borromean Islands (see p127) – although they can easily be reached from other resorts around the lake – it has something of a literary tradition. Hemingway was among the rash of writers to seek inspiration on Maggiore's shores. He first set foot in Stresa in 1918 to convalesce from a war wound, and part of one of his novels, *A Farewell to Arms*, is set here.

ORIENTATION

The tourist office sits on the lake in Piazza Marconi next to the ferry-landing stage. To get to the town centre, cross Corso Italia and go down Via Mazzini to Piazza L Cardona, the main square. The centre is a 600m walk southeast of the station. Turn right out of the station and walk along Via Principe di Piemonte. Turn left when you reach Via Duchessa di Genova, then right at Corso Italia on the lakefront. After about 200m you will reach Piazza Marconi.

INFORMATION

Banks and ATMs abound on Corso Italia, the road running along Stresa's waterfront.

Hospital (☎ 0323 54 11; Via Crocetta, Verbania) 15km north of Stresa in Verbania.

Newdata Internet Point (☎ 0323 303 23; www.newdata.too.it; Via De Vit 15a; per 30 mins/€4; ♥ 9.30am-12.30pm & 3.30-6.30pm Mon-Sat, 3.30-6.30pm Sun)

Police Station (☎ 335 651 75 85; Piazza Marconi; ♥ 10.30am-noon & 6.15-7pm Mon-Fri, 10am-noon Sat)

Post Office (☎ 0323 300 65; Via Anna Bolongaro 44; ♥ 8.30am-7pm Mon-Fri, 8.30am-1pm Sat)

Tourist Office (☎ 0323 313 08; proloco.stresa@libero.it; Piazza Marconi 16; ♥ 10am-12.30pm & 3-6.30pm Mar-Oct, 10am-12.30pm & 3-6.30pm Mon-Fri, 10am-12.30pm Sat Nov-Feb)

SIGHTS

Apart from visiting the Borromean Islands (see p127), you can ride the **Funivia Stresa-Mottarone** (☎ 0323 302 95; Piazzale della Funivia; adult return Alpino/Mottarone €6.50/11.50; ♥ every 40 minutes 9.20am-5pm) to the top of Monte Mottarone (1491m). The cable car takes 20 minutes to reach the top. At the Alpino mid-station (803m), 700 Alpine species flourish in the **Giardino Botanico Alpinia** (☎ 0323 302 95; adult/child €1.50/1.20; ♥ 9.30am-6pm Tue-Sun Apr–mid-Oct), a botanical garden dating to 1934.

Parents with children might also enjoy the **Parco Zoologico di Villa Pallavicino** (☎ 0323 324 07; adult/child €6.70/4.70; ♥ 9am-6pm Mar-Nov) at Stresa's southern end. A kid-friendly park spread over 20 hectares, it boasts more than 40 species of exotic birds and animals that roam relatively freely.

ACTIVITIES

Sunbathing on the **Lido** near the cable-car station is fun but for the more energetic there are ample opportunities to exercise.

For the cycling fraternity Monte Mottarone has a number of good biking trails. **Mountain bikes** (☎ 0323 303 99, ☎ 338 839 56 92; www.bicico.it) can be rented from the lower Stresa cable-car station. Rates include a helmet and road book detailing a 25km panoramic descent (two to three hours) from the top of Mottarone back to Stresa. A one-way trip with a bike, on the cable car to Alpino/ Mottarone, costs €5.50/9.

With eight **golf courses** in the lakes area, enthusiasts are spoilt for choice. For an 18-hole course with a view try the **Golf Club des Iles Borromees** (☎ 0323 92 92 85; Localitá Motta Rossa; green fees weekday/weekend €40/60; ☼ Feb-Dec) six kilometres from Stresa. By car, follow the signs for Gignese and then for the clubhouse.

Those who prefer their **walking** uninterrupted by irksome holes should ask at the cable-car station for a copy of *Trekking on the Slopes of Mont Mottarone*. It's a free brochure compiled by the Club Alpino Italiano (CAI), which outlines a two-hour walk from Stresa to the Alpine garden, and a four-hour walk to the top of Mottarone. Walks further afield are mapped out in the free multilingual *Nature Hikes* brochure, available at tourist offices.

Most winters, skiers and boarders can cruise down the slopes of Mottarone from late December to early March. Although not extensive, there is **skiing** for all levels. A one-day ski pass costs €16. Gear can be hired from the station at the top of Mottarone.

TOURS

A day trip that's well worth the money is the **Lago Maggiore Express** into Switzerland and back. From Stresa you head to Domodossola, where you change onto a charming little train for Locarno (take your passports) and a ferry back to Stresa. The package costs €27/13.50 per adult/child; Navigazione Lago Maggiore sells tickets from their office on Piazza Marconi.

FESTIVALS & EVENTS

Lago Maggiore's major musical festival is the internationally renowned **Settimane Musicali di Stresa** (☎ 0323 310 95; www.settimanemusicali.net). From late July until early September the lakes echo with the sound of music as orchestras, choirs and ensembles present a programme ranging from Mozart to Stravinsky.

SLEEPING & EATING

There are hundreds of camp sites and hotels along the lake's western shore. Hotels on the water's edge tend to be more expensive than those further back. Booking ahead is always a good idea.

STRESA

INFORMATION	
Newdata Internet Point	1 D3
Police Station	2 D2
Post Office	3 D3
Tourist Office	4 D2
SIGHTS & ACTIVITIES (pp124–5)	
Funivia Stresa-Mottarone	5 A1
Lido	6 A1

SLEEPING 🛏 (pp125–6)	
Grand Hotel des Iles Borromees	7 B2
Hotel Elena	8 D3
Hotel Luina	9 D3
Hotel Saini Meublè	10 D3
EATING 🍴 (p126)	
La Grigliata	11 C3
Osteria degli Amici	12 D3
TRANSPORT (pp126–7)	
Landing Stage	13 D2

NORTHERN PIEDMONT & THE LAKES

TERRE D'AQUA

The plains that extend across much of northern Italy are flat, featureless and wet. In other words, they are perfect for the cultivation of rice. Italy produces 60% of Europe's annual rice output, and more than half of it (some 660,000 tonnes) is cultivated in Piedmont. Little more than a blip on the world market, the €250-million business is an important contributor to the region's economic and gastronomic way of life.

The rice capital of Europe is Vercelli, while cultivation extends across the provinces of Novara, Alessandria and, in neighbouring Lombardy, Pavia.

Rice was introduced to Europe by Arab traders between the 11th and 12th centuries, first to Spain and then on to Sicily. From there it spread northwards, arriving in Piedmont's more humid climes in the 15th century. At the time, much of the area was covered in woods but the medieval green lobby was no match for the farming interests and the trees got the chop. Since then much of the Po Valley has worked to the rhythm of the rice cycle.

The cycle begins in March when the paddy fields are prepared for their annual dousing. Banks have to be rebuilt and the frozen soil broken up before the taps are turned on in mid-April. Sowing quickly follows and then it's pretty much plain sailing until harvesting and threshing in September and October.

There are more than 100 varieties of rice cultivated in the Vercelli area, of which Baldo, Arborio and Nuovo Maratelli are all suitable for risotto, while Sant'Andrea is better suited for soups and rice cakes.

To visit a working rice farm, head for the **Cascina Veneria** (☎ 0161 31 42 33; Fraz. Veneria) in the tiny village of Veneria, 10km west of Vercelli. Here you can peruse a choice of rice and risotto products that would put your local supermarket to shame. It was at this historic farm that the neo-realist film *Riso Amaro* (Bitter Rice) was filmed in 1949. Directed by Giuseppe De Santis, it stars Vittorio Gassman and Silvana Mangano in a tale of stolen jewellery and high passions in the paddy fields.

Hotel Saini Meublè (☎ 0323 93 45 19; www .hotelsaini.it; Via Garibaldi 10; s €68-78 d €82-93) Open year-round, this welcoming three-star has stone walls in the reception area that seem more suited to a mountain refuge, while the bedrooms are comfy, if a little anonymous. Breakfast is included in room rates.

Hotel Luina (☎ 0323 302 85; luinastresa@yahoo.it; Via Garibaldi 21; s €31-46 d €49-68) In the heart of Stresa's cobbled streets, Luina is a simple but friendly place with quiet rooms and a restaurant. Some rooms have a lake view.

Hotel Elena (☎ 0323 310 43; www.hotelelena.com; Piazza Cadorna; s €57-68 d €68-83) Adjoining a café, old-fashioned Hotel Elena is slap bang on Stresa's pedestrian central square. Rooms are small but well kept and each has a balcony overlooking the square.

Grand Hotel des Iles Borromees (☎ 0323 93 89 38; www.borromees.it; Corso Umberto I; s/d €277/374; P ☒ ☐ ☒) Rockefeller, Hemingway, Clark Gable and Mussolini are among the guests to have stayed at Stresa's most fabulous hotel, built in 1861 and furnished as it would have been in the *belle époque*.

Osteria degli Amici (☎ 0323 304 53; Via Anna Maria Bolongaro 33; 1st/2nd courses from €5.50/10, pizza €4-8)

Dine under vines on one of Stresa's most delightful terraces. Expect to queue.

La Grigliata (☎ 0323 331 10; Via Principe Tomaso 61; 1st/2nd courses from €6.50/7, pizza from €5) Laid-back and, when the football's on the big screen, full of locals, this simple trattoria specialises in grilled meats. Don't expect silver service but for a cheerful chomp it's fine.

GETTING THERE & AWAY

Boat

Ferries and hydrofoils around the lake are operated by **Navigazione Lago Maggiore** (☎ 0323 303 93, ☎ 800 55 18 01; www.navigazionelaghi. it in Italian), which has its main ticket office and landing stage on Piazza Marconi. Boats connect Stresa with Arona (adult/child return €8/4, 40 minutes, nine daily), Angera (€8/4, 35 minutes, nine daily), Baveno (€5/2.60, 20 minutes, eight daily) and Pallanza (€7/3.60, 35 minutes, five daily).

Various excursions are also available to Isola dei Pescatori and Isola Bella (adult/child €6/3), plus Isola Madre (€9/5); and to Isola dei Pescatori and Villa Taranto (€10/5). More expensive one-day passes include admission to the various villas.

Bus

Buses leave from the waterfront for destinations including Milan, Novara and Lago d'Orta. The daily Verbania Intra-Milan bus service operated by **SAF** (☎ 0323 40 15 26; www.saf duemila.com) links Stresa with Arona (€1.75, 20 minutes), Verbania Pallanza (€1.75, 20 minutes), Verbania Intra (€1.75, 25 minutes) and Milan (€5.60, 1½ hours). Getting to Turin from here is difficult and is best achieved by travelling through either Milan or Novara.

You can also go direct from Stresa to Milan's Malpensa airport with **Alibus** (☎ 0322 84 48 62; €10.50, one hour 50 minutes, five times daily mid-April–mid-October). Buy your ticket on the bus.

Car & Motorcycle

Travelling with your own wheels, the A33 straddles the shore from Arona in the south and continues north for Domodossola and Switzerland. The A26 motorway also parallels the southwestern shore of the lake.

Train

Stresa sits on the Domodossola–Milan line and is well served by hourly trains from both Milan (€6.92, one hour) and Domodossola (€2.65, 30 minutes). For Turin, change at Milan (€7.40, three hours).

Borromean Islands (Isole Borromee)

The Borromean Islands can be reached from various points around the lake, but Stresa makes a good departure point. The four islands, Bella, Madre, Pescatori (or Superiore) and San Giovanni, are all within 30 minutes of Stresa and form the lake's most beautiful corner. San Giovanni is off-limits to tourists.

BELLA

Named after Charles III's wife, the *bella* (beautiful) Isabella, in the 17th century, Isola Bella has courted a number of famous holiday-makers including Wagner, Stendhal, Byron and Goethe. **Palazzo Borromeo** (☎ 0323 305 56; www.borromeoturismo.it, Italian only; adult/child €9/4; 9am-5.30pm mid-Mar–Sep, 9am-5pm Oct) is its main drawcard. Built in the 17th century for the Borromeo family, the sumptuous palace contains works by Anthony Van Dyck as well as Flemish tapestries and sculptures by Canova. Mussolini tried to stave off WWII here at the Conference of Stresa in April 1935. The fossilised boat

displayed behind glass in one of the palace grottoes is 3000 years old. The actual grottoes, studded with pebbles from the lake bed, took 25 years to complete and were used by the Borromeo family as their cool (literally) hang-out. What little is left of the island swarms with stalls selling ice cream, pizza slices and tacky island souvenirs.

MADRE

Isola Madre provides fertile ground for Italy's tallest palm trees. The entire island is taken up by the fabulous, 16th- to 18th-century **Palazzo Madre** (☎ 0323 312 61; adult/child €8.50/4; 9am-5.30pm Apr-Sep, 9am-5pm Oct) and its peacock-filled gardens, which are even more lavish than those of Palazzo Borromeo. Period furnishings cram the palace interior; highlights include Countess Borromeo's doll collection, a neoclassical puppet theatre featuring a cast of diabolical marionettes, including the Devil and his hellish monsters and a seven-headed dragon. A combined ticket covering admission to the Borromeo and Madre palaces costs €12/7 per adult/child.

DEI PESCATORI

Beyond an 11th-century apse and a 16th-century fresco in the **Chiesa di San Vittore**, there are no real sights to see on **Isola dei Pescatori**, making it most visitors' port of call for lunch. Despite the many places to eat, there are no snack stalls and the tiny island retains some of its original fishing-village atmosphere. Count on eating much the same in whichever restaurant you choose – grilled fish 'fresh from the lake' for around €14. If

---

DETOUR

Rising above the lake's tranquil waters, the magnificent Rocca di Angera provides quite an eyeful when viewed from Arona's waterfront. The medieval castle today shelters the 12-room **Museo della Bambola** (Dolls Museum; ☎ 0331 93 13 00; www.borromeoturismo .it; adult/child €8.50/4; 9am-5.30pm Mon-Sat, 9am-6pm Sun, mid-Mar–end Oct), which chronicles the history of the doll with a collection of more than 1000 precious pieces.

To make the five-minute crossing there are more than 15 ferries a day from the landing stage near the tourist office. A return ticket costs €1.30.

FACTORY OUTLETS

It's possible to save yourself a whole heap of euros by shopping at one of the area's numerous factory outlets. Big business in these parts, outlets are peppered throughout the whole of Piedmont, although most of the big names are clustered around Verbania and Stresa. There is a second concentration in the Biella-Vercelli-Novara triangle.

Names to look out for in the Verbania province include:

- **Alessi** (☎ 0323 86 86 48; Via Privata Alessi 6, Crusinallo) Designer kitchenware.
- **Bialetti** (☎ 0323 65 31; Piazza Siro Collini; Omegna) Italy's best cafetieres.
- **Lagostina** (☎ 0323 65 21; Via IV Novembre 39; Omegna) Top-notch pots and pans.
- **Sergio Tacchini** (☎ 0323 86 49 93; Via Marconi 40; Gravellona Toce) Sportswear.

In the Biella, Vercelli and Novara area:

- **Mattel** (☎ 0322 23 13 11; Via Vittorio Veneto 119, Oleggio Castello) Games.
- **Cashmere & Co** (☎ 0331 96 32 71; Corso Sempione 188, Castelletto Ticino) Socks.
- **Lanerie Agnona** (☎ 0163 20 21 11; Via Casazza 7, Agnona di Borgosesia) Wool and cashmere.

The tourist office in Stresa has a comprehensive list. Most outlets are open approximately 9am to 12.30pm and 3pm to 7pm Tuesday to Saturday; some open on Sunday.

you want to stay on the island the romantic **Albergo Verbano** (☎ 0323 304 08; www.hotelverbano.it; s/d €100/145 half-board per person minimum 3 nights €125; ⏳ Mar-Dec) will impress your sweetheart.

Arona

pop 15,900 / elevation 212m
An attractive town on the southern shores of the lake, Arona's one great drawcard is the gigantic **Statua di San Carlo** (Piazzale San Carlo; admission €3.50; ⏳ 9am-12.30pm & 2-6.30pm Mar-Oct, 9.15am-12.30pm & 2-4.45pm Sun only Jan-Feb & Dec, Sat & Sun Nov), 2km north of the town centre. Standing 35m high, the statue depicts local boy and 17th-century saint Carlo Borromeo reaching out to bestow a priestly blessing. A staircase running up the hollow centre allows you to climb to just below the neck, where a couple of hatches afford magnificent views.

Carlo Borromeo was born in Arona's former fortress, which, until its destruction in 1800, fortified the **Rocca di Arona**. Novelist Stendhal described its demolition after witnessing events. Ruins of the 9th-century fortress, an early Romanesque chapel and a couple of storehouses are all that remain in the parkland today (off-limits to visitors).

The **tourist office** (☎ 0322 24 36 01; Piazzale Duca d'Aosta; ⏳ 9am-12.30pm & 3-6pm Mon-Fri, 9am-12.30pm Sat) is opposite the train and bus stations at the southern edge of the waterfront.

SLEEPING & EATING
Below the castle, an attractive waterfront unfolds with an appealing line-up of hip and trendy cafés and lakeside hotels.

Hotel Florida (☎ 0322 462 12; fax 0322 462 13; Piazza del Popolo 32; s €45-50 d €65-70) A warm welcome awaits you at this lakeside hotel. The large rooms are furnished according to the old school, and the breakfast room displays a bizarre mix of wall hangings, from Mordillo posters to fishing accoutrements.

Ristorante del Barcaiolo (☎ 0322 24 33 88; Piazza del Popolo 23; mains €12; ⏳ Thu-Tue) Hidden beneath the 14th-century porticoes that line pretty Piazza del Popolo, this busy place serves massive portions of everything from freshly caught fish to lamb chops.

Further down the lakefront, there is a trio of trendy places: mellow and elegant **Café de la Sera** (☎ 0322 24 15 67; Lungo Lago Marconi 85; 1st/2nd courses €6.50/7), which offers a simple choice of four dishes for each course; **Ul Boc** (☎ 0322 446 58; Lungo Lago Marconi 71; ⏳ 8am-3am Thu-Tue) with a dazzling Art Deco–inspired decor and a younger clientele; and **Gym Café** (☎ 0322 24 36 84; Lungo Lago Marconi 47) for those who prefer a 1950s US-diner feel.

GETTING THERE & AWAY
To reach Arona by car, take either the SS33, which passes through town or the A26,

which thunders past on its way to Milan and Domodossola.

From the **train station** (Piazzale Duca d'Aosta) there are regular trains to Domodossola (€3.50, 55 minutes, about 20 daily), Novara (€2.65, 40 minutes, six daily) and Milan (€4.25, 50 minutes, about 20 daily). For Turin, change at Novara (€6.25).

Verbania & Around

pop 30,300 / elevation 197m

The biggest town on the lake, Verbania is a not unattractive place that bursts into colour around April and May, when it plays host to a fanfare of floral exhibitions.

Split into three distinct districts, it is Intra (the Swiss end with an attractive old town and car ferry port to cross the lake) and Pallanza (the middle chunk) that are of the most interest.

In Pallanza there is a **tourist office** (☎ 0323 55 76 76; Viale delle Magnolie; ☺ 9am-12.30pm & 3-6pm Mon-Sat, 9am-12.30pm Sun) on the waterfront and a second **office** (☎ 0323 50 32 49; Corso Zanitello 6-8; ☺ 9am-12.30pm & 3-6pm Mon-Sat, 9am-12.30pm Sun) down the lakeside path towards Intra. A third **office** (☎ 0323 50 44 48; ☺ 9am-12.30pm & 2-5.30pm Fri-Sun) greets you at the car ferry terminal.

In Pallanza the green-fingered can stroll the grounds of the late 19th–century **Villa Taranto** (☎ 0323 40 45 55; www.villataranto.it; adult/child €8/5.50; ☺ 8.30am-7.30pm mid-Mar–Nov). In 1931 royal archer and Scottish captain Neil McEacharn bought the villa from the Savoy family and planted some 20,000 species over 30 years, creating what are today considered to be among Europe's finest botanical gardens.

Fans of fauna rather than flora might enjoy the **Centro Studi Sulle Migrazione** (Migration Study Centre; ☎ 0323 49 65 96; Via Canale 48) in Fondotoce, a small town half way between Stresa and

---

BEACH-WATCH BLUES

In 1999 Verbania became the first lakeside resort in Italy to receive the prestigious blue-flag beach rating. Awarded by the Foundation for Environmental Education in Europe, the little blue banner represents a much sought-after hallmark of environmental quality. To achieve it a resort has to satisfy up to 27 criteria covering water quality, environmental management, beach security and services.

Verbania. This bird research station runs a tagging operation to monitor migration patterns. Real enthusiasts should contact the centre for details of the work-experience placements on offer between April and May, and then August and October.

SLEEPING & EATING

Ostello Verbania (☎ 0323 50 16 48; Via alle Rose 7, Verbania; dm B&B €18.50; ☺ reception 7am-11am & 3.30-11.30pm Mar-Oct & Christmas) Backpackers should make a beeline for Verbania's only hostel. Rates include sheet hire.

Ostello del Castello (☎ 0323 51 65 79; Piazza Castello 9, Verbania Intra; 1st/2nd courses from €6.50/12; ☺ Mon-Sat) With its flower-topped pergola terrace overlooking a quaint old-town square, Ostello del Castello's location (20m from the ferry port) is hard to beat. Wine is plentiful and dishes are rustic and regional.

La Latteria (☎ 0348 371 24 06; Piazza San Rocco 20, Verbania Intra; 1st/2nd courses from €6.50/12; ☺ Tue-Sat) Around the corner, next to the Chiesa San Vittore, is Verbania Intra's other tasty find – a cow-inspired trattoria overlooking a quite traffic-free square.

GETTING THERE & AWAY

The only car ferry connecting the western and eastern shores for motorists sails between Verbania Intra (the Swiss end of Verbania) and Laveno. Ferries run every 20 minutes; one-way transport costs €5.10 for a small car and driver, or €3.10 for a bicycle and cyclist.

Continuing northwards along the shores of the lake, you come to **Cannero Riviera**, a tranquil lakeside village. Just off the coast lie some tiny islets that, before being taken over by the Borromeo family in the 15th century, served as a den for thieves, who operated in the area during the 12th century.

More interesting is **Cannobio**, 5km short of the Swiss border. The tiny toy town's spotless cobblestone streets retain something of a village flavour. It has an active sailing and surfing school, **Tomaso Surf & Sail** (☎ 0323 722 14; www.tomaso.com) next to a patch of gritty beach at the village's northern end, and mountain bikes can be hired (€3/11 per hour/day) from **Cicli Prezan** (Viale Vittorio Veneto 9), opposite the **tourist office** (☎ /fax 0323 712 12; Viale Vittorio Veneto 4; ☺ 9am-noon & 4.30-7pm Mon-Fri, 9am-noon Sat & Sun).

Hotel Pironi (☎ 0323 721 84; hotel.pironi@cannobio .net; Via Marconi 35, Cannobio; s/d from €80/130) Languishing in a 15th-century *palazzo* (palace)

**NORTHERN PIEDMONT
& THE LAKES**

DETOUR

Driving south from Verbania, about a couple of kilometres out of town, turn right following signs to Mergozzo. Almost immediately steer left and follow the road round. After another couple of kilometres you'll find yourself in front of the tiny **Lago Mergozzo**. Beloved by windsurfers, it's not exactly a secret but nonetheless offers something of a retreat from the crowds of Lago Maggiore. It was from the marble quarries surrounding the lake that the marble used in Milan's Duomo was taken.

Right on the waterfront, **Picolo Lago** (☎ 0323 58 67 92; www.piccololago.it; Via Filippo Turati 87; s/d €70/110; **P**) is a smart hotel-cum-restaurant that dishes up high-calibre cuisine and has 12 bright modern rooms overlooking the lake. You can even learn the secrets of the kitchen on a day-long cookery course.

---

amid Cannobio's cobbled maze, this is one of several charming hotels in Cannobio.

Cà Bianca (☎ 0323 78 80 38; Via Casali Cà Bianca 1, Cannero; 1st/2nd courses €8/12, menus from €25; ⏱ Thu-Tue) An atmospheric hotel that radiates elegance and timeless charm, this is a beautiful place to come to of a summer evening. Pasta is strictly *in casa* (homemade) and the *gnocchi al radicchio e gorgonzola* (gnocchi with chicory and gorgonzola cheese) is a real mouth-melter. Look for the house on the water, 1km north of Cannero Riviera.

LAGO D'ORTA

Only 15km long and about 2.5km wide, Lago d'Orta is separated from its eastern neighbour, Lago Maggiore, by Monte Mottarone (1491m). The lake is surrounded by lush woodlands and, unlike its cousins, does not swarm with visitors 365 days a year.

Orta San Giulio

pop 1133 / elevation 293m

A mite twee, Orta is a picturesque spot with no real sights but lots of cobbled lanes to stroll and medieval squares to sip coffee on.

Orta's **tourist office** (☎ 0322 901 55; Via Bossi 11; ⏱ 10am-7pm Mon-Sat, 10am-6pm Sun, winter hours vary) is right in the heart of the cobbled quarter.

From the main waterfront square, regular launches make the short trip to the **Isola**

San Giulio, named after a Greek evangelist who earned his saintly status by ridding the island of an assortment of snakes and monsters late in the 4th century. The island (dubbed the 'island of silence') is dominated by the 12th-century **Basilica di San Giulio** (⏱ 9.30am-12.15pm & 2-6.45pm Mon-Sat, 9.30-10.45am & 2-6.45pm Sun). From there, a single footpath, La Via del Silenzio (The Way of Silence), encircles the island. There is one museum to see, the **Museo del Regio Esercito Italiano** (☎ 0322 90 52 24; museo_regio_esercito@libero.it; adult/child €5/2.60; ⏱ 9.30am-6pm), which dedicated to military history from 1861 to 1945, and one pocket-sized pebble beach to speak of.

Sacro Monte (☎ 0322 91 19 60), behind Orta San Giulio, is dotted with a series of 20 small chapels erected to St Francis of Assisi over a 200-year period from 1591. Each one depicts an event from the animal world's favourite saint. It makes for a pleasant stroll above the town.

SLEEPING & EATING

Piccolo Hotel Olina (☎ 0322 90 56 56; Via Olina 40; s/d €50/70) Rooms here are cosy but charming. There are self-catering apartments to rent too, plus a tasty restaurant.

Hotel San Rocco (☎ 0322 91 19 77; www.hotelsanrocco.it; Via Gippini 11; s/d from €153/221; **P** ✖ ⊟ ⊠) Giuseppine nuns lived a life of seclusion at this 17th-century convent until 1960, when it was transformed into a luxurious place to stay. Moor your motorboat outside and cruise into this pool-filled oasis of luxury.

Villa Crespi (☎ 0322 91 19 02; www.slh.com/crespi; s/d from €140/195; **P** ✖ ⊟ ⊠) Secular decadence was lived out to the full by 19th-century Lombard industrialist Benigno Crespi, who made a fortune trading cotton, and had this oriental extravaganza built in 1879. Its lavish gardens and opulent Moorish interior are breathtaking.

GETTING THERE & AWAY

Orta Miasino train station, a short walk from the centre of Orta San Giulio, is just off the Novara–Domodossola train line.

Navigazione Lago d'Orta (☎ 0322 84 48 62) runs boats to numerous other lakeside spots, including the Isola San Giulio (single/return €1.50/3) and Omegna (€3.50/5), from its landing stage on Piazza Motta. Island boats simply leave when there are sufficient passengers to warrant the five-minute crossing.

Around Orta

Omegna's **tourist office** (☎ 0323 619 30; Piazza XXIV Aprile 17; ☺ 9am-12.30pm & 2.30-5.30pm Mon-Fri) has further details on the following activities as well as lists of camp sites and accommodation in the area.

On the northern tip of Lago Orta, **Omegna** is popular for its historic Thursday market and is home to the cult kitchenware company Alessi. The highly sought-after designer gear can be admired at the **Museo Alessi** (☎ 0323 86 86 11; www.alessi.com; Via Privata Alessi 6; admission free; ☺ first Mon of the month by appointment only, guided tours in English 10.30am) set inside the company's colourful headquarters designed by Milanese architects Alessandro and Francesco Mendini. A veritable temple to design, the high-tech displays feature prototypes and kitchen classics, ranging from trendy trays to cafetieres.

Children bored of gawping at knives and forks might perk up at the **Parco della Fantasia** (☎ 0323 88 72 33; www.rodariparcofantasia.it; Via XI Settembre 9; adult/child free/€3; ☺ 2.30-6pm Wed-Sun), a park aimed at combining fun with learning.

The colourful **Forum di Omegna** (☎ 0323 866141; www.forumomegna.org; Parco Maulini 1; adult/child €2.50/1.50; ☺ 10.30am-12.30pm & 3-6.30pm Tue-Sat, 3-6.30pm Sun) celebrates local industry with a permanent collection that showcases household articles and handicrafts, both past and present, of the area. Design junkies can feast on cult objects by, among others, Alessi, Bialetti and Lagostina.

Pizzeria Pomodoro (☎ 0323 622 17; albergo .pomodoro@libero.it; Piazza Martiri 4; pizza from €5) Opposite the market square and right on the lakeside this colourful pizzeria serves up bubbling pizza downstairs and offers bright unfussy **rooms** (s/d €47/66) upstairs.

The small village of **Armeno**, at the foot of Monte Mottarone, is worth visiting, not least for its **umbrella museum**. From here, the narrow road that perilously wiggles over to Stresa makes for a splendid drive.

VALSESIA

The Valsesia is one of the less crowded of Piedmont's valleys. The spectacular mountain scenery lends itself perfectly to adventure tourism and forms a magnificent backdrop for summer sports of every description. Forming part of the Monte Rosa ski area, it's particularly favoured by whitewater enthusiasts, who flock to the Sesia's wild rapids between May and September.

The valley contains two protected areas, the **Parco Naturale del Monte Fenera** extends for 3365 hectares near the town of Valduggia, while to the north, Europe's highest protected area, lies the 6511-hectare **Parco Naturale dell'Alta Valsesia**.

Varallo

pop 7795/ elevation 451m

A charming little town, Varallo marks the start of the Valsesia. Often regarded as little more than a stepping stone to the valley's deeper reaches, it's worth a little exploration in its own right. It's not a big place and although much of its outer suburbs are given over to the area's traditional industries (wood, lace and wrought iron) the historic centre is atmospheric and appealing.

The **tourist office** (☎ 0163 56 44 04; www.tu rismovalsesiavercelli.it; Corso Roma 38; ☺ 9am-1pm & 2.30-6.30pm Mon-Fri, 9.30am-1pm & 2.30-7pm Sat) can furnish heaps of information on the town and surrounding area.

SIGHTS

Most people who come to Varallo make a quick beeline for the **Sacro Monte di Varallo** (☎ 0163 539 38; riservasacromonte@laproxima.it; admission free) a series of 45 chapels dating to the 16th century. Inside each numbered chapel, life-size statues capture a biblical episode, be it the original sin or Christ's crucifixion. Work started on the first chapel in 1491 and the entire project took 250 years to complete.

The wooded complex, above the town, is protected by the Riserva Naturale Speciale del Sacro Monte di Varallo and a half-day stroll here is a must. In summer, and infrequently in winter, a **cable car** (adult/child under 6 return €2/free) links the Sacro Monte with Piazza G Ferrari in town.

Opposite the cable-car station the **Chiesa Madonna Delle Grazie** (Via Ferrari; ☺ 6.30am-noon & 3-6pm Mon-Sat, 8am-noon & 2.30-6pm Sun) is a beautiful 15th-century church that boasts a 21-panel fresco depicting the passion of Christ. Painted in 1513 by Gaudenzio Ferrari, it's a wonderful example of the maestro's work.

ACTIVITIES

The River Sesia provides the perfect conditions for a wide variety **river sports**. To canoeing, kayaking and white-water rafting you can add canyoning, river trekking, hydrospeed and tubing. The gentler arts of fishing are also popular.

The tourist office has details on white-water sport associations along the valley, including **Riverside** (☎ 335 662 45 34; Località Valmaggia), which runs week-long canoeing courses from €210. A day's rafting starts at €40.

For those who prefer their fun on dry land, there are plenty of opportunities for **cycling** and **hiking**.

SLEEPING & EATING

Ostello Città di Varallo (☎ 0163 510 36; ostello@ comunevarallo.com; Via Scarognini 37; dm bed €12.50; ☻ 5-10.30pm) One of two youth hostels in the Valsesia, this modest hostel provides basic accommodation deep in Varallo's cobbled heart. To get there from the town centre, cross the river and follow the signs.

Albergo Italia (☎ 0163 511 06; www.albergoitalia .net; Corso Roma 6; s €40-50 d €65-75) Formerly a 17th-century convent, the Italia became a hotel in the 18th century. Well versed in the art of hospitality, it offers modern and comfortable rooms and a delightfully named *Sala di Conversazione e Musica*, where guests are invited to practise the ancient art of conversation.

Ristorante Pizzeria La Sfinge (☎ 0163 515 88; Via Osella 27; pizza from €4, 1st/2nd courses from €5/8) Enter this riverside restaurant from the small courtyard and you'll find a laid-back unpretentious restaurant that serves unoriginal but tasty pasta and good-sized pizzas. There are also **rooms** (€35) available.

GETTING THERE & AWAY

Autoservizi Novarese (☎ 011 90 31 003) operates buses from Varallo to Turin (€6.25, 2¼ hours, two daily). **ATAP** (☎ 015 84 88 411) buses for Alagna (one hour, five times daily) depart from outside the train station in Piazza Marconi.

If travelling by car, a narrow winding road links the valley directly with the pretty **Lago d'Orta** (see p130).

Alagna
pop 431 / elevation 1191

Alagna is Valsesia's main ski resort and a departure point for excursions into the Monte Rosa massif to the northwest.

Ranging from tough off-piste descents to nursery slopes for beginners, the skiing suits all levels. For the experts, the **heli-skiing** is a tempting prospect. **Lyskamm Viaggi** (☎ 0163 92 29 93; www.alagna.it; Fraz. Centro 44) offer a one-day €230 excursion that involves flying to the 4200m Colle del Lys, from where you ski down to Zermatt and back to Alagna via the interconnected slopes.

For more down-to-earth skiing, a ski pass costs €31/181 per day/week, while lessons start at €28 per hour.

In summer there are well-marked walking trails in the foothills around the village. For a workout, head up to **Punta Indren** (3260m), a cable-car station from where the views are out of this world and a number of marked paths lead deep into the mountains.

The **tourist office** (☎ 0163 92 29 88; Piazza Grober 1; www.alagna.it; ☻ 9am-noon & 3-6pm Wed-Mon) has accommodation and skiing information.

Hotel Monterosa (☎ 0163 92 32 09; www.hotel monterosa-alagna.it; Piazza degli Alberghi; d €80-120; **P**) Alagna's first hotel, the Monterosa has been accommodating guests for 150 years, and even today the restaurant in the Salone Margherita is decorated in 19th-century finery. Rooms are modern, a little small, and inoffensively decorated.

THE WALSER CONNECTION

In the 13th century the higher reaches of the Valsesia were subject to something of an invasion by stealth. Fed up with a life of serfdom in their Swiss homeland, the Walsers, a fiercely independent religious sect of German descent, decided to up sticks and search for pastures new. Seeking absolute isolation they ended up in the uninhabited wilds of the upper Valsesia.

It was a tough and insulated existence that fostered a deep sense of pride within the community. Outside contacts were rare and it wasn't until they'd secured the rights to their lands that they even started trading with their neighbours in Varallo. More than seven centuries later, it's still possible to hear the Walser's Germanic dialect spoken in the valley.

You can learn more about the Walsers Italian adventures at the **Museo Walser** (☎ 341 137 74 04; admission free; ☻ 2-6pm Sat & Sun Sep-Jun, 2-6pm Mon, 10am-noon & 2-6pm Sat & Sun Jul, 10am-noon & 2-6pm daily Aug) in the hamlet of Pedemonte near Alagna.

Alagna is linked to Varallo by buses, which depart from Piazza Mercato (€2.65, one hour, five daily).

Valsesia's second youth hostel is to be found in the tiny ski resort of **Carcoforo** on the edges of the **Parco Naturale Alta Valsesia**.

Ostello Alpenrose (☎ 0163 956 46; Località Tetto Minocco 12; dm bed €12-17) Open year-round this makes an excellent base for exploring the beautiful surrounding countryside. You'll need your own wheels to get here.

VAL D'OSSOLA

Stretching from Lago Maggiore to Piedmont's northernmost tip, and the Simplon (Sempione) Pass through to Switzerland, Val d'Ossola offers some reaches that still today remain relatively unexplored and unspoilt. Following the course of the River Toce, it's lined by menacing peaks that rise to over 3000m. In the smaller side valleys you'll find a glorious unpolluted landscape of gorges and waterfalls, lakes and lush meadows.

Domodossola
pop 18,796 / elevation 272m

There are two reasons to come to this medieval town, now swamped by dusty sprawl. The first is to visit the 16th-century Sacro Monte Calvario, the other is to pick up the dinky tourist train that pops over to Locarno in Switzerland and back again.

Domodossola's **tourist office** (☎ 0324 24 82 65; www.prodomodossola.it; Piazza Matteotti 24; ☒ 9am-noon & 2.30-6.30pm Mon-Fri, 9am-noon Sat) is situated in the train station and has plenty of information on walking and cycling itineraries in the area and nearby valleys.

SIGHTS & ACTIVITIES
Situated on a hill within walking distance of town, the **Sacro Monte Calvario** (☎ 0324 24 19 76; www.sacromontedomodossola.it) lies at the heart of a special 25-hectare nature reserve. The 15 numbered chapels and 17th-century sanctuary contain some fine frescoes and heart-stopping statues. Not to be missed is chapel No IV, which contains a splendid 17th-century creation of Christ meeting his mother as he struggles under the weight of the cross. To reach the Sacro Monte either head uphill from Via Mattarella on foot or take one of the buses that departs from outside the train station four times daily.

To pop over the border into Switzerland, hop on the **Vigezzina train** (adult/child return €18.80/9.40), which takes you on a thrilling ride over the gorges of the Val Vigezzo to the border, and on to Locarno. There are eight departures a day, and journey time to Locarno is an hour and a half.

SLEEPING & EATING
Antica Trattoria Da Sciolla (☎ 0324 24 26 33; www .ristorantedasciolla.it; s/d €30/55) This welcoming place in the historical centre is a real find. The **restaurant** (mains from €8) is proud of its wonderful traditional fare (the partridge with orange sauce is a marvel), while its stylish rooms are both classy and unpretentious.

GETTING THERE & AWAY
Domodossola is on the main train line that links Milan and Switzerland. From the train station in Piazza Matteotti there are regular trains for Turin (€18.50, three hours) and Verbania (€2.25, 30 minutes).

Autolinee Comazzi (☎ 0324 24 03 33) operates buses in the valleys and down to Novara and Verbania.

The Valleys
From Domodossola, **Val Vigezzo** bears east towards Switzerland. A passage through to Italy's largest wilderness area, **Parco Nazionale della Val Grande**, it boasts incredible landscapes and local fame as a source of chimney sweeps (see p134).

To the west, **Valle Anzasca** carves its way through to the Alp's second-highest peak, (4633m). At the foot of the massif lies the valley's main ski resort **Macugnaga**. For summer skiing take the cable car up to the Monte Moro pass (2868m) on the crest between Switzerland and the Valle Anzasca, from where the views are quite amazing.

Quark (☎ 0324 652 84; Località Isella, Macugnaga; per week €258) An *agriturismo* in the hamlet of Isella, this working farm offers two self-contained apartments for weekly rent. You can help the farmhands milk the cows.

For the **Parco Regionale dell'Alpe Veglia e Alpe Devero**, you'll need to visit **Val Devero**, a small valley branching northwest off Val d'Ossola. Continue north up the SP659 and you arrive at **Cascata del Toce**, a 143m waterfall that marks the source of the River Toce, 6 km from the town of **Formazza** in the Val Formazza.

SWEEPING OUT OF THE VALLEY

Ever since the 17th century the town of Santa Maria Maggiore (population 1261) has enjoyed, or endured, the reputation as a producer of chimney sweeps. An unpleasant occupation that entrapped a large number of children, it was a skill that the valley folk took with them as they fled the poverty of the mountains in the 17th, 18th and 19th centuries. In 1837, more than 500 of 964 emigrants who set off for France, Holland and Germany were chimney sweeps.

It's a sad history of emigration and exploitation that is told at the **Museo dello Spazzacamino** (Chimneysweep Museum; ☎ 0324 950 91; Piazza Risorgimento; ☼ 3.30-6.30pm Tue-Sat, 10am-noon & 3.30-6.30pm Sun & Mon Jul & Aug, 10am-noon Sun & Mon Sep & Jun).

In Santa Maria Maggiore, **Hotel Miramonti** (☎ 0324 950 13; www.miramontihotels.com; Piazzale Diaz 1; s/d €40/80) is a homely three-star hotel that has comfortable rooms decorated in a style that grandmother would approve of.

NOVARA

pop 102,233 / elevation 159m

The most-likely reason for coming to Novara is to change trains. Industrial and largely unlovely, Piedmont's second city is a major rail hub that has little to tempt visitors. While it's true that the medieval core is well preserved and in places rather grand, it's not exceptional by Piedmontese standards and the dreary plains that surround the city make it unlikely you'll want to base yourself here.

Like many towns in these parts, Novara's history is bloody. First settled in the 5th century BC, it featured heavily in the complicated European wars of the 16th, 17th and 18th centuries with the usual cast, the Spanish, Austrian, French and Savoys, playing their habitual roles. A noteworthy event here was the abdication here of King Carlo Alberto in favour of his son Vittorio Emanuele II.

Orientation

Novara's train station is on Piazza Garibaldi, from where it's a short walk up Corso Garibaldi to the geometric historic centre. The main strip Corso Cavour runs north to south, crossed by cobbled Via Negroni and Corso Italia.

Information

Novara has a **police station** (☎ 0321 38 81; Piazza del Popolo 2) and **hospital** (☎ 0321 37 31; Corso Mazzini 18). For Internet access, try the **Internet Train** (☎ 0321 44 24 12; Corso Garibaldi 10; per 30 min €3; ☼ 9am-9pm Mon-Fri, 9am-7.30pm Sat, 3-7.30pm Sun). Postal services are available at the Novara **post office** (☎ 0321 67 53 11; Viale Manzoni 7; ☼ 8.30am-7pm Mon-Fri, 8.30am-1pm Sat). You'll

find tourist information at the **tourist kiosk** (☎ 0321 33 16 20; Corso Garibaldi; ☼ 10am-1pm & 2-7pm Mon-Sat 10am-1pm Sun) and the **tourist office** (☎ 0321 39 40 59; www.turismonovara.it; Via Quintino Sella 40; ☼ 9am-1pm & 2-6pm Mon-Fri).

Sights

Novara's most distinctive landmark is the **Basilica di San Gaudenzio** (☎ 0321 62 98 94; Via San Gaudenzio; admission free; ☼ 7am-noon & 3-7pm) and its towering dome. Lancing upwards to a height of 121m, the dome was designed by Alessandro Antonelli (1798–1888), the architect best known for his Mole in Turin (see p65).

Further south and worth a quick look, the **Broletto** (☎ 0321 62 30 21; Palazzo dei Paratici, Via Rosselli 20; admission free; ☼ 9am-noon & 3-6pm Tue-Sun) is a medieval complex that houses the archaeology, history and art sections of the **Museo Civico**. Works by minor 13th- to 18th-century Lombard and Piedmontese artists feature in what is otherwise a fairly unoriginal museum collection.

The **Duomo** (☎ 0321 66 16 60; Piazza Repubblica; admission free; ☼ 7am-noon & 3-6.30pm) owes its extravagant neoclassical design (including a 10m-high doorway) to Antonelli, although the interior retains elements of an earlier Romanesque church. Across a courtyard stands Novara's oldest monument, the 5th-century **Baptistry** (☎ 0321 66 16 11; Piazza del Duomo; admission free; ☼ 3.15-6.15pm Sat & Sun). Inside look out for the gruesome 11th-century frescoes depicting the Apocalypse.

Sleeping & Eating

Novara's hotels are aimed at business travellers, so tend to be on the expensive and impersonal side.

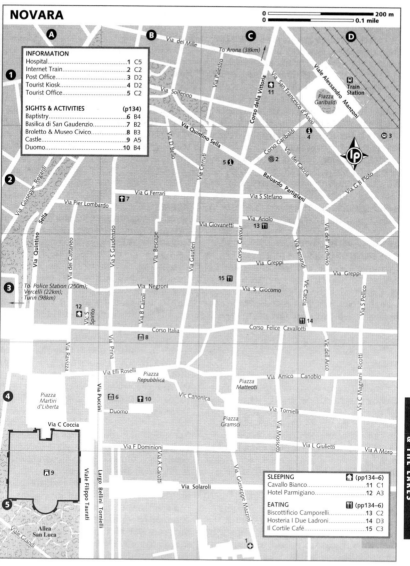

NOVARA

INFORMATION
Hospital.................................1 C5
Internet Train.......................2 C2
Post Office...........................3 D2
Tourist Kiosk........................4 D2
Tourist Office......................5 C2

SIGHTS & ACTIVITIES   (p134)
Baptistry.............................6 B4
Basilica di San Gaudenzio......7 B2
Broletto & Museo Civico........8 B3
Castle.................................9 A5
Duomo...............................10 B4

SLEEPING   (pp134–6)
Cavallo Bianco....................11 C1
Hotel Parmigiano................12 A3

EATING   (pp134–6)
Biscottificio Camporelli.........13 C2
Hosteria I Due Ladroni...........14 D3
Il Cortile Café.....................15 C3

Hotel Parmigiano (☎ 0321 62 32 31; fax 0321 62 05
00; Via Dei Cattaneo 4/6; s €50-70 d €77-110) Despite its
cheesy name, this friendly three-star is a good
bet. On the edge of the *centro storico* (historic
centre), it has decent rooms with parquet
floors and spanking new bathrooms.

Cavallo Bianco (☎ 0321 356 33; www.cavallobianco
.com in Italian; Corso della Vittoria 6; s/d €36/51) Ideal

for the train station, this is a modest family-run pensione with functional, clean
rooms. You can also grab a bite to eat in
the ground-floor **restaurant** (mains €6).

Hosteria I Due Ladroni (☎ 0321 62 45 81; Corso
Cavallotti 15; meals around €15; ☽ Mon-Fri & Sat evening)
A hugely popular choice for locals, this is a
little more than your average *osteria* (wine

bar serving food). The fashionable wood decor is inviting and the *antipasti* (starter) spread a winner. To enjoy a taste of the local land, tuck into a steaming plate of *paniscia* (risotto with veggies, salami and wine).

Il Cortile Café (☎ 0321 39 88 32; Corso Cavour 9; cheese platter €7; ⊗ Tue-Sun) This is the place for an aperitif and a designer plate of something. Well-dressed slickers head to the black and steel-grey minimalist bar, while outside in the stylish courtyard the volume falls and the pace slackens.

Biscottificio Camporelli (☎ 0321 62 06 89; Vicolo Monte Ariolo 3-5; ⊗ 8.30am-12.30pm & 3-7pm Mon-Sat) Novara is known in sweetie circles for its deliciously light *biscottini* (little biscuits). At this historic biscuit-maker, they've been perfecting their baking skills since 1852.

Getting There & Away
CAR & MOTORCYCLE
By motorway you can take either the A4 or the A26, which snakes north for Lago Maggiore and the Swiss border. Alternatively take the SS11, which goes from Novara to Milan in an easterly direction, and to Vercelli and Turin to the west. From the lakes, the SS32 goes from Arona to Novara.

TRAIN
Novara is an important rail junction and there are regular services to most parts of Piedmont including Alessandria (€3.90, one hour 15 minutes, eight daily), Arona (€2.65, 40 minutes, seven daily), Domodossola (€4.70, one hour 55 minutes, nine daily), and Turin (€3.85, one hour 15 minutes; more than 20 daily). For Varallo (€3.50, one hour 20 minutes, 12 daily) a bus substitutes the train.

VERCELLI
pop 47,955 / elevation 130m
Already an important Christian centre, the rice arrived in the 15th century along with the Savoys. The destruction of the surrounding woodlands followed as every available hectare was razed to make way for the paddy fields. Useful as well as fruitful, the fields were deliberately flooded by the town's cunning burghers to stop the Austrians marching in during the war of the Risorgimento.

Orientation
Vercelli's train station on Piazza Roma stands north of the historic centre at the top of Viale Garibaldi, which runs south to Piazza Paietta (sometimes spelt Pajetta). The main shopping street, Corso Libertá, branches off eastwards from Piazza Paietta.

Information
For emergencies go to the **police station** (☎ 0161 22 54 11; Via San Cristoforo 2). Medical treatment is available at the **hospital** (☎ 0161 59 31 11; Corso M Abbiate 21). Vercelli has a **post office** (☎ 0161 26 40 90; Via Ponti 9; ⊗ 8.30am-7pm Mon-Fri, 8.30am-1pm Sat), and tourist information is available at the **tourist office** (☎ 0161 580 02; fax 0161 25 78 99; Viale Garibaldi 90; ⊗ 9am-1pm & 3-6pm Tue, Thu & Fri, 10am-1pm & 2-6pm Sat).

Sights
Vercelli's treasures are impressive, even if they're not widely advertised. The **Basilica di Sant' Andrea** (Via Ferraris; ⊗ 7am-11.45am & 3-5.45pm Mon-Sat, 7am-12.30pm, 3-7pm Sun Oct-May, 7am-11.45pm & 3-6.45pm Mon-Sat, 7am-noon, 3-5.20pm Sun Jun-Sep) is considered an architectural masterpiece. One of the first churches to combine Gothic and Romanesque features, it was built in record time between 1219 and 1227, thanks, in part, to funds sent over from England. Adjoining the cathedral is the abbey, notable for its cloisters and the capitular room, regarded by many as one of the most beautiful in Italy.

From the Basilica it's just a short walk to the **Cattedrale di Sant' Eusebio** (Piazza S Eusebio; ⊗ 7.30am-noon & 3-6pm daily). Originally a 4th-century church built at the behest of Eusebio, Vercelli's and Piedmont's first archbishop, it endured various metamorphoses over the centuries, culminating in the addition of the dome in 1860. Inside is one of the biggest silver crucifixes (3.25m high and 2.35m across) you're ever likely to see.

Tucked away behind the cathedral, the **Museo del Tesoro del Duomo** (☎ 0161 516 50; Piazza d'Angennes; adult/child €3/free; ⊗ 9am-noon Wed, 9am-noon & 3-6pm Sat, 3-6pm Sun) contains some fascinating medieval manuscripts, including the so-called Vercelli Book, a 10th-century collection of Anglo Saxon poetry.

The principal art gallery in town, the **Museo Francesco Borgogna** (☎ 0161 25 27 76; Via Borgogna 8; admission €5.50; ⊗ 3-5.30pm Tue-Fri, 10am-12.30pm Sun), is Piedmont's second biggest. The collection consists largely of works by local artists from the 16th to 19th centuries.

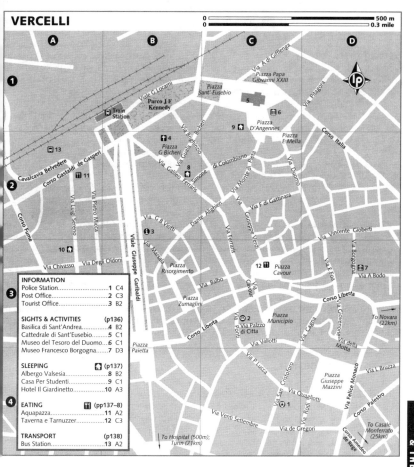

VERCELLI

INFORMATION
Police Station.......................1	C4
Post Office...........................2	C3
Tourist Office.......................3	B2

SIGHTS & ACTIVITIES (p136)
Basilica di Sant'Andrea...........4	B2
Cattedrale di Sant'Eusebio......5	C1
Museo del Tesoro del Duomo...6	C1
Museo Francesco Borgogna......7	D3

SLEEPING (p137)
Albergo Valsesia....................8	B2
Casa Per Studenti..................9	C1
Hotel Il Giardinetto...............10	A3

EATING (pp137–8)
Aquapazza...........................11	C1
Taverna e Tarnuzzer..............12	C3

TRANSPORT (p138)
Bus Station..........................13	A2

Sleeping & Eating

There isn't a huge choice of hotels in the centre of Vercelli, so it can be tricky to find a room if you turn up unannounced.

Hotel Il Giardinetto (☎ 0161 25 72 30; girardi .dan@libero.it; Via Luigi Sereno 3; s/d €66/77; 🏋) It's difficult to believe, as the photos at reception suggest, that Ayrton Senna or Sylvester Stallone stayed in this decent, but in no way outstanding, three-star pad. Rooms are fine but the lack of a lift is a pain.

Albergo Valsesia (☎ 0161 25 08 42; Via Galileo Ferraris 104; s/d without bathroom €30/50) Not two yards from the Basilica di San Andrea and within a stone's throw of the train station, this is one of the cheapest sleeps in town. Rooms are basic and the shared facilities clean.

Casa Per Studenti (☎ 0161 25 54 25; suorloreto@libero .it; Piazza d'Angennes 4; s&d without bathroom €25) English is spoken at this nun-run hostel, hidden away in a grand 17th-century *palazzo*. The sisters' preferred guests are young solo travellers or self-sufficient groups.

Aquapazza (☎ 0161 21 74 20; Corso Gastaldi de Gasperi 25; pasta & risotto from €4, pizza from €3.50; 🕙 Thu-Tue) Resembling an upmarket office canteen, this bustling eatery efficiently serves a bewildering array of pasta, risotto and pizza. Not surprisingly, the risotto is memorable. Local specialities to try include risotto with salami or sausage and beans.

Taverna e Tarnuzzer (☎ 0161 25 31 39; Piazza Cavour 27; 🕙 7.30am-8.30pm Tue-Sun) Vercelli's most historic café sells cakes and choccies galore.

A peculiar detail to note is the brass figurine on the tap top.

Getting There & Away

Vercelli, just off the A26 motorway and the SS11, is relatively well connected. **ATAP** (☎ 0161 25 00 15) buses depart from the **bus station** (☎ 0161 25 00 15; Calvacavia Belvedere) for Biella (€2.95, 50 minutes, 10 daily), Ivrea (€3.50, one hour 20 minutes, 11 daily) and Varallo (€3.90, one hour 30 minutes, 10 daily).

There are also frequent trains to Turin (€4.70, one hour), Casale Monferrato (€2, 30 minutes) and Novara (€2, 15 minutes).

IVREA

pop 25,100 / elevation 253m

Ivrea's fame rests on two things – oranges and typewriters. The first features in the town's madcap annual festival, which involves large numbers of highly charged citizens dressing up in medieval garb and pelting each other with oranges. The second made the fortune of Olivetti, Ivrea's most famous company.

A mildly charming plains town, Ivrea lies 55km northeast of Turin and 38km west of Novara. Divided in two by the River Dora Baltea, it is the historic old town on the north bank, with its arcaded squares and medieval red-brick **castle**, that offers the most obvious attractions. The modern south bank is of little interest, except for its Olivetti-inspired modern-architecture museum.

Ivrea's **tourist office** (☎ 0125 61 81 31; www .canavese-vallilanzo.it; Corso Vercelli 1; ⏰ 9am-12.30pm & 2.30-6pm Mon-Fri, 10am-noon & 3-6pm Sat) has information on the town and surrounding province, but be warned, it's a considerable way out of the town centre.

Sights

In the 1950s and 1960s, Olivetti, the typewriter giant founded by entrepreneur Camillo Olivetti (1868–1943) in Ivrea in 1896, enjoyed respectively, a 27% and 33% share of the world typewriter and calculator markets. Today its factory and offices, with their glass facades, form part of **MAAM** (Museo a Cielo Aperto dell'Architettura Moderna; ☎ 0125 64 18 15; mam@comune.ivrea.to.it; Via Jervis 26; admission free; ⏰ museum 24 hrs, info centre 9am-1pm Tue-Sat), an open-air museum of modern architecture. Numbered information panels (in English)

THE BATTLE OF ORANGES

The story goes that back in the 12th century, a miller chose Violetta, another miller's pretty young daughter, for his wife. However Ranieri, the nasty Count of Biandrate who ruled at the time, like many feudal overlords, reserved for himself the right to the first round with any local woman who was about to be married. A feisty individual, the miller's daughter was so upset by this that she sparked a revolt against the tyrant by the impoverished townspeople. On foot and armed only with stones, they launched themselves against the tyrant's troops, pelting them as they rode around the town in horse-drawn carts. This desperate uprising went down in the town's folk history and centuries later provided an excuse for rival gangs from different parts of town to stage an annual riot around carnival.

When Napoleon occupied this part of Italy at the beginning of the 19th century, his administrators ordered everyone to wear red revolutionary bonnets. They also put a stop to the fatal nature of the brawling, ordering that from then on the re-enactment of the famous uprising was to be carried out with oranges.

And so today, for three consecutive days, nine teams of 'revolutionaries' (3500 in all) wait on foot at four different squares for 30 roaming carts, each laden with 10 helmeted 'soldiers', and they pound each other with 400,000kg of oranges, imported from Sicily for the occasion. *Anyone* slipping and sliding on the slimy carpet of squashed orange (well mixed with horse manure) without some kind of red headgear is considered fair game for a massive orange assault by the 'rebel' squads, and will be pelted.

The Battle of Oranges is part of the **Ivrea Carnival**, which traditionally starts on the Thursday before Lent with a masked ball on Piazza Ottinetti. Sunday afternoon sees the main costumed procession with drums, flag bearers and a band – and the start of the orange battles! The final battle of Shrove Tuesday is followed on Ash Wednesday by a great open-air feast of polenta and salted cod, in the Borghetto quarter of town. This marks the start of Lent.

lead visitors on a tour of the facades of the Olivetti buildings (all still in use). You can walk around at will, or you can book a guided tour through the **Coop Sociale Alce Rosso** (☎ 0125 491 84; www.alcerosso.it; Villa Girelli, Strada Privata Bidasio).

To further investigate the company's past, the **Associazione Archivio Storico Olivetti** (☎ 0125 52 81 19; www.arcoliv.org; Villa Casana, Via delle Miniere 31; admission free; ☼ 9am-noon & 2-5pm Mon-Fri by appointment only) guards the company's archives, which runs to thousands of documents, periodicals and even audio recordings of debates and meetings.

Ivrea's medieval red-brick **castello** (castle; ☎ 0125 444 15; Piazza Castello; guided visits €2; ☼ 10am-noon & 3-6.30pm Sun May–mid-Oct) is a solemn affair that stands at the top of the historical centre. Dating to 1358, it was struck by lightning in 1676 in an incident that left many dead and the main tower irreparably damaged. Between 1750 and 1970 it served as a prison.

Nearby, the Romanesque 11th-century **Duomo** (Piazza Duomo; ☼ 8am-6pm) sits on the site of a Roman temple dedicated to Apollo.

Each March Ivrea's grand **Teatro Giacosa** (☎ 0125 402 67; www.teatrogiacosa.it; Piazza Teatro) plays host to the Euro Jazz Festival, a three-day ride of soulful sounds.

Sleeping & Eating

Albergo Nord (☎ 0125 401 35; Corso Nigra 63; s/d €35/46) In the modern part of town next to the train station, this modest family-run hotel offers basic accommodation at no-frills rates. Rooms are small but clean and come with a TV. It's no place for night owls, however, as the front doors are locked at 11pm.

Trattoria Residence Monferrato (☎ 0125 64 10 12; monferrato@iol.it; Via Gariglietti 1; 1st/2nd courses €6.20/7; ☼ Mon-Sat, lunch Sun) Typical Piemontese cuisine characterises this great value trattoria, with a handful of kitchenette-equipped **rooms** (s/d €45/55) above. Its eight-dish *antipasti* (nine if you opt for snails too), for €15.50, is a meal itself and ensures you'll never forget the place.

Enoteca Vino e Dintori (☎ 0125 64 12 23; Via Arduino 126; ☼ Tue-Sat) Simple wooden tables stage serious wine-tasting in Ivrea. The traditional wine bar hosts thematic tasting evenings on Friday and Saturday, focusing on regional specialities (frequent risotto evenings) as well as wine.

Arduino (☎ 0125 443 71; Piazza Gioberti 139) The dimly lit ochre ambience thumps to the

---

KOSHER CUISINE

La Miniera (☎ 0125 586 18; www.laminiera .it in Italian; Via delle Miniera 9, Calea di Lessolo; meals including wine €23-28, breakfast €6; ☼ B&B Mar–mid-Aug & mid-Sep–Dec, kitchen Fri-Sun) The tasty Piemontese kitchen of Signora Roberta Anau is the place for extraordinary kosher cuisine and traditional Piedmont dishes, fresh from the farm. **Accommodation** (s/d with shared bathroom €23/46, d with bathroom €66) is inside the main house or in a separate little cottage with a wood-burning stove, a trickling stream outside and fabulous green views. Only lunch is served on Sunday. Reservations are essential. From Lessolo, 10km west of Ivrea, follow the signs for Calea, from where La Miniera is 1.5km up a dirt track.

---

beat of a young, out-for-fun crowd at this fashionable historic-centre wine bar. Aperitifs pave the way for late-night drinking against a high-volume soundtrack.

Getting There & Away

To reach Ivrea by car, take the A5 or the SS26, which parallels it.

From Ivrea **train station** (cnr Corso Jervis & Corso Nigra), in the new town, there are direct trains to and from Chivasso (€2.45, 40 minutes, at least hourly) and Turin (€3.90, one hour, eight daily). Both the historic centre and MAAM are an easy walk from here.

Around Ivrea

Piedmont's most important bird-watching wetland lies 16km south of Ivrea. The **Parco Naturale del Lago di Candia** (☎ 011 861 211 111; www.parks.it/parco.lago.candia/index.html) covers a 336-hectare site just outside the village of Candia. The lake and marshes are home to around 80 species of nesting birds as well as a wide range of aquatic flora. The best time to visit is autumn and spring away from the thriving summer mosquito community.

From here it's only a short 10km skip west to the 300-room **Castello Ducale d'Aglié** (☎ 0124 33 01 02; castle adult/child €4/2, park €2, combination ticket €5; ☼ castle 8.30am-6.30pm Tue-Sun, park 9am-1pm & 2-7pm Tue-Sun May-Oct) and its glorious park. The castle itself belonged to Count Filippo Aglié, who transformed the original castle into a sumptuous palace. King Carlo Felice continued the makeover in the mid-18th century.

Particularly noteworthy is the elaborately frescoed ballroom.

Stashed away in the **Enoteca Regionale della Serra** (☎ 0161 985 01; Via al Castello 2; 9.30am-noon & 3-6.30pm Fri-Sun Oct-Mar, 3-7pm Thu, 9.30am-noon & 3-7pm Fri-Sun Apr-Sep), in the castle of **Roppolo**, is a collection of wine from the Vercelli and Canavese areas. Roppola is on the SS 228, 16km south east of Ivrea.

BIELLA
pop 48,091/ elevation 420

A commercial and workaday town, Biella's wealth is based on wool. It is said that designer Valentino shops here, so if you're looking for a little cashmere number, this is your place. There are a number of factory outlets in town where the prices are tempting and quality assured.

Textiles apart, there's not an awful lot to keep you here. The most atmospheric part of town is the medieval Piazzo district up at the top of the hill. Down below the historic centre is a popular spot for an afternoon stroll.

Information
Internet access is available at **Internet Point** (☎ 015 206 62; Via Duoma 10a; per 15mins/1hr €1/3.50; 10am-1pm & 3-8pm Tue-Sat, 10am-1pm Mon) and tourist information can be found at the **tourist office** (☎ 015 35 11 28; www.atl.biella.it; Piazza V Veneto 3; 8.30am-1pm & 2.30-6pm Mon-Fri, 8.30am-12.30pm & 2.30-6.30pm Sat).

Sights & Activities
Biella's attractions are centred on the cobbled quarter around Corso Italia. Construction of the **Cattedrale di Santo Stefano** (☎ 015 225 92; Piazza Duomo; admission free; 7am-noon & 3-7pm) began in 1402, after the town's population made a deal with the Madonna di Oropa that if she rid the area of plague, they'd build her a church. The plague died out and up went the cathedral. Next door, the 11th-century red-brick **Battistero** is considered one of Piedmont's most important Romanesque monuments. To go inside you'll need to ask at the cathedral.

The 16th-century complex incorporating the **Chiesa di San Sebastiano** and the adjoining **Chiostro di San Sebastiano** houses the small **Museo del Territorio Biellese** (☎ 015 252 93 45; www .museodelterritorio.biella.it; Via Quintino Sella; admission free; 10am-noon & 3-7.30pm Sat & Thu, 3-10pm Fri, 3-7pm Sun). Here you'll find medieval maps, colourful frescoes and an Egyptian mummy.

To head up the hill to the Piazzo quarter, with its porticoes and panoramas, you can either take the long way and walk, or jump on the **funicular railway** (Piazza Curiel; one way €0.67; 7am-midnight Mon-Thu, 7-2am Fri & Sat), which will whisk you up in about two minutes.

Two top outlets that might tempt shoppers are **Fila Sport** (☎ 015 231 38; Viale C. Battisti 28; 3-7.30pm Mon, 9.30am-12.30pm & 3-7.30pm Tue-Fri, 9.30am-7.30pm Sat), where you can pick up the entire Fila range, including the Ferrari Grand Prix collection and **Dressage** (☎ 015 40 26 18; Via Torrione 22; 9.30am-12.30pm & 3.30-7.30pm Tue-Sat), which specialises in cashmere.

Sleeping & Eating
Biella is not exactly overloaded with good-quality accommodation.

Augustus Hotel (☎ 015 275 54; www.augustus.it; Via Italia 54; s/d €78/99;   ) A recently renovated four-star, the Augustus Hotel sports corporate blues and oranges, and a lack of character. However, it's comfortable, rooms have mod cons, and it's right in the middle of the historic centre. Rates include breakfast.

Tenuta La Mandria (☎ 015 253 60 78; www.te nutalamandria.com; Via Castellengo 106; s/d €30/60) This *agriturismo*-cum-riding-school is set in a large estate, 7km southeast of Biella. Perfect for horse lovers, it offers courses for all

---

AUTHOR'S CHOICE

A reason in itself for coming to town is the beer brewed at the **Birreria Menabrea** (☎ 015 252 24 35; Via Germanin 4; mains around €8; Tue-Sat), Biella's historic beer-maker. Three times the legendary lagers have been named the best in the world. In 1997, 1998 and 2000 judges at the World Beer Championship in Chicago decided that there simply was no better beer around.

The brewery was founded in 1846 and by 1899 it was already winning awards. More than a century later, the barrels are still full and the punters are still drinking. To sup a pint or two with a hearty plate of good old pub grub, head for the brick-vaulted *osteria* next to the main brewery. A hugely popular dining spot it's often heaving, so make sure you book ahead.

And the secret of its success? The purity of the local water? The age-old brewing techniques? Quite frankly, who cares? Cheers!

PARCO NAZIONALE DEL GRAN PARADISO

Gran Paradiso was Italy's first national park, established in 1922 after Vittorio Emanuele II gave his hunting reserve to the state. By 1945 the ibex (wild goat) had been almost hunted to extinction in the park and there were only 419 left. Today, as the result of a conservation policy, almost 4000 live here.

The national park incorporates the valleys around the Gran Paradiso (4061m), two of which, Soana and Orco, are in Piedmont. On the Aosta side of the mountain, the park includes the Valsavarenche, Val di Rhêmes and the beautiful Valle di Cogne.

The main entry point to the park from Piedmont, is Noasca (48km northwest of Turin and 45km east of Ivrea) in the Valle Orco. The **park headquarters** (☎ 0124 90 10 70; www.pngp.it; Via Umberto 1, 1, Noasca; 🕑 9am-noon & 2-6pm) are open year-round and have a wealth of information on the range of activities available including, in winter, cross-country skiing and snow trekking, and in the warmer months hiking, climbing and cycling. The best time to spot the indigenous chamois and ibex is spring, when they venture down into the valleys looking for grass.

To get to the park from Turin, head north on the SS460. At Pont Canavese bear right for Val Soana or continue straight for Valle Orco.

Information is also available from the park's Turin-based **headquarters** (☎ 011 860 62 11; Via Della Rocca 47).

levels, has decent rooms and serves plentiful local food. To get here, follow signs for Candelo and then for the homestead itself.

Getting There & Away

Biella is 31km north east of Ivrea and can be reached by the SP338, which travels through pretty hillside scenery. To get to the lakes, take the SS142 for Gattinara and then Arona.

From the **train station** (Piazza San Paolo) catch trains to Novara (€3.50, 50 minutes, hourly).

Around Biella
SANTUARIO DI OROPA

Piedmont's most famous shrine, **Santuario di Oropa** (Via Santuario di Oropa 48; www.santuariodioropa .it), is a steep 12km climb from Biella. Sitting in stately majesty at an altitude of 1200m, it's a place whose impact relies more on size than artistic splendour. But size counts and it's an impressive spectacle.

According to tradition the sanctuary dates to the 4th century, when it was built on the wishes of Saint Eusebio, the first Archbishop of Vercelli. The basilica was added in the 17th century, along with many of the outbuildings designed by Filippo Juvarra, and an assortment of big-name baroque architects.

The wooded slopes surrounding the sanctuary also provide fertile soil for amusement. Guided tours are available to the **Sacro Monte**, a group of 19 chapels dedicated to the life of the Virgin Mary, while the **Giardino Botanico** will lure garden lovers. Walkers and skiers

can take to the paths and pistes of Monte Mucrone (2335m). To visit the heights, either don the walking boots or take the cable car from behind the sanctuary. A return ticket to Lago Mucrone (1902m) costs €8.50.

For further information or to book one of the rooms available, contact the sanctuary **tourist office** (☎ 015 2555 12 00; 🕑 8am-7pm; s/d €28/42).

On weekdays there are buses to Oropa (€1.40, 40 minutes, seven daily) from Biella train station.

SORDEVOLO

Located 7km west of Biella, this tiny hilltop village sheds its sleepy demeanour every five years, when thousands of visitors pile in for **La Passione** (☎ 015 256 24 86; www.passionedicristo .org). A tradition going back more than 200 years, the three-hour passion play involves up to 400 actors reciting a 16-century script. The next edition is set for 2005.

Floral fans can feast on two lovely gardens in the area. In the village itself, the gardens of the 19th-century **Villa Cernigliaro** are an attractive sight, while nearby in Pollone, **Parco Burcina** makes a colourful impression.

GATTINARA

Almost halfway between Biella and Arona, the **Enoteca di Gattinara e dei Nebbioli del Nord Piemonte** (☎ 0163 83 40 70; Corso Valsesia 112; 🕑 10am-12.30pm & 4-7.30pm Tue-Sun) highlights local wines made from the Nebbiolo grape.

Directory

CONTENTS

Accommodation	142
Business Hours	143
Children	144
Climate Charts	144
Courses	144
Customs	144
Dangers & Annoyances	144
Disabled Travellers	144
Discount Cards	144
Embassies & Consulates	145
Festivals & Events	145
Food	146
Gay & Lesbian Travellers	146
Holidays	146
Insurance	146
Internet Access	146
Legal Matters	147
Maps	147
Money	147
Post	147
Shopping	148
Solo Travellers	148
Telephone	148
Time	148
Tourist Information	148
Visas	149
Work	149

PRACTICALITIES

- Plugs have two or three round pins; the electric current is 220V, 50Hz
- Use the metric system for weights and measures.
- Buy or watch videos on the PAL system.
- For local and regional news, try *La Stampa* (www.lastampa-nordovest.it in Italian), a 50-page broadsheet going strong since 1867.
- Tune into: Radio Torino Populare (97 FM in Turin, 88.6 FM in Ivrea and Biella; www.rtp97.it in Italian) or Radio Piemonte Stereo (90.7 FM; www.radio eradio.com in Italian) for news, events and chat; music stations Radio Veronica One (93.6 FM; www.radioveronica.it in Italian) and Radio Energy (93.9 FM; www .radioenergyison.it in Italian) for local DJ-spun music; and Turin-based Radio Blackout 2000 (97 FM; www.arpnet .it/b2000 in Italian) for music and gossip with a student slant.
- Watch Italy's commercial stations Canale 5, Italia 1, Rete 4 and La 7, as well as state-run RAI 1, RAI 2 and RAI 3 (programme listings for all three at www.rai.it in Italian).

ACCOMMODATION

Accommodation ranges from rock bottom to ravishing. Hotels form the bulk of town accommodation, and *agriturismi* (farmstays) rule rural Piedmont. High-altitude travellers can overnight in *rifugi* (mountain huts).

A *camera singola* (single room) is more expensive per person than a *camera doppia* (double room with twin beds) or a *camera matrimoniale* (double room with a double bed). Many *agriturismi* only have doubles.

Local tourist offices have accommodation lists. Online, Regione Piemonte (www .regione.piemonte.it/turismo/ricettivita .htm in Italian) has a searchable database.

Agriturismi & B&Bs

Piedmont's most idyllic accommodation – a winery, truffle-hunting domain or working dairy – is represented by **Agriturismo Piemonte** (☎ 011 53 49 18; www.agriturismopiemonte.it in Italian; Via San Tommaso 22b, Turin), an association of 75-odd *agriturismi* (farmstays) offering green activities as well as enticing sleeping and eating. It publishes an annual guide of its properties in English.

Farmstays offer bed and breakfast (€15 to €70), with some offering a lip-smacking evening meal for an extra fee (€10 to €35). Farms range from crumbling abodes with few frills and shared bathrooms, to palatial state-of-the-art estates with period furnishings, private designer bathrooms and a swimming pool in the grounds. Most properties are out-of-town havens of peace.

Bed and breakfast in Turin and the other provincial capitals (single/double €40/70) is limited. Online, scour the Piedmont section of **Bed & Breakfast Italia** (☎ 06 687 86 18; www.bbitalia.it).

Camping
Camp sites *(campeggi)* range from complexes with swimming pools, restaurants and supermarkets to fields where bush-squatting campers can pitch up for a small (or no) fee. Sites are generally open from March to October and cost upwards of €4.50 per adult and €4.50 per tent pitch.

Wild camping is not permitted in protected areas.

Hostels
The **Associazione Italiana Alberghi per la Gioventù** (AIG; ☎ 06 487 11 52; www.ostellionline.org), affiliated to **Hostelling International** (HI; www.iyhf.org), runs youth hostels in Turin, Alessandria, Verbania, Bergolo and Pietroporzio. To stay in any of these hostels, you need an HI card. Otherwise, there are privately run hostels in Varallo and Vercelli.

Accommodation is in dormitories (€10.50 to €14 per person without breakfast) or family rooms (€11.50 to €17 per person without breakfast). Breakfast/dinner costs around €1.55/8.50, and some hostels charge €1 to €1.50 for hot water and heating.

Some hostels have a lock-out period between 10am and 3.30pm, impose an evening curfew and close in winter – see regional chapters for details.

Hotels
Piedmont boasts a wide choice of *alberghi* (hotels), although travellers seeking five-star luxury will be disappointed: there are just three five-star hotels in Piedmont (six more will open by the Olympic kick-off in 2006). Breakfast is included in the rates of mid-range and top-end hotels, and most accept major credit cards. Many Turin hotels offer special weekend rates (p143).

Turin touts many budget hotels. Most demand cash payment and don't serve breakfast. Many are on the upper floor of an ageing building serviced by a rattling iron cage–style lift – or no lift at all. Check until what time reception is open to as close around 11pm. Sporadic low water pressure (read: less than a pathetic dribble out of the shower head) in some of these budget joints is a common complaint among Lonely Planet readers.

A WEEKEND IN TURIN
City-breakers arriving in Turin on Friday or Saturday can take advantage of the city's *weekend a Torino* deal, whereby selected hotels offer cheaper rates to guests staying in a double room for two nights. Rates include breakfast; a Torino Card; a bottle of champagne, chocolates, fruit or other gift on your pillow; and – not for romance-seekers – a bed in the room for one child aged under 12. Book at least seven days in advance.

Rental Accommodation
Tourist offices have lists of agencies through which you can rent apartments and villas on a short- and long-term basis in Turin, major towns and resort areas.

Rifugi
A network of *rifugi* sustains the flow of walkers in the Alps. Some have dormitories, others only a handful of beds. Most open July to September. A night's kip costs from €7.50 to €20, plus €3/11 for breakfast/dinner.

Many are run by the **Club Alpino Italiano** (CAI; ☎ 011 54 60 31; cai.torino@iol.it; Via Barbaroux 1, Turin). Contact details for refuges in the national parks are online at www.parks.it.

BUSINESS HOURS
Shops open from 9am or 10am to around 1pm and 3.30pm to 7.30pm (or 4pm to 8pm) Monday to Saturday; many are closed Monday morning. In Turin, larger shops and department stores open Sunday afternoon and until 10pm some evenings. Many supermarkets operate 'nonstop', meaning 9am to 7.30pm Monday to Saturday.

Opening hours of museums and galleries vary; many close on Monday or Tuesday. Banks open from 8.30am to 1.30pm and 3.30pm to 4.30pm weekdays. Post offices open from 8.30am to 5pm or 6pm Monday to Friday and 8.30am to 1pm on Saturday. Pharmacies open from 9am to 12.30pm and 3.30pm to 7.30pm Monday to Friday and Saturday mornings. A couple in Turin run a night service.

Bars and cafés open from 7.30am to 8pm. Clubs and discos open around 10pm; in Turin the scene stays busy until 3am or 4am.

Many businesses and shops close for part of August.

DIRECTORY

CHILDREN

Practicalities

Bambini (children) are welcomed with open arms, but nappy-changing facilities, high chairs and cots are far from commonplace. *Agriturismi* are a convenient option: when making your reservation, check whether your host cooks evening meals, allowing you to feast in the kitchen while the kids sleep up top (bring your own baby monitor).

Pharmacies sell baby formula, sterilising solutions and nappies. Nappies are also sold at supermarkets, as is fresh milk.

Children under three enter museums and other sights for free; those aged three to 12 pay half-price. The same applies to public transport. In ski resorts, kids get discounted lift passes and ski hire.

The **City of Turin** (Città di Torino; www.comune.torino .it) publishes a list of Turin-based babysitters, childcare agencies, doctors and kiddie restaurants; follow the 'English Version/Turin for Children/Useful Numbers' link.

Sights & Activities

Piedmont has lots to keep kids smiling. For sights and activities specific to Turin, see p70. For entertainment elsewhere, see p14. If all else fails, take them to a chocolate shop (p76) or festival (p145).

Rural Piedmont offers fantastic opportunities for children. Many farms in Agriturismo Piemonte (p142) invite little hands to help with farmyard chores.

For more information, see Lonely Planet's *Travel with Children* or the websites www.travelwithyourkids.com and www .familytravelnetwork.com.

CLIMATE CHARTS

For a weather forecast, follow the *'meteo'* link on the Regione Piemonte website (www.regione.piemonte.it). For ski resort weather reports, see www.torino2006.org.

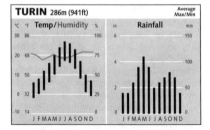

TURIN 286m (941ft)

COURSES

Most courses delve into the region's rich culinary recipes and produce (p51) or teach non-Italians how to wrap their tongue around Italian (p70). The Parco Nazionale del Gran Paradiso (p141) organises week-long art and photography courses.

CUSTOMS

There is no limit on the amount of euros brought into the region. Goods brought in and exported within the EU incur no additional taxes, provided duty has been paid somewhere within the EU and the goods are for personal consumption.

Duty-free sales within the EU no longer exist. Visitors coming from non-EU countries can import, duty-free, 1L of spirits, 2L wine, 60mL perfume, 250mL eau de toilette, 200 cigarettes and other goods up to a total of €175.50; anything over this limit must be declared on arrival and the appropriate duty paid. On leaving the EU, non-EU citizens can reclaim any Value Added Tax (VAT) on expensive purchases.

DANGERS & ANNOYANCES

See the Turin chapter for city-centred dangers and annoyances (p57). Elsewhere in the region, the swarms of mosquitoes that buzz above the plains of eastern Piedmont are about as annoying as you'll get.

DISABLED TRAVELLERS

Piedmont offers disabled travellers assistance through Turin-based **Informa Handicap** (☎ 011 442 16 31; informahandicap@comune.torino.it; Via Palazzo di Città 11; ☽ 9am-noon & 1.30-4pm Mon-Fri).

Online, **Consulta Persone in Difficoltà** (☎ 011 319 81 45; www.comune.torino.it/itidisab in Italian; Via San Marino 10, Turin) publishes four excellent sightseeing itineraries.

The Parchi e Riserve Astigiani (p105) and Parco Nazionale Gran Paradiso (p141) have marked walking trails for blind people.

DISCOUNT CARDS

The Torino Card (48/72 hours for €15/17) includes free admission into 120 museums and monuments in Piedmont, and 50% discount on selected theatre and concert tickets, bicycle hire, guided visits and so on. In Turin, card holders travel for free on public transport, get a 50% discount on suburban transport and a free ride on a River Po boat, the Sassi-Superga tram and the Mole Antonelliana's panoramic lift. In Turin the tourist office, some hotels and the Automobile Club Torino (p152) sell the card.

Students holding an International Student Identity Card (ISIC) and under 26s with a Euro<26 card get discounts. **Centro Turistico Studentesco e Giovanile** (CTS; ☎ 011 812 45 34; www .cts.it; Via Montebello 2h) in Turin sells both cards.

For rail-pass details, see p153.

EMBASSIES & CONSULATES
Italian Embassies & Consulates
Australia Canberra (☎ 02-6273 3333; www.ambitalia .org.au; 12 Grey St, Deakin ACT 2600); Sydney (☎ 02-9392 7900; itconsydn@itconsyd.org; Level 43, The Gateway, 1 Macquarie Place NSW 2000)
Canada (☎ 604-684 7288; consolato@italianconsulate .bc.ca; Standard Bldg 1100-510 West Hastings St, Vancouver, BC V6B 1L8)
France (☎ 01 49 54 03 00; ambasciata@amb-italie.fr; 51 Rue de Varenne 75007, Paris)
Germany (☎ 030-254 40 0; www.botschaft-italien.de in Italian & German; Dessauer Strasse 28-29, Berlin 10963)
Ireland (☎ 01-660 1744; www.italianembassy.ie; 63-65 Northumberland Rd, Dublin 4)
Netherlands (☎ 070-302 10 30; www.italy.nl; Alexanderstraat 12, The Hague, 2514 JL)
Switzerland (☎ 031 350 07 77; Elfenstrasse 14-3000, Bern, 16)
UK (☎ 020-7312 2200; www.embitaly.org.uk; 14 Three Kings Yard, London, W1K 4EH)
USA Washington (☎ 202-328 5500; www.italyemb .org; 1601 Fuller St, NW Washington, DC 20009); New York (☎ 212-737 9100; www.italconsulnyc.org; 690 Park Ave, 10021)

Embassies & Consulates in Italy
Most countries have an embassy or consulate in Turin or Milan as well as in Rome.
Australia (☎ 02 77 70 41; australian-consulate -general@austrade.gov.au; 3rd floor, Via Borgogna 2, Milan, 20122)
Canada (☎ 02 6 75 81; Via Vittorio Pisani 19, Milan, 20124)
France (☎ 011 573 23 11, 011 561 95 29; Via Roma 366, Turin, 10123)
Germany (☎ 011 53 10 88; Corso Vittorio Emanuele II 98, Turin, 10121)
Ireland (☎ 02 551 87 569; Piazza F Pietro in Gessate 2, Milan, 20122)
Netherlands (☎ 02 485 58 41; nlgovmil@iol.it; Via San Vittore 45, Milan, 20123)
Switzerland (☎ 011 71 55 70; Via Sacra San Michele 66, Turin, 10141)

> ### TOP FIVE – FESTS FOR KIDS (BIG & SMALL)
>
> - **CioccolaTò** (www.cioccola-to.com, Italian only; Mar) Chocolate, chocolate and more chocolate for three chocolate-caked weeks throughout the region.
> - **Carnevale** (Feb or Mar) Before Lent, towns stage carnivals and enjoy their last fling before Easter. Ivrea Carnival (p138), with its wild Battle of Oranges, kicks off on the Thursday before Lent.
> - **Burattinarte** (May-Jun) Puppet theatre takes to the street and stage of Alba, Bra and the Langhe hills.
> - **Palio d'Asti** (Sep) Twenty-one jockeys race on horseback around Asti's central square.
> - **Palio degli Asini** (Oct) Alba's annual donkey derby.

UK (☎ 011 650 92 02; www.britain.it; Via Saluzzo 60, Turin, 10125)
USA (☎ 02 29 03 51; www.usembassy.it; Largo Donegani 1, Milan)

FESTIVALS & EVENTS
Piedmont's cultural year oozes colour. Events are also listed in the regional chapters. Piedmont hosts the **XX Winter Olympic Games** from 10 to 26 February 2006 and the **IX Paralympic Winter Games** from 10 to 19 March 2006.

FEBRUARY/MARCH
Settimana Santa (Holy Week) Holy Week is marked by solemn processions and Passion plays.

MAY
Folkermesse (www.ethnosuoni.it in Italian; May-Aug) One of Europe's largest folk-music festivals brings an eclectic electric bunch of concerts to the region.

JULY/AUGUST
Lago Maggiore Jazz Festival (Jul-Aug) BB King and Ray Charles are among the big shots to have played at this European jazz festival, held in venues around Lago Maggiore.
Festival dei Laghi (Jul-Aug) Dance rules at the Lake Festival, a dance event originally conceived to showcase stately homes and gardens around Lago Maggiore and Lago d'Orta.
Festenàl (mid-Jul–Aug) High-altitude tribute to European ethnic music, with concerts held in Alpine villages in the region's mountains.

Le Fenestrelle (Jun-Aug) Two valleys, 13 lakes, 4000 fortress steps and several mines in the Chisone and Germanasca Valleys set the scene for this unique theatre festival.
Grinzane Festival (www.grinzane.it; Jul-Sep) Literary readings, theatre performances and workshops to celebrate literary culture in the Langhe, Roero and Monferrato.

SEPTEMBER

Two Lakes Jazz Festival (www.jazzfest.it in Italian) Some of Europe's best jazz masters bring seven days of jamming sessions, concerts and workshops to the Parco Naturale dei Laghi di Avigliana in the Valle di Susa.

OCTOBER/NOVEMBER

Feminine Blues (www.centrojazztorino.it/blues.html in Italian) Female blues singers converge on Piedmont.

DECEMBER

Natale (Christmas) The weeks leading up to Christmas host numerous processions and religious events. Churches build elaborate cribs; local communities re-enact nativity scenes; and Christmas markets set central squares buzzing.

See p71 for a rundown on Turin-specific events.

FOOD

For a titillating look at Piedmont cuisine, see p46.

Restaurant listings for Turin in this book are given in the order: budget (€5 to €15), mid-range (€15 to €25) and top end (over €25); eating choices are listed in order of preference within each section. Elsewhere, the best places to feast are listed first.

GAY & LESBIAN TRAVELLERS

Homosexuality is well tolerated in Turin (p72), but less so in rural Piedmont where public displays of affection by homosexual couples can attract a negative response.

HOLIDAYS

Most Italians take their annual holiday in August. *Settimana Santa* (Easter Week) is another busy holiday period for Italians.

National public holidays:
New Year's Day 1 January
Epiphany 6 January
Easter Monday March/April
Liberation Day 25 April
Labour Day 1 May
Feast of the Assumption 15 August
All Saints' Day 1 November
Feast of the Immaculate Conception 8 December

Christmas Day 25 December
Feast of Santo Stefano 26 December

INSURANCE

A travel-insurance policy to cover theft, loss and medical problems is a good idea. Some policies specifically exclude dangerous activities, which can include scuba diving, motorcycling, and even trekking.

You may prefer a policy that pays doctors or hospitals directly rather than you having to pay on the spot and claim later. If you have to claim later ensure you keep all documentation.

Check that the policy covers ambulances or an emergency flight home.

In Italy, medical care is freely available to EU nationals carrying an E111 form. Emergency cover (including accidents) in Italy is available, by law, free of charge to all travellers.

For car insurance, see p153.

INTERNET ACCESS

Internet cafés, where you can surf from €3 to €5 per hour, abound in towns. Rural

---

TOP FIVE FILM FESTS

■ **International Women's Cinema Festival** (mid-Mar) Turin screens eight days of film dedicated to, and by, women of the world.

■ **Short Film in Bra** (www.cortoinbra.it, www.slowfoodonfilm.it; Apr) Biennial international short-film festival in Bra, with a particularly tasty zoom-in on food and gastronomy in film; organised with Slow Food (p51).

■ **Turin International Gay & Lesbian Film Festival** (www.turinglfilmfestival .com; end Apr) Five-day film festival in Turin with a strictly homosexual focus; dubbed 'from Sodom to Hollywood'.

■ **Cinemambiente** (www.cinemambiente.it; Oct) Italy's premier environmental film festival, Turin.

■ **Turin Film Festival** (www.torinofilmfest .org; Nov) Italy's most important film festival (after Venice), filling cinemas for a week in the Piedmont capital.

Piedmont however remains off the beaten electronic track.

If you plan to carry your notebook or palmtop computer with you, invest in a universal AC adaptor for your appliance and a European plug adaptor. For more on travelling with a computer, see www.telea dapt.com.

AOL (www.aol.com) and **CompuServe** (www .compuserve.com) have an Italy dial-in node (☎ 702 000 50 32).

For a list of websites specific to Piedmont, see p10.

LEGAL MATTERS

The average tourist has no reason to brush with the law, unless robbed or pickpocketed. Should you need to report a crime, call the *carabinieri* (military police) for nonviolent thefts and incidents that don't endanger life, and the *polizia statale* (state police) for everything else. The police are headquartered in a *questura*, details of which are given in Emergency sections in this guide.

While a few grams of cannabis or marijuana are permissible for personal use, drugs are frowned upon. Police can hold you for as long as it takes to analyse your case (by law police can detain you for any alleged offence for up to 48 hours without a magistrate being informed, and interrogate you without the presence of a lawyer). If the police decide you are a pusher, you can end up in prison (where you can be held legally for up to three years without being brought to trial).

While driving, the legal blood-alcohol limit is 0.05%.

MAPS

Michelin's *North-West Italy* (1:400,000; No 428 in its orange-jacketed series) covers all of Piedmont. Those intent on penetrating Piedmont's backwaters should buy *Piemonte e Valle d'Aosta* (1:200,000; €7) by the Tour-

ing Club Italiano (TCI; www.touringclub.it). Bookshops sell both.

Free maps dished out by tourist offices range from the sublime to the useless; see p56 for Turin city maps.

Tabacco publishes the best walking maps in its 1:25,000-scale topographical series. These are available at most bookshops.

MONEY

The euro is the official currency, one euro being divided into 100 cents. Coin denominations are one, two, five, 10, 20 and 50 cents, €1 and €2. Notes are €5, €10, €20, €50, €100, €200 and €500. Exchange rates are given on the inside front cover of this book, and a guide to costs can be found on p9.

You'll find Visa, MasterCard, Eurocard, and other major credit cards are widely accepted – except at some toll booths on the motorway and in many budget hotels, pizzerias and smaller *trattorie*, which only accept cash. ATMs are abundant in town centres.

If your credit card is lost, stolen or swallowed by an ATM, cancel the card immediately on the following numbers:
MasterCard ☎ 800 870 866
Visa ☎ 800 877 232
American Express ☎ 06 722 82

You can change money in banks, at the post office or in a *cambio* (exchange office). Out of hours, try a 24-hour banknote-exchange machine – Turin has a couple.

To cash travellers cheques, you need your passport as ID. If you lose your travellers cheques call:
American Express ☎ 800 872 000
Thomas Cook/MasterCard ☎ 800 872 050
Visa ☎ 800 874 155

POST

Italy's postal service is slow, unreliable and expensive.

Francobolli (stamps) are sold at post offices and tobacconists. To send a letter weighing up to 20g by *posta ordinaria* (regular airmail) costs €0.41 within Europe and €0.52 to other destinations. Count on up to two weeks for it to arrive in the UK or USA, and two to three weeks to reach Australia.

Posta prioritaria (priority mail) guarantees delivery within Europe (€0.62 for a

---

THE LEGAL AGE...

- To vote: 18 years old
- To consent to sex: 16 years old (heterosexual and homosexual)
- To drive: 18 years old
- To drink: 18 years old

letter up to 20g) in three days and to the rest of the world (€0.77) within four to eight days. For urgent mail, use *postacelere*, the Italian post office's courier service. Important or valuable items are best sent by *posta raccomandata* (registered mail; €2.58/2.94 for a letter up to 20/100g) or *posta assicurata* (insured mail), the cost of which depends on the value of the object being sent (10% of the object's value within Europe).

For more information, call ☎ 803 160 or see www.poste.it.

SHOPPING
Pretty much anything can be snapped up in Turin (p85), the shopping hub of Piedmont. Tasty food and wine shops aside, the city is known for its fashion boutiques (p86) and markets (p85). Smaller towns are less of a shoppers paradise. For opening hours see quick reference page.

SOLO TRAVELLERS
Piedmont is a pleasure to explore alone, although solo women will probably draw the attention of Italian men. Shake off an unwanted Romeo by ignoring him, telling him you have a *marito* (husband) or *fidanzato* (boyfriend), or walking away. If things turn nasty, approach the nearest police.

The same 'streetwise' rules apply in Turin as in any city. Avoid walking alone in deserted and dark streets; look for hotels within easy walking distance of places where you can eat at night, and don't hitchhike alone.

TELEPHONE
Mobile Phones
Italy uses GSM 900/1800 (compatible with the rest of Europe and Australia, but not with North American GSM 1900 or the system in Japan). Mobile-phone numbers start with a four-digit prefix, such as 0330, 0335 or 0347. Drop the initial zero when calling a mobile number from abroad.

TIM (Telecom Italia Mobile; www.tim.it in Italian) and Vodaphone Omnitel offer *prepagato* (prepaid) accounts for GSM phones (frequency 900mHz). **Wind** (www.wind.it) is the only dualband operator.

Phone Codes
Italy has no area codes; the 'code' (eg ☎ 011 for Turin) is an integral part of the telephone number and must always be dialled.

> **PHONEBOOK**
>
> Track down telephone numbers of hotels, restaurants, businesses and so on in Italy's electronic **Yellow Pages** (www.paginegialle.it, includes English search function). Otherwise call one of the following
>
> ■ Directory enquiries ☎ 12
> ■ International directory enquiries ☎ 176
> ■ Operator-assisted calls (collect calls) to Europe ☎ 15
> ■ Operator-assisted calls (collect calls) to elsewhere ☎ 170
> ■ Info 412 (cinemas, pharmacies, weather & traffic reports) ☎ 142

To call Italy from abroad, dial Italy's country code (☎ 39) and the telephone number (*including* the initial 0). For mobile phones, drop the 0. *Numeri verdi* (toll-free numbers) kick off with ☎ 800, and the prefixes ☎ 848 or ☎ 199 indicate national numbers charged at a local rate.

To make an international call from Italy, dial ☎ 00, the country code, city code and telephone number.

Phonecards
State-run Telecom Italia (www.telecomitalia.it) has a liberal sprinkling of orange public payphones in the streets and train stations of Turin and other large towns. Phones accept Telecom Italia phonecards (values of €5, €10 and €20), sold at post offices, tobacconists, newspaper stands, and vending machines at train stations and in Telecom offices.

A local/national call from a public phone costs €0.10/0.20 for three to six minutes, depending on the time of day.

TIME
Piedmont is one hour ahead of GMT. Daylight-saving time, when clocks are moved forward one hour, starts on the last Sunday in March. Clocks are put back an hour on the last Sunday in October. Italy operates on a 24-hour clock.

TOURIST INFORMATION
Local Tourist Offices
Tourist offices sit on a goldmine of practical information, be it in verbal or brochure form. Tourist offices in Turin's city centre open

seven days a week; elsewhere they are open from at least 8.30am to 12.30pm or 1pm, and 3pm to 7pm Monday to Friday; many open on Saturday or Sunday in summer. Staff speak English and often French.

Tourist Offices Abroad

Information on Piedmont is available from the following Italian state tourist offices:

Australia (☎ 02-9262 1666; enitour@ihug.com.au; Level 26, 44 Market St Sydney, 2000)

Canada (☎ 416-925 4882; enit.canada@on.aibn.com; Suite 907, South Tower, 17 Bloor St E, Toronto, Ontario M4W 3R8)

France (☎ 01 42 66 66 68; enit.parigi@wanadoo.fr; 23 Rue de la Paix, Paris, 75002)

Germany Berlin (☎ 030-247 83 97; enit-berlin@t-online .de; Karl Liebknecht Strasse 34, 10178) Munich (☎ 089-531 31 7; enit-muenchen@t-online.de; Goethestrasse 20, 80336) Frankfurt (☎ 069-259 12 6; enit.ffm@t-online.de; Kaiserstrasse 65, 60329)

Netherlands (☎ 020-616 82 44; enitams@wirehub.nl; Stadhouderskade 2, Amsterdam, 1054 ES)

Switzerland (☎ 01 211 79 17; enit@bluewin.ch; Uraniastrasse 32, Zurich, 8001)

UK (☎ 020-7408 1254; italy@italiantouristboard.co.uk; 1 Princes St, London, W1B 2AY)

USA Chicago (☎ 312-644 0996; www.italiantourism.com; 500 North Michigan Avenue, Suite 2240, IL 60611) Los Angeles (☎ 310-820 1898; 12400 Wilshire Blvd, Suite 550, CA 90025) New York (☎ 212-245 4822; 630 Fifth Ave, Suite 1565, NY 10111)

VISAS

Italy is one of 15 countries to sign the Schengen Convention, an agreement whereby Schengen countries have abolished checks at common borders. Legal residents of one Schengen country do not require a visa for another Schengen country. Citizens of the UK and Ireland are also exempt from visa requirements for Schengen countries. Nationals of Australia, Canada, Israel, Japan, New Zealand, Switzerland and the USA do not require visas for tourist visits of up to 90 days to any Schengen country.

The standard tourist visa is valid for up to 90 days. A Schengen visa issued by one Schengen country is generally valid for

---

PIEDMONT'S PATRON SAINTS

Individual towns have public holidays – and throw fantastic festivals – to celebrate the days of their patron saints, including:

- **San Gaudenzio** Novara, 22 January
- **Sant Petro** Biella, 12 March
- **San Vittore** Verbania, 13 April
- **Sant Secondo** Asti, 1 May
- **San Giovanni** Turin, 24 June
- **San Savino** Ivrea, 7 July
- **Sant'Eusebius** Vercelli, 2 August
- **San Baudolino** Alessandria, 9 November

---

travel in other Schengen countries. However, individual Schengen countries may impose additional restrictions on certain nationalities. It is therefore worth checking visa regulations with the consulate of each country you plan to visit.

It's now mandatory that you apply for a Schengen visa in your country of residence. You can apply for no more than two Schengen visas in any 12-month period and they are not renewable inside Italy. If you are going to visit more than one Schengen country, you should apply for the visa at a consulate of your main destination country or the first country you intend to visit.

WORK

EU citizens wanting to work (legally) need a *permesso di soggiorno* (work permit). In Turin, apply to the **Ufficio Stranieri** (Foreigners Office; ☎ 011 442 94 00; stranieri@comune.torino.it; Via Cottolengo 26; ⏱ 2-5.30pm Mon & Wed).

Work can be picked up during the ski season in the Alpine resorts or during southern Piedmont's grape harvests. In Turin, scour the classifieds and job ads in the local edition of the *Secondamano* (www .secondamano.it in Italian) newspaper for possible English-teaching opportunities.

The 2006 Winter Olympics may present job opportunities; see www.torino2006.org.

Transport

CONTENTS

Getting There & Away	**150**
Entering the Country	150
Air	150
Land	151
Getting Around	**152**
Bicycle	152
Boat	152
Bus	152
Car & Motorcycle	152
Local Transport	153
Train	153

TRANSPORT

THINGS CHANGE...

The information in this chapter is particularly vulnerable to change. Check directly with the airline or a travel agent to make sure you understand how a fare (and ticket you may buy) works and be aware of the security requirements for international travel. Shop carefully. The details given in this chapter should be regarded as pointers and are not a substitute for your own careful, up-to-date research.

GETTING THERE & AWAY

ENTERING THE COUNTRY

There are no special complications to entering Italy. As a rule a valid passport is all you need to enter the country.

Italy is a signatory of the Schengen Convention, so there are no checks at borders with other Schengen countries (all EU member countries except the UK, Ireland, Iceland, Norway and the newest 10 countries). Legal residents of one Schengen country do not need a visa for another. UK and Irish nationals are also exempt from visa requirements for Schengen countries. Nationals of Australia, Canada, Israel, Japan, New Zealand, Switzerland and the USA do not require visas for tourist stays of up to 90 days to any Schengen country. South African nationals require visas for Italy.

Passports

Citizens of EU member states can travel to Italy with their national ID cards. Travellers from the UK and non-EU countries must have a passport that's valid for three months beyond your intended stay. Entry stamps may not be stamped in your passport, but if you're planning on staying for any length of time you should insist on having one.

AIR
Airports & Airlines

Turin's **International Airport** (code TRN; ☎ 011 567 63 61; www.turin-airport.com) in Caselle, 16km north of the city, is the region's most important, serving domestic and international flights. Piedmont's smaller second airport, **Cuneo Levaldigi Airport** (code CUF; ☎ 0171 37 43 74; www.aeroporto.cuneo.it) is 20km north of Cuneo. Air Excel runs daily flights from Cuneo to Rome and weekday flights to Strasbourg. See Cuneo on p118 for more information.

Milan's two airports are also important gateways to the region, in particular the lakes. From **Malpensa** (code MXP; ☎ 02 7485 22 00; www.malpensa.com) it is 50km to Stresa on Lago Maggiore; from **Linate** (code LIN; ☎ 02 7485 23 90; www.sea-aeroportimilano.it) it is 90km.

Airlines flying to and from the area include:

Aer Lingus (code EIN; ☎ 02 5810 57 36; www.flyaerlingus.com) Dublin International Airport.

Air Dolomiti (code EN; ☎ 045 860 52 11; www.airdolomiti.it) Munich International Airport.

Air France (code AF; ☎ 02 76 07 31; www.airfrance.com) Charles de Gaulle Airport, Paris.

Air One (code AP; ☎ 02 756 01 60; www.air-one.it) Auckland International Airport.

Alitalia (code AZ; ☎ 06 656 41, 848 86 56 41; www.alitalia.com) Fiumicino, Rome.

American Airlines (code AA; ☎ 02 6269 41 76; www.aa.com) Chicago O'Hare Airport.

British Airways (code BA; ☎ 06 147 812 266; www.britishairways.com) Heathrow Airport, London.

Brussels Airlines (code SAB; ☎ 02 696 823 64; www.flysn.com) Brussels National Airport.

Delta Air Lines (code DL; ☎ 800 47 79 99; www.delta.com) John F Kennedy Airport, New York

EasyJet (code U2; ☎ 848 88 77 66; www.easyjet.com) Stansted Airport, London.

Finnair (code FIN; ☎ 02 6968 23 64; www.finnair.com) Helsinki Vantaa International Airport.

Iberia (code IBE; ☎ 02 88 99; www.iberia.com) Madrid Barajos Airport.

KLM (code KL; ☎ 02 21 89 81; www.klm.com) Schiphol, Amsterdam.

Lufthansa (code LH; ☎ 02 806 630 25; www.lufthansa .com) Frankfurt Airport.

Luxair (code LGL; ☎ 06 6501 80 80; www.luxair.lu) Luxembourg International Airport.

Meridiana (code IG; ☎ 199 11 13 33; www.meridiana.it in Italian) Linate Airport, Milan.

Northwest Airlines (code NWA; ☎ 02 21 89 81; www .nwa.com) Minneapolis International Airport.

Ryanair (code FR; ☎ 353-818 30 30 30 in English, 0899 88 99 73 in Italian; www.ryanair.com) Stansted Airport, London.

SAS (code SAS; ☎ 02 720 001 93; www.scandinavian .net) Arlanda Airport, Stockholm.

United Airlines (code UA; ☎ 02 6963 37 07; www.ual .com) Washington Dulles International Airport.

Virgin Express (code TV; ☎ 02 482 960 00, 800 097 097; www.virgin-express.com) Brussels National Airport.

Tickets

The Internet is fast becoming the smoothest way of finding and booking plane tickets. Online agents that specialise in cheap flights include www.travelocity.co.uk and www .cheaptickets.com.

High season is June to September, while the low season, November to March, is interrupted by price hikes around Christmas and Easter. Expect price hikes across the board for the 2006 Winter Olympics.

AUSTRALIA

Reliable ticket agencies include:

Flight Centre (☎ 1300 36 26 65; www.flightcentre .com.au)

STA Travel (☎ 1300 36 03 90; www.statravel.com.au)

CONTINENTAL EUROPE

The following are all well-known ticket agencies operating in the countries listed.

Denmark, Sweden, Norway & Finland

Kilroy Travel Group (www.kilroygroups.com)

France

Look Voyages (☎ 0892 89 01 01; www.lookvoyages .fr in French)

OTU Voyages (☎ 0820 81 78 17; www.otu.fr in French)

> **DEPARTURE TAX**
>
> Italian departure tax stands at €10. It is generally included in the price of the ticket.

Germany

STA Travel (www.statravel.de in German)

Virgin Express (www.virgin-express.com) Offices in Germany, Belgium, Denmark, France and Greece.

The Netherlands

My Travel (www.mytravel.nl)

Spain

Viajes Zeppelin (☎ 902 38 42 53; www.viajeszeppelin .com in Spanish)

REST OF ITALY

Two of the biggest national travel agencies are:

CTS Travel (☎ 06 44 11 11; www.cts.it in Italian)

Nouvelles Frontieres (☎ 199 50 50 90; www.nfi.it in Italian)

UK & IRELAND

Expert ticket agencies include:

STA Travel (☎ 0870 160 05 99; www.statravel.co.uk)

Trailfinders (☎ 020 7292 18 88; www.trailfinders.com)

USA

Cheap deals are available through:

Priceline (www.priceline.com)

STA Travel (☎ 800 781 40 40; www.statravel.com)

LAND

Before attempting to cross the Italian border, check the visa and entry requirements.

If you are entering Switzerland, remember to have your passport with you. It is not an EU country, so there are custom controls and no euros. Nationals of Britain, Australia, Canada, Japan, New Zealand, South Africa and the USA do not need visas to enter Switzerland. Also make sure your car insurance covers Switzerland.

Bus

Most national and international buses terminate at and depart from Turin's **bus station** (☎ 011 433 25 25; Corso Castelfidardo).

For the UK and Continental Europe, **Eurolines** (☎ 055 35 71 10; www.eurolines.it) links Turin with a number of European cities including London, Paris, Barcelona and Prague.

TRANSPORT

Within Italy there are a whole host of private companies serving Piedmont. The major ones are:

Marino (☎ 011 53 52 47; www.marinobus.it) Bari, Brindisi, Taranto and Lecce by way of Milan and Novara.

Sadem (☎ 011 300 06 11; www.sadem.it in Italian) For Valle d'Aosta, Lombardy and Emilia Romagna.

Sena (☎ 800 93 09 60; www.sena.it) Overnight buses to Calabria via Modena, Bologna and Florence.

Car & Motorcycle

Piedmont is directly connected with neighbouring France and Switzerland. In winter driving conditions can be hazardous, so make sure you have a set of snow chains in the car.

When driving in Europe always carry proof of ownership of a private vehicle. Third-party motor insurance is also a minimum requirement and it's a good idea to carry a European Accident Statement form in case of accidents. For further details see following.

To and from France there are two major crossings: the **Fréjus Tunnel** (Traforo del Frejus; www.tunneldufrejus.com; car one-way €28.80), which connects with the A32 autostrada at the head of the Valle di Susan near Bardonecchia; and the **Mont Blanc Tunnel** (Traforo del Monte Bianco; www.tunnelmb.com; car one-way €28.80) in neighbouring Valle d'Aosta, which links Chamonix with the A5. In the northern reaches of Piedmont, nothwest of Domodossola, the **Simplon (Sempione) Pass** connects Switzerland with the SS9.

The other major pass between Piedmont and France is the **Colle della Maddalena** (p119).

From Lombardy in the east, the A4 links Milan and Turin, while for Genoa and the south, the A26 merges with the A12, the main coastal route to Tuscany.

Train

Turin is an important rail junction, with regular departures for major cities including Rome, Milan and Venice. International trains currently run to Paris, Lyons and Barcelona. They are operated by:

Artesia (☎ 01 4281 05 89; www.sncf.com)

Elipsos Internacional (☎ 902 2402 02; www.renfe.es)

For further rail information, visit the **Rail Europe Travel Centre** (☎ 0870 84 88 84; www.raileurope.co.uk).

GETTING AROUND

BICYCLE

There are no special road rules for cyclists but you'd be wise to wear a helmet and carry lights. Bicycles can be transported on regional trains for as little as €3.50.

Rental charges vary but count on about €15 per day for a mountain bike. To buy a similar model you'll be looking at €220 plus. For more information, refer to p69.

BOAT

Cross-lake services on Lago Maggiore are run by **Navigazione Lago Maggiore** (☎ 0323 303 93; www.navigazionelaghi.it in Italian) and on Lago d'Orta by **Navigazione Lago d'Orta** (☎ 0322 84 48 62). For further details see p121 in the Northern Piedmont & the Lakes chapter.

BUS

In an area as mountainous as Piedmont, buses provide an essential service. On the whole they are cheap, with tickets widely available at newsagents, bus stations and travel agents. Reservations are rarely necessary.

Major operators and the areas they serve include:

Cavourese (☎ 0121 690 31; www.cavourese.it) Val Chisone.

GTT (☎ 800 99 00 97; www.satti.it) Turin and environs.

Sadem (☎ 011 53 89 67; www.sadem.it) Chivasso and Carmagnola.

Sapav (☎ 800 80 19 01; www.sapav.it) Valle di Susa and Val Chisone.

CAR & MOTORCYCLE

Driving in Piedmont is the best way to get the most out of the region. Italy's national motoring organisation, the **Automobile Club Italiano** (ACI; 24hr info line ☎ 166 66 44 77; www.aci.it in Italian) has a Turin office.

Bring Your Own Vehicle

Apart from regular licence and insurance obligations, there are no special requirements for bringing a car into Italy.

Piedmont's roads are liberally lined with petrol stations, where you'll be disheartened at the high cost of petrol – reckon on about €1.10 for a litre of unleaded (benzina senza piombo) or €0.90 for a litre of diesel (gasolio). Breakdown pick-up charges are also horribly high so ensure that you're covered by insurance. For breakdown assistance call ☎ 116.

Driving Licence
All EU member states' driving licences are fully recognised throughout Europe. If you have a non-EU licence you'll need an International Driving Permit, available from your national automobile association. It's valid for 12 months and must be kept with your regular licence. Costs vary from country to country, but count on about €10.

Hire
To rent a car in Italy you have to be aged 21 or over – 23 for some companies – and have a valid driving licence and credit card. Always make sure you understand exactly what you're paying for (unlimited kilometres, tax, insurance, collision damage waiver etc) and what your liabilities are. In some cases you're liable for penalties of between €260 and €520 if the car is stolen. Average rental charges stand at about €65 per day.

Major companies include:

Avis (☎ 011 50 11 07; www.avis.com; Stazione Porto Nuova)

Europcar (☎ 011 650 36 03; www.europcar.com; Stazione Porta Nuova)

Hertz (☎ 011 50 20 80; www.hertz.com; Via Magellano 12)

Maggiore (☎ 011 661 46 29; www.maggiore.it; Stazione Porta Nuova)

Insurance
Third-party car insurance is a minimum requirement in Italy but to drive your own vehicle in Italy you'll also need an International Insurance Certificate, known as a *Carta Verde* (Green Card); your car insurance company can issue this.

Car-rental charges usually cover insurance costs but always check what your liabilities are.

Purchase
You have to be a resident in Italy to buy a car or motorcycle legally. If you're desperate and you know a resident who'll do the honours for you, check out www.quattroruote.it for second-hand car prices.

Road Rules
Contrary to popular belief, Italy's road rules follow international norms. Drive on the

right and overtake on the left; wear seat belts; drive with your headlights on outside built-up areas; carry a warning triangle; and don't drink and drive. Spot checks are becoming more frequent, and the blood-alcohol limit is 0.05%.

Speed limits, unless otherwise indicated by local signs, are: 130km/h on autostrade; 110km/h on main roads; 90km/h on secondary roads; and 50km/h in built-up areas.

LOCAL TRANSPORT
Turin apart, most of Piedmont's towns and cities are easily covered on foot. All, however, have decent bus services, some also have trams and you'll even find the odd cable car in action. Tickets are usually valid for a set time and cover all means of public transport, within a defined urban area.

The standard practise is to buy your ticket before you board the bus (or tram) and validate it on board. Tickets are available from newsagents, tobacconists (*tabacchi*), ticket booths or dispensing machines.

Taxis are universally expensive and should you use one, insist that the meter is switched on and that you pay the meter fare and not an agreed price.

TRAIN
Trains in Italy are run by **Trenitalia** (☎ 89 20 21; www.trenitalia.com). The network is comprehensive but there are some mountainous areas where you're better off taking a bus.

Trains are divided into the stop-at-every-station *regionali*, the faster Intercity (IC) and super-fast Eurostar (ES), with ticket prices corresponding to the type of train you take. Reservations are not usually necessary and are not even available on *regionali* trains. If you do make one you'll pay an extra €3 on top of the ticket price.

HITCHING

Hitching is not particularly common in Piedmont, and with an effective public transport system, it's largely unnecessary. Travellers who make friends with locals will find it easy to get a lift but once on the road most drivers are loath to slow down, let alone stop, for anybody.

Health

CONTENTS

Before You Go	**154**
Insurance	154
Recommended Vaccinations	154
Internet Resources	154
In Transit	**154**
Deep Vein Thrombosis (DVT)	154
Jet Lag	154
In Piedmont	**155**
Availability & Cost of Health Care	155
Travellers' Diarrhoea	155
Environmental Hazards	155
Travelling with Children	156
Women's Health	156
Sexual Health	156

BEFORE YOU GO

While Piedmont has excellent health care, prevention is the key to staying healthy while abroad. A little planning before departure, particularly for pre-existing illnesses, will save trouble later. Bring medications in their original, labelled containers. A signed and dated letter from your physician describing your medical conditions and medications, including generic names, is a good idea. If carrying syringes or needles, be sure to have a physician's letter documenting their medical necessity. If you are embarking on a long trip, have your teeth checked (dental treatment is particularly expensive in Italy) and take your optical prescription with you.

INSURANCE

If you're an EU citizen, an E111 form, available from health centres (and post offices in the UK), covers you for most medical care but not emergency repatriation home or nonemergencies. Citizens from other countries should find out if there is a reciprocal arrangement for free medical care between their country and Italy. If you do need health insurance, make sure you get a policy that covers you for the worst possible scenario, such as an accident requiring an emergency flight home. Find out in advance if your insurance plan will make payments directly to providers or reimburse you later for overseas health expenditures.

RECOMMENDED VACCINATIONS

No jabs are required to travel to Italy. The World Health Organization (WHO), however, recommends that all travellers be covered for diphtheria, tetanus, measles, mumps, rubella, polio and hepatitis B.

INTERNET RESOURCES

The WHO's publication *International Travel and Health* is revised annually and is available online at www.who.int/ith. Other useful websites include:

- www.ageconcern.org.uk – advice on travel for the elderly
- www.fitfortravel.scot.nhs.uk – general travel advice for the layman)
- www.mdtravelhealth.com – travel health recommendations for every country; updated daily
- www.mariestopes.org.uk – information on women's health and contraception

IN TRANSIT

DEEP VEIN THROMBOSIS (DVT)

Blood clots may form in the legs during plane flights, chiefly because of prolonged immobility (the longer the flight, the greater the risk). The chief symptom of DVT is swelling or pain of the foot, ankle, or calf, usually but not always on just one side. When a blood clot travels to the lungs, it may cause chest pain and breathing difficulties. Travellers with any of these symptoms should immediately seek medical attention. To prevent the development of DVT on long flights you should walk about the cabin, contract the leg muscles while sitting, drink plenty of fluids and avoid alcohol and tobacco.

JET LAG

To avoid jet lag try drinking plenty of nonalcoholic fluids and eating light meals. Upon arrival, get exposure to natural sunlight and readjust your schedule (for meals, sleep etc) as soon as possible.

IN PIEDMONT

AVAILABILITY & COST OF HEALTH CARE

If you need an ambulance anywhere in Italy call ☎ 118. For emergency treatment, go straight to the *pronto soccorso* (casualty) section of a public hospital, where you can also get emergency dental treatment.

Excellent health care is readily available throughout Italy but standards can vary. Pharmacists can give valuable advice and sell over-the-counter medication for minor illnesses. They can also advise when more specialised help is required and point you in the right direction. In major cities you are likely to find English-speaking doctors or a translator service available.

TRAVELLERS' DIARRHOEA

If you develop diarrhoea, be sure to drink plenty of fluids, preferably in the form of an oral rehydration solution such as Dioralyte. If diarrhoea is bloody, persists for more than 72 hours, or is accompanied by fever, shaking, chills or severe abdominal pain, you should seek medical attention.

ENVIRONMENTAL HAZARDS
Heatstroke

Heatstroke occurs following excessive fluid loss with inadequate replacement of fluids and salt. Symptoms include headache, dizziness and tiredness. Dehydration is already underway by the time you feel thirsty – aim to drink sufficient water to produce pale, diluted urine. To treat heatstroke drink water and/or fruit juice, and cool the body with cold water and fans.

Hypothermia

Hypothermia occurs when the body loses heat faster than it can produce it. As ever, proper preparation will reduce the risks of getting it. Even on a hot day in the mountains, the weather can change rapidly so carry waterproof garments, warm layers and a hat, and inform others of your route. Hypothermia starts with shivering, loss of judgment and clumsiness. Unless re-warming occurs, the sufferer deteriorates into apathy, confusion and coma. Prevent further heat loss by seeking shelter, warm dry clothing, hot sweet drinks and shared bodily warmth.

Bites, Stings & Insect-Borne Diseases

Italy's only dangerous snake, the viper, is found throughout the country. To minimise the possibilities of being bitten, always wear boots, socks and long trousers when walking through undergrowth where snakes may be present. Don't put your hands into holes and crevices, and be careful when collecting firewood. Viper bites do not cause instantaneous death and an antivenin is widely available in pharmacies. Keep the victim calm and still, wrap the bitten limb tightly, as you would for a sprained ankle, and attach a splint to immobilise it. Seek medical help, if possible with the dead snake for identification. Don't attempt to catch the snake if there is a possibility of being bitten again. Tourniquets and sucking out the poison are now comprehensively discredited.

Always check all over your body if you have been walking through a potentially tick-infested area as ticks can cause skin infections and other more serious diseases such as Lyme disease and tick-borne encephalitis. If a tick is found attached, press down around the tick's head with tweezers, grab the head and gently pull upwards. Avoid pulling the rear of the body as this may squeeze the tick's gut contents through the attached mouth parts into the skin, increasing the risk of infection and disease. Lyme disease begins with the spreading of a rash at the site of the bite, accompanied by fever, headache, extreme fatigue, aching joints and muscles and severe neck stiffness. If untreated, symptoms usually disappear but disorders of the nervous system, heart and joints can develop later. Treatment works best early in the illness – medical help should be sought. Symptoms of tick-borne encephalitis include blotches around the bite, which is sometimes pale in the middle, and headaches, stiffness and other flu-like symptoms (as well as extreme tiredness) appearing a week or two after the bite. Again, medical help must be sought.

Rabies is still found in Italy but only in isolated areas of the Alps. Any bite, scratch or even lick from a mammal in an area where rabies does exist should be scrubbed with soap and running water immediately and then cleaned with an alcohol solution. Medical help should be sought.

HEALTH

TRAVELLING WITH CHILDREN

Make sure children are up to date with routine vaccinations, and discuss possible travel vaccines with your doctor or local travel vaccination centre well before departure as some vaccines are not suitable for children under a year. Lonely Planet's *Travel with Children* includes travel-health advice for younger children.

WOMEN'S HEALTH

Emotional stress, exhaustion and travelling through different time zones can all contribute to an upset in the menstrual pattern.

If using oral contraceptives, remember some antibiotics, diarrhoea and vomiting can stop the pill from working. Time zones, gastrointestinal upsets and antibiotics do not affect injectable contraception.

Travelling during pregnancy is usually possible but consult your doctor before planning your trip. The riskiest times for travel are during the first 12 weeks of pregnancy and after 30 weeks.

SEXUAL HEALTH

Condoms are readily available but emergency contraception is not, so take the necessary precautions.

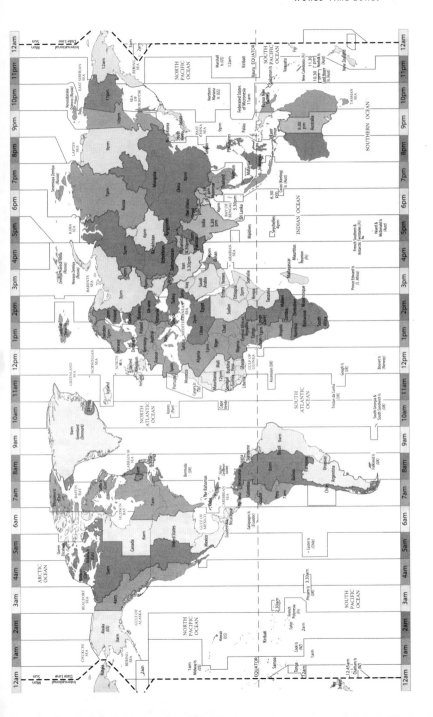

Language

PRONUNCIATION

Stress is indicated in our pronunciation guide by italics. Word stress generally falls on the second-last syllable, as in spa-*ghet*-ti, but when a word has an accent, the stress falls on that syllable, as in cit-*tà* (city).

ACCOMMODATION

I'm looking for a ...	Cerco ...	*cher*·ko ...
guesthouse	una pensione	oo·na pen·*syo*·ne
hotel	un albergo	oon al·*ber*·go
youth hostel	un ostello per la gioventù	oon os·*te*·lo per la jo·ven·*too*

Do you have any rooms available?
Avete camere libere?
a·*ve*·te *ka*·me·re *lee*·be·re

I'd like (a) ...	Vorrei ...	vo·*ray* ...
bed	un letto	oon *le*·to
single room	una camera singola	oo·na *ka*·me·ra *seen*·go·la
double room	una camera matrimoniale	oo·na *ka*·me·ra ma·tree·mo·*nya*·le
room with a bathroom	una camera con bagno	oo·na *ka*·me·ra kon *ba*·nyo

How much is it ...?	Quanto costa ...?	*kwan*·to *ko*·sta ...
per night	per la notte	per la *no*·te
per person	per persona	per per·*so*·na

CONVERSATION & ESSENTIALS

Hello.	Buon giorno.	bwon *jor*·no
	Ciao. (inf)	chow
Goodbye.	Arrivederci.	a·ree·ve·*der*·chee
	Ciao. (inf)	chow
Yes/No.	Sì/No.	see/no
Please.	Per favore/	per fa·*vo*·re/
	Per piacere.	per pya·*chay*·re
Thank you.	Grazie.	*gra*·tsye
That's fine/ You're welcome.	Prego.	*pre*·go
Excuse me.	Mi scusi.	mee *skoo*·zee
Sorry (forgive me).	Mi scusi/ Mi perdoni.	mee *skoo*·zee/ mee per·*do*·nee

My name is ...
Mi chiamo ...   mee *kya*·mo ...

EMERGENCIES

Help!		
	Aiuto!	a·*yoo*·to
I'm lost.		
	Mi sono perso/a.	mee *so*·no *per*·so/a
Go away!		
	Lasciami in pace!	la·*sha*·mi een *pa*·che
	Vai via! (inf)	va·ee *vee*·a

Call ...!	Chiami ...!	kee·*ya*·mee ...
	Chiama ...! (inf)	kee·*ya*·ma ...
a doctor	un dottore/ un medico	oon do·*to*·re/ oon *me*·dee·ko
the police	la polizia	la po·lee·*tsee*·ya

I'm from ...
Vengo da ...   *ven*·go da ...
I (don't) like ...
(Non) Mi piace ...   (non) mee *pya*·che ...

DIRECTIONS

Where is ...?
Dov'è ...?   do·*ve* ...
Go straight ahead.
Si va sempre diritto.   see va *sem*·pre dee·*ree*·to
Vai sempre diritto. (inf)   va·ee *sem*·pre dee·*ree*·to
Turn left/right.
Giri a sinistra/destra.   *jee*·ree a see·*nee*·stra/*de*·stra

HEALTH

I'm ill.	Mi sento male.	mee *sen*·to *ma*·le
It hurts here.	Mi fa male qui.	mee fa *ma*·le *kwee*

I'm ...	Sono ...	*so*·no ...
asthmatic	asmatico/a	az·*ma*·tee·ko/a
diabetic	diabetico/a	dee·a·*be*·tee·ko/a
epileptic	epilettico/a	e·pee·*le*·tee·ko/a

I'm allergic ...	Sono allergico/a ...	*so*·no a·*ler*·jee·ko/a ...
to antibiotics	agli antibiotici	a·lyee an·tee·bee·*o*·tee·chee
to aspirin	all'aspirina	a·*la*·spe·*ree*·na
to penicillin	alla penicillina	a·la pe·nee·see·*lee*·na
to nuts	ai noci	a·ee *no*·chee

LANGUAGE DIFFICULTIES

Do you speak English?
Parla inglese?   *par*·la een·*gle*·ze

How do you say ... in Italian?
Come si dice ...   *ko*·me see *dee*·che ...
in italiano?   een ee·ta·*lya*·no
What does ... mean?
Che vuol dire ...?   ke vwol *dee*·re ...
I (don't) understand.
(Non) Capisco.   (non) ka·*pee*·sko
I don't understand.
Non capisco.   non ka·*pee*·sko
Please write it down.
Può scriverlo, per favore?   pwo *skree*·ver·lo per fa·*vo*·re
Can you show me (on the map)?
Può mostrarmelo   pwo mos·*trar*·me·lo
(sulla pianta)?   (soo·la *pyan*·ta)

NUMBERS

0	*dze*·ro	**13**	tre·*dee*·chee
1	*oo*·no	**14**	kwa·*tor*·dee·chee
2	*doo*·e	**15**	*kween*·dee·chee
3	tre	**16**	se·dee·chee
4	*kwa*·tro	**17**	dee·cha·*se*·te
5	*cheen*·kwe	**18**	dee·*cho*·to
6	say	**19**	dee·cha·*no*·ve
7	*se*·te	**20**	*ven*·tee
8	*o*·to	**21**	ven·*too*·no
9	*no*·ve	**22**	ven·tee·*doo*·e
10	*dye*·chee	**30**	*tren*·ta
11	oon·*dee*·chee	**100**	chen·*to*
12	do·*dee*·chee	**1000**	mee·*le*

QUESTION WORDS

Who?	*Chi?*	kee
What?	*Che?*	ke
When?	*Quando?*	*kwan*·do
Where?	*Dove?*	*do*·ve
How?	*Come?*	*ko*·me

SHOPPING & SERVICES

I'd like to buy ...
Vorrei comprare ...   vo·*ray* kom·*pra*·re ...
How much is it?
Quanto costa?   *kwan*·to *ko*·sta
I'm just looking.
Sto solo guardando.   sto *so*·lo gwar·*dan*·do
I'll take it.
Lo/La compro.   lo/la *kom*·pro

Do you accept	*Accettate carte*	a·che·*ta*·te *kar*·te
credit cards?	*di credito?*	dee *kre*·dee·to

more	*più*	pyoo
less	*meno*	*me*·no
smaller	*più piccolo/a*	pyoo *pee*·ko·lo/la
bigger	*più grande*	pyoo *gran*·de

TIME & DATES

What time is it?	*Che ore sono?*	ke *o*·re *so*·no
It's (8 o'clock).	*Sono (le otto).*	*so*·no (le *o*·to)

today	*oggi*	*o*·jee
tomorrow	*domani*	do·*ma*·nee
yesterday	*ieri*	ye·ree

Monday	*lunedì*	loo·ne·*dee*
Tuesday	*martedì*	mar·te·*dee*
Wednesday	*mercoledì*	mer·ko·le·*dee*
Thursday	*giovedì*	jo·ve·*dee*
Friday	*venerdì*	ve·ner·*dee*
Saturday	*sabato*	*sa*·ba·to
Sunday	*domenica*	do·*me*·nee·ka

TRANSPORT
Public Transport

What time does	*A che ora parte/*	a ke *o*·ra *par*·te/
the ... leave/	*arriva ...?*	a·*ree*·va ...
arrive?		
boat	*la nave*	la *na*·ve
(city) bus	*l'autobus*	*low*·to·boos
(intercity) bus	*il pullman*	eel *pool*·man
train	*il treno*	eel *tre*·no

I'd like a ...	*Vorrei un*	vo·*ray* oon
ticket.	*biglietto ...*	bee·*lye*·to ...
one-way	*di solo andata*	dee *so*·lo an·*da*·ta
return	*di andata e*	dee an·*da*·ta e
	ritorno	ree·*toor*·no
1st class	*di prima classe*	dee *pree*·ma *kla*·se
2nd class	*di seconda*	dee se·*kon*·da
	classe	*kla*·se

I want to go to ...
Voglio andare a ...   vo·lyo an·*da*·re a ...

SIGNS

Ingresso/Entrata	Entrance
Uscita	Exit
Informazione	Information
Aperto	Open
Chiuso	Closed
Proibito/Vietato	Prohibited
Camere Libere	Rooms Available
Completo	Full/No Vacancies
Polizia/Carabinieri	Police
Questura	Police Station
Gabinetti/Bagni	Toilets
Uomini	Men
Donne	Women

LANGUAGE

Glossary

abbazia – abbey
affittacamere – rooms for rent
agriturismo (s), **agriturismi** (pl) – tourist accommodation on working farms
albergo (s), **alberghi** (pl) – hotel
anfiteatro – amphitheatre
autostrada (s), **autostrade** (pl) – motorway (highway)

benzina (senza piombo) – petrol (unleaded)
bivacchi – unattended mountain hut

cappella – chapel
carabinieri – police with military and civil duties
carta – menu
carta d'identità – identity card
carta geografica – map
centro – city centre
centro storico – historic centre
chiesa (s), **chiese** (pl) – church
cima – summit
città – town, city
comune – equivalent to a municipality or county; town or city council; historically, a self-governing town or city
corso – main street

degustazione – tasting (of wine, grappa, cheese or chocolate)
deposito bagagli – left luggage
duomo – cathedral

enoteca – wine shop where you can also taste
estiva – summer

ferrovia – train station
festa – feast day; holiday
fiume – river
fontana – fountain

gabinetto – toilets, WC
garni – B&Bs
giardino (s), **giardini** (pl) – gardens

isola – island

lago – lake
largo – (small) square
lavanderia – laundrette
locanda – inn, small hotel

lo ski – downhill skiing

mercato – market
monte – mountain
municipio – town hall

Natale – Christmas

oggetti smarriti – lost property
ostello per la gioventù – youth hostel

palazzo (s) **palazzi** (pl) – mansion, palace; large building of any type, including an apartment block
palio – contest
passeggiata – traditional evening stroll
piazza – square
pinacoteca – art gallery
ponte – bridge
porta – gate, door
portico – portico; covered walkway, usually attached to the outside of buildings
porto – port
posta – post office

quartieri – districts
questura – police station

reale – royal
rifugio (s), **rifugi** (pl) – mountain huts; accommodation in the Alps
riva – river bank
rocca – fortress

santuario – sanctuary
sci alpinismo – ski mountaineering
sci di fondo – cross-country skiing
stazione – station
strada – street, road

teatro – theatre
tempio – temple
terme – thermal baths
torre – tower
torrente – stream

ufficio postale – post office
ufficio stranieri – foreigners bureau

via – street, road
viale – avenue
vigili del fuoco – fire brigade
vigili urbani – traffic police, local police

Behind the Scenes

THIS BOOK
This 1st edition of *Piedmont* was researched and written by Nicola Williams and Duncan Garwood.

THANKS from the Authors
Nicola Williams Paola Galasso (Regione Piemonte) went beyond the call of duty in helping out. Superstar Paola aside, thanks to Angelo Pittro, Luisella Arzani, Elisa Bigotti and Eleonora Bianco (EDT); Linda Brizzolara and Loris Gherra (Toroc); Nadia Bottazzi (ICIF); and Slow Food. Elsewhere, thanks to LP's Laetitia for roping me into this project; to Matthias for kidding around Piedmont for me; and to little Mischa Lüfkens and his big brother, to whom my chunk of this book is dedicated.

Duncan Garwood An awful lot of people helped me on this job. A big thank you to Paola Galasso for showing me round Turin and answering my sometimes ridiculous requests; Angelo Pittro and Luisella Arzani for their help and generosity; and Paola Musolino for seeing me at such short notice.

Tourist-office staff were generally very helpful. Particularly so Erika Arancio (Acqui Terme), Nella Carnevale (Alba), Erica Mondino (Cuneo), Maria Luisa Surico (Pinerolo), Cristina (Bardonecchia), Simona Cresta (Alessandria) and the folk at Vercelli, Varallo and Alba.

Back home I'd like to thank Rebecca Lennox for her understanding and Lesley Mills for her *agriturismo* tips; Viviana, Rosella and Gerardo for their generous support; Daddy for keeping me company on the road; and as always, Lidia for just being there, and Ben for looking after her while I was away.

SEND US YOUR FEEDBACK
We love to hear from travellers – your comments keep us on our toes and help make our books better. Our well-traveled team reads every word on what you loved or loathed about this book. Although we cannot reply individually to postal submissions, we always guarantee that your feedback goes straight to the appropriate authors, in time for the next edition. Each person who sends us information is thanked in the next edition – and the most useful submissions are rewarded with a free book.

To send us your updates – and find out about LP events, newsletters and travel news – visit our award-winning website: **www.lonelyplanet.com**.

Note: We may edit, reproduce and incorporate your comments in Lonely Planet products such as guidebooks, websites and digital products, so let us know if you don't want your comments reproduced or your name acknowledged. For a copy of our privacy policy visit www.lonelyplanet.com/privacy.

CREDITS
This title was commissioned and developed in Lonely Planet's London office by Laetitia Clapton and Michala Green. Cartography was coordinated by Kusnandar, who was assisted by Jolyon Philcox, Jimi Ellis and Daniel Fennessy, and developed by Mark Griffiths. Bruce Evans was the Managing Editor

THE LONELY PLANET STORY
The story begins with a classic travel adventure: Tony and Maureen Wheeler's 1972 journey across Europe and Asia to Australia. There was no useful information about the overland trail then, so Tony and Maureen published the first Lonely Planet guidebook to meet a growing need.

From a kitchen table, Lonely Planet has grown to become the largest independent travel publisher in the world, with offices in Melbourne (Australia), Oakland (USA), London (UK) and Paris (France).

Today Lonely Planet guidebooks cover the globe. There is an ever-growing list of books and information in a variety of media. Some things haven't changed. The main aim is still to make it possible for adventurous travellers to get out there – to explore and better understand the world.

At Lonely Planet we believe travellers can make a positive contribution to the countries they visit – if they respect their host communities and spend their money wisely.

and Ray Thomson the Project Manager. The editing was coordinated by Craig Kilburn, with assistance from Andrea Dobbin, Victoria Harrison, Simon Sellars and Suzannah Shwer. The book was laid out by Michael Ruff who was assisted by Adam Bextream. Annika Roojun designed the cover.

ACKNOWLEDGMENTS

This guide was made possible by the contribution of the Piedmont region's communications initiative FESR, in cooperation with the Ministry for the Economy, Production Activities and the European Union.

Index

A

accommodation 142-3, *see also* individual locations
Acqui Terme 108-9
Agnelli, Giovanni 16, 21-2, 68, 96
air travel 150-1
airports 150-1
Alagna 132-3
Alba 110-12, **110**
Alessandria 107-8
Alessi 28, 131
animals 29-30
    conservation 32
    Museo Civico di Storia Naturale 116
Antonelli, Alessandro 26, 134
aperitifs 48, 81
architecture 26-7, 138
Armeno 131
Arona 128-9
arts 24-8
Asti 103-6, **104**
Asti Spumante 48
Avigliana 98

B

Barbaresco 113
Barbaresco wine 47
Bardonecchia 99
    Olympic events 42-3
Barolo 115
Barolo wine 47
Basilica di Superga 66
Battle of Oranges 138
beer 48
Bergolo 109
Bialetti, Alfonso 27
bicerin 75
Biella 140-1
bird watching 139
boat travel, *see* ferries
Bonaparte, Napoleon 19-20
books 10
border crossings 151-2
Borromean Islands (Isole Borromee) 127-8
Bosco del Lago 105
Bra 114-15
Brigate Rosse (Red Brigades) 22
business hours 143
bus travel
    to/from Piedmont 151-2
    within Piedmont 152

000 Map pages
000 Location of colour photographs

C

Canale 113
Canelli 114
Cannobio 129-30
car travel
    hire 153
    insurance 153
    to/from Piedmont 152
    within Piedmont 152-3
Casale Monferrato 106-7
Castellamonte, Carlo di 26
Castello di Rivoli 67-8
Castello Ducale d'Aglié 139-40
Castelmagno cheese 46, 119
castles
    Borgo Medievale 67
    Castello del Valentino 67
    Castello de La Mandria 68
    Castello di Manta 116
    Castello di Moncalieri 68
    Castello di Rivoli 67-8
    Castello di Roddi 114
    Castello Ducale d'Aglié 139-40
    Castello Grinzane Cavour 114
    Castello Reale di Carlo Felice di Casa Savoia 113
    Castello Reale di Casotto 120
    Castello Reale di Racconigi 116
    itinerary 12
    Ivrea Castello 139
    La Castiglia 115
    Reggia Venaria Reale 68
Cavour, Camillo Benso di 20, 65
Certosa di Pesio 120
Centro Cicogne e Anatidi (Stork Sanctuary) 116
Centro Studi Sulle Migrazione (Bird Migration Study Centre) 129
Cesana 97
Cesana Torinese
    Olympic events 43-4
Cesare, Balbo 20
Cherasco 115
children, travelling with 70, 131, 144
    food 50
    itinerary 14
    Parco Zoologico di Villa Pallavicino 124
Chiomonte 98
chocolate 47, 76, 111
churches & cathedrals
    Abbazia di Santa Maria di Staffarda 116
    Basilica di Sant' Andrea 136
    Basilica di San Gaudenzio 134
    Basilica di San Giulio 130
    Basilica di Superga 66

Capella Sol LeWitt-David Tremlett 115
Cappella della Santa Sindone 63
Cattedrale di Sant' Eusebio 136
Cattedrale di Santo Stefano 140
Cattedrale di San Lorenzo 111, 8
Certosa di Pesio 120
Chiesa Collegiata di San Secondo 104
Chiesa della Gran Madre di Dio 66
Chiesa di Santa Cristina 65
Chiesa di Santa Croce Juvarra 67
Chiesa di Santa Teresa 65
Chiesa di San Carlo 65
Chiesa di San Filippo Neri 63-4
Chiesa di San Francesco 118
Chiesa di San Giovanni 115
Chiesa di San Lorenzo 59
Chiesa di San Maurizio 93
Chiesa di San Sebastiano 140
Chiesa e Convento di Santa Maria 66
Chiesa Madonna Delle Grazie 131
Duomo (Novara) 134
Duomo di San Donato 93
Duomo di San Giovanni Battista 63
Sacra di San Michele 98
Sacro Monte 130
Sacro Monte Calvario 133
Sacro Monte di Varallo 131
cinema 11, 19, 28, 84, 146
    Museo Nazionale del Cinema 66
Cinzano 114
CioccolaTò festival 76
Clavière 97
climate 144
coffee 48-9, 70, 6
consulates 145
Conte, Paolo 25
courses 70, 144
    cooking 51-2
    language 70
credit cards 147
culture 23-8
    food 51
Cuneo 116-18, **117**
customs 26
customs regulations 144
cycling 69, 93, 108, 111
    within Piedmont 152

D

Dei Pescatori 127-8
design 27-8, 85-6, 131
disabled travellers 144
Domodossola 133
drinks 47-8

driving licence 153
Dronero 119
Duomo di San Giovanni Battista 63

E
economy 16
electricity 142
embassies 145
enoteca 51, 87, *see also* wine
    Enoteca Colline del Moscato 114
    Enoteca del Piemonte 87
    Enoteca Regionale Cavour 114
    Enoteca Regionale della Serra 140
    Enoteca Regionale del Barbaresco
        113
    Enoteca Regionale del Barolo 115
    Enoteca Regionale del Monfer-
        rato 107
    Enoteca Regionale del Roero 113
    Enoteca Regionale di Acqui Terme
        109
    Enoteca Regionale di Canelli 114
Entracque 119-20
environment 30-2
    floods 32
events 11

F
fashion 86
Felice, Carlo 113
Ferrero 111
ferries 126, 152
festivals 11, 71, 145-6, *see also* special
    events
    food 49
FIAT 20-2, 24, 68, 70
    Lingotto Fiere 67
Fiera del Tartufo Bianco d'Alba 112
Filiberto, Emanuele 19
food 11, 46-7, 87, 146
    courses 51-2
    customs 51, 52, 53
    festivals 49
    for children 50
    itinerary 14
    osteria 50
    pizzeria 49
    ristorante 50
    trattoria 50
    Università di Scienze Gastronom-
        iche 103
    vegetarian travellers 50
football 84
Fortezza di Fenestrelle 95
Forte di Exilles 98
Forte di Fenestrelle 95
Fréjus Tunnel 22

G
Garessio 120
Garibaldi, Giuseppe 20
gay travellers 72, 146
geography 29
Gianduja 23

Giolitti, Giovanni 21
golf 36, 69, 97, 125
Govone 113
Gramsci, Antonio 24
grappa 48, 107, 113, 6
Grinzane Cavour 114
Grotta di Bossea 120

H
health 154-6
history 17-22
holidays 146
horse riding 35

I
Il Monregalese 120
insurance 146
    health 154
Internet access 146-7
Internet resources 10-11
Isola Bella 127
Isola Madre 127
Isola San Giulio 130
Isole Borromee (Borromean Islands)
    127-8
itineraries 12-14
    author's favourite trip 15
Ivrea 138-40

J
Juvarra, Filippo 26, 67, 68, 141
Juventus 21, 84

L
Lago d'Orta 130-1
Lago Maggiore 124-30, 7
Lago Maggiore Jazz Festival 145
Lago Mergozzo 130
Langhe, the 112-15, 8
language 158-9, 160
    food vocabulary 52-3
Lavazza 70, 75
legal matters 147
Lega Nord (Northern League) 21
lesbian travellers 72, 146
Levi, Primo 25
Limone Piemonte 119
Lingotto Fiere 22, 67
literature 24-5

M
MAAM contemporary art museum
    138-9
Macugnaga 133
magic 59
Mango 114
maps 147
Martini and Rossi 21, 114
Mole Antonelliana 6, 66
Mondovì 120
money 9-10, 143, 144-5, 147
    Torino Card 63
Monferrato 106
Monviso 116
Moscato 114

Moscato wine 47-8
motorcycle travel
    insurance 153
    to/from Piedmont 152
    within Piedmont 152-3
mountain biking 34, 124-5
Mt Blanc Tunnel 22
Museo Egizio 64
Museo Nazionale del Cinema 66
Museo Nazionale del Risorgimento 64
museums & galleries
    Antiquarium di Villa del Foro 108
    Civico Museo Etnografico e Museo
        del Legno 93
    Complesso di San Pietro in
        Consavia 104
    Galleria Civica d'Arte Moderna e
        Contemporanea 65
    Galleria Sabauda 64
    MAAM 138-9
    Museo Alessi 131
    Museo Borsano 109
    Museo Civico (Cuneo) 117-18
    Museo Civico (Novara) 134
    Museo Civico d'Arte Antica 62
    Museo Civico di Casa Cavassa 115
    Museo Civico di Storia Naturale 116
    Museo Civico Federico Eusebio 111
    Museo Civico Pietro Micca 65
    Museo d'Arte e Storia Ebraico 106
    Museo dei Campionissimi 108
    Museo del Cappello 107-8
    Museo del Costume Tradizionale
        delle Genti Alpine 95-6
    Museo del Dinamitificio Nobel 98
    Museo del Regio Esercito Italiano
        130
    Museo del Territorio Biellese 140
    Museo del Tesoro del Duomo 136
    Museo dell'Automobile 67
    Museo della Bambola 127
    Museo della Battaglia di Marengo
        108
    Museo della Grappa Mazzetti 107
    Museo della Marionetta 65
    Museo dello Spazzacamino 134
    Museo di Antichità 63
    Museo di Arte e Ammobiliamento 67
    Museo Egizio 64
    Museo Francesco Borgogna 136
    Museo Martini di Storia
        dell'Enologia 114
    Museo Nazionale dell'Arma di
        Cavalleria 93
    Museo Nazionale della Montagna
        66
    Museo Nazionale del Cinema 66
    Museo Nazionale del Risorgimento
        64
    Museo Regionale di Scienze
        Naturali 66-7
    Museo Storico Nazionale
        dell'Artiglieria 65

Museo Valdese 94
Museo Walser 132
Pinacoteca Giovanni e Marella
    Agnelli 67
Scopriminiera 96
mushing 35, 97

N
Napoleon Bonaparte 19-20
national parks & nature reserves 31
    Parchi e Riserve Astigiani 31, 105
    Parchi e Riserve Naturali Cuneesi 31
    Parchi e Riserve Naturali del Lago
        Maggiore 31
    Parco Fluviale del Po Torinese
        31, 116
    Parco Naturale dei Laghi di
        Avigliana 98
    Parco Naturale dell'Alta Valsesia
        31, 131
    Parco Naturale della Val Troncea 95
    Parco Naturale delle Alpi Marittime
        31, 119
    Parco Naturale del Lago di Candia
        31, 139
    Parco Naturale del Monte Fenera 131
    Parco Naturale di Rocchetta 105
    Parco Naturale Orsiera Rocciavrè 31
    Parco Nazionale della Val Grande
        31, 133
    Parco Nazionale del Gran Paradiso
        31, 141
    Parco Regionale dell'Alpe Veglia e
        Alpe Devero 133
    Riserva Naturale Speciale della Val
        Sarmassa 105
    Riserva Naturale Speciale Vallean-
        dona Valle Botto 105
Neive 113, 7
newspapers 142
Nizza Monferrato 109
Novara 134-6, **134**

O
Olivetti 27, 138-9
Olympics, *see* Winter Olympics
Omegna 131
Orta San Giulio 130
osteria 50
Oulx 98-9
outdoor activities 33-6, 131-2
    Paesana 116

P
Paesana 116
palaces
    La Palazzina di Caccia di Stupinigi 67
    Palazzo Bricheràsio 65
    Palazzo Carignano 64

Palazzo Cavour 65
Palazzo Coardi di Carpeneto 67
Palazzo Lascaris di Ventimiglia 65
Palazzo Madama 59-62
Palazzo Madre 127
Palazzo Municipale 104
Palazzo Reale 62-3
Palazzo Madama 59-62
Palazzo Reale 62-3
Palio 105
Palio degli Asini 111
Parchi e Riserve Astigiani 31, 105
Parchi e Riserve Naturali Cuneesi 31
Parchi e Riserve Naturali del Lago
    Maggiore 31
Parco Fluviale del Po Torinese 31, 116
Parco Naturale dei Laghi di Avigliana 98
Parco Naturale dell'Alta Valsesia
    31, 131
Parco Naturale della Val Troncea 95
Parco Naturale delle Alpi Marittime
    31, 119
Parco Naturale del Lago di Candia
    31, 139
Parco Naturale del Monte Fenera 131
Parco Naturale di Rocchetta 105
Parco Naturale Orsiera Rocciavrè 31
Parco Nazionale della Val Grande
    31, 133
Parco Nazionale del Gran Paradiso
    31, 141
Parco Regionale dell'Alpe Veglia e
    Alpe Devero 133
Parco Zoologico di Villa Pallavicino 124
parks & gardens
    Giardini Reali 63
    Giardino Botanico Alpinia 124
    Parco Burcina 141
    Parco della Fantasia 131
    Parco Valentino 67
    Villa Cernigliaro 141
    Villa Taranto 129
passports 150
Pavese, Cesare 24, 113-14
Piazza Castello 59-63
Pinerolo 93-4, **94**
    Olympic events 45
pizzeria 49
planning 9-11, 144-5 *see also*
    itineraries
    holidays 146
plants 30, 32
politics 22
Ponzone 109
population 24
postal services 147-8
Pragelato 95-6
    Olympic events 44
Prali 94-5
public transport 153 *see also* indi-
    vidual destinations
    within Piedmont 153
Punta Indren 132

R
radio 142
Red Brigades (Brigate Rosse) 22
rice 126
Riserva Naturale Speciale della Val
    Sarmassa 105
Riserva Naturale Speciale Valleandona
    Valle Botto 105
risotto 46
ristorante 50

S
Sacra di San Michele 98
Sacred Mountains 30
safe travel
    road 153
    Turin 57-9
sailing 129
Saluzzo 115-16
Santa Maria Maggiore 134
Santo Stefano Belbo 113-14
Santuario di Oropa 141
San Sicario 97
    Olympic events 43-4
Sauze d'Oulx 99
    Olympic events 43
Savoy, House of 18-20, 67-8
    Galleria Sabauda 64
    Palazzo Reale 62-3
    Piazza Castello 59-63
Sestriere 96-7
    Olympic events 44
shopping 128, 140, 148
Shroud of Turin 63, 64
skiing 33, 120, 125
    Alagna 132-3
    cross-country 99
    Macugnaga 133
    Valle di Susa 98-9
    Val Chisone 93-7
    Via Lattea 96-9
Slow Food 51, 114
snails 46, 115, 119, 8
Sordevolo 141
special events 145-6, *see also* festivals
sport 84
Stresa 124-7, **125**
Susa 98

T
telephone services 148
television 142
thermal springs 36, 109
time 148, 157
Torino Atrium 63
Toroc (Winter Olympics Organizing
    Committee) 45
Torre Pellice 94
Torre Troyana o dell'Orologio 104
tourist information 148-9
tours 11, 125
train travel
    to/from Piedmont 152

trattoria 50
truffles 7, 46, 111, 112, 7
Turin 54-89, **58, 60-1**, 6
  accommodation 71-5
  activities 69
  attractions 59-68
  children, travelling with 70
  cinemas 84
  drinking 81-2
  emergency 56
  festivals 71
  food 75-81
  gay and lesbian Turin 72
  itineraries 57
  live music 83-4
  markets 85
  medical services 56
  nightclubs 83
  Olympic events 42
  quirky Turin 70
  shopping 85-7
  sport 84
  theatre 84
  tourist information 57
  tours 70-1
  travel to/from 87-8
    travel within 88-9
    walking tour 69-70, **69**

U
Umberto, Bossi 21
Unesco sites 27

V
Valle Anzasca 133
Valle Corsaglia 120
Valle Gesso 119-20
Valle Pesio 120
Valle Tanaro 120
Valle Vermenagna 119
Valsesia 131-3
Val d'Ossola 133
Val Germanasca 95, 96
Val Grana 119
Val Maira 119
Val Pellice 95
Val Stura 119
Val Vigezzo 133
Varallo 131-2
vegetarian travellers 50
Verbania 129-30
Vercelli 136-8, **136**

Vernante 119
Via Lattea 96-9
Victor Emmanuel II 20
video systems 142
visas 149, *see also* passports
Vittorio Amedeo II 19

W
Waldensians 94-5
walking 33-5, 69, 111, 125
Walsers 132
white-water sports 35-6
wine 47-8, 51, 87, 107, 112-15, *see
  also* enoteca
  Museo Borsano 109
Winter Olympics 37-45, **41**
  competitors 38-9
  events 39-40
  Olympic flame 38
  Olympic logo 41
  statistics 42
  tickets 45
  venues 42-5
women travellers 148
work 149
WWI 21-2
WWII 22

MAP LEGEND

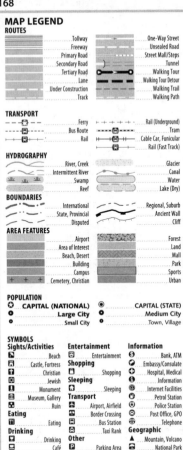

ROUTES

..................Tollway
..................Freeway
..................Primary Road
..................Secondary Road
..................Tertiary Road
..................Lane
..................Under Construction
..................Track

..................One-Way Street
..................Unsealed Road
..................Street Mall/Steps
..................Tunnel
..................Walking Tour
..................Walking Tour Detour
..................Walking Trail
..................Walking Path

TRANSPORT

..................Ferry
..................Bus Route
..................Rail

..................Rail (Underground)
..................Tram
..................Cable Car, Funicular
..................Rail (Fast Track)

HYDROGRAPHY

..................River, Creek
..................Intermittent River
..................Swamp
..................Reef

..................Glacier
..................Canal
..................Water
..................Lake (Dry)

BOUNDARIES

..................International
..................State, Provincial
..................Disputed

..................Regional, Suburb
..................Ancient Wall
..................Cliff

AREA FEATURES

..................Airport
..................Area of Interest
..................Beach, Desert
..................Building
..................Campus
..................Cemetery, Christian

..................Forest
..................Land
..................Mall
..................Park
..................Sports
..................Urban

POPULATION

○ CAPITAL (NATIONAL)
● Large City
○ Small City

◉ CAPITAL (STATE)
● Medium City
○ Town, Village

SYMBOLS

Sights/Activities
..................Beach
..................Castle, Fortress
..................Christian
..................Jewish
..................Monument
..................Museum, Gallery
..................Ruin

Eating
..................Eating

Drinking
..................Drinking
..................Café

Entertainment
..................Entertainment

Shopping
..................Shopping

Sleeping
..................Sleeping

Transport
..................Airport, Airfield
..................Border Crossing
..................Bus Station
..................Taxi Rank

Other
..................Parking Area

Information
..................Bank, ATM
..................Embassy/Consulate
..................Hospital, Medical
..................Information
..................Internet Facilities
..................Petrol Station
..................Police Station
..................Post Office, GPO
..................Telephone

Geographic
..................Mountain, Volcano
..................National Park
..................Pass, Canyon
..................River Flow

LONELY PLANET OFFICES

Australia
Head Office
Locked Bag 1, Footscray, Victoria 3011
☎ 03 8379 8000, fax 03 8379 8111
talk2us@lonelyplanet.com.au

USA
150 Linden St, Oakland, CA 94607
☎ 510 893 8555, toll free 800 275 8555
fax 510 893 8572, info@lonelyplanet.com

UK
72–82 Rosebery Ave,
Clerkenwell, London EC1R 4RW
☎ 020 7841 9000, fax 020 7841 9001
go@lonelyplanet.co.uk

France
1 rue du Dahomey, 75011 Paris
☎ 01 55 25 33 00, fax 01 55 25 33 01
bip@lonelyplanet.fr, www.lonelyplanet.fr

Published by Lonely Planet Publications Pty Ltd
ABN 36 005 607 983

© Lonely Planet 2004

© photographers as indicated 2004

Cover photograph: Springtime flowers in vineyard below Cantina Aldo Conterno, Monforte d'Alba, Piedmont, Mick Rock/Cephas Picture Library (front); Houses on the banks of Lago Maggiore below Carmine Superior, Piedmont, Sandra Bardwell (back). Many of the images in this guide are available for licensing from Lonely Planet Images: www.lonelyplanetimages.com.

Printed through The Bookmaker International Ltd
Printed in China

Lonely Planet and the Lonely Planet logo are trademarks of Lonely Planet and are registered in the US Patent and Trademark Office and in other countries.

FEB 1 2005